The Netherlands in Perspective

The Netherlands
in Perspective

The Dutch Way
of Organizing a Society and its Setting

WILLIAM Z. SHETTER

nederlands centrum buitenlanders

Graphic design
MFS Grafische Vormgeving, Utrecht

Printed by
Krips, Meppel

Published by
Nederlands Centrum Buitenlanders
Postbus 638
3500 AP Utrecht
The Netherlands
tel. (030) 239 49 59
fax. (030) 236 45 46

ISBN 90 5517 079 8
Ordernumber 971.0798

To the reader

This book, which first saw the light of day in 1987, is now appearing in an entirely new format. It is still *The Netherlands in Perspective*, but it now has a new subtitle. Among other reasons, this signals the fact that it has changed its 'home' and is now under the care of the **Nederlands Centrum Buitenlanders**.

In taking on this new venture, the NCB hopes the book will reach the same audience as before: those residing and working in the Netherlands, plus those who are undertaking serious study of the country abroad. Since part of the NCB's mission is reaching all residents of the Netherlands from other countries for whatever reason, the Center hopes with this publication to cast its net wider and reach all minorities, and those who have sought refuge in the Netherlands for political reasons and need to learn more about their new country.

The book has been rearranged, cut down from 27 to 20 chapters, and drastically streamlined to approximately two-thirds its former length. We hope that in this tighter, briefer format it will prove even more useful and accessible. What we are presenting here, in other words, is a mixture of the older and the newer.

Nevertheless this is not yet another 'guidebook' to the Netherlands, but a selective presentation emphasizing what is characteristic. It presents what contributes to understanding of the unity of land and people that in Dutch is coming to be called *Nederlandkunde*. The most important aim of this presentation is to interpret each facet in the light of others, until a 'depth perspective' begins to emerge. If we have done this right, seemingly unrelated things more and more fall into place. We are looking at facets of a society that to its members is, after all, a reasonably logical whole. This is a systematic view of the geographical, social, cultural and historical aspects of the Netherlands in constant interaction with each other.

As the opening chapter will point out, the Netherlands as a highly urbanized society can perhaps provide a model for the future of a rapidly urbanizing world. It is a 'social experiment', a society in a constant process of evolving and adapting new forms. The presentation is being done not by a Dutch citizen but by an outsider looking in, because of a conviction that seeing any society truly 'in perspective' can only be done successfully by someone who can view it from the detached vantage point of the outsider. By implication, the Dutch seem to agree with this, being notoriously poor at presenting their country and its society to the world. In fact, a Dutch newspaper recently summed up an all too common view of their culture among the Dutch with the cynical aphorism *Nederlandse cultuur is klagen over de Nederlandse cultuur* 'Dutch culture is: complaining about Dutch culture'.

In the ten years since the book's first appearance, much has changed. The perception of the country is changing, and there is more and more talk of the

Netherlands being 'full' (a term with some interesting modern connotations that are explored in chapter 15). The continued development of the European Union has resulted in vastly increased debates about the future of Dutch language and culture in the context of the new Europe. In the light of new realities in society, physical planners have had to revise their whole system of proposals for how to structure their already cramped space in the coming years. The political system seems to be in the process of thoroughly revising itself. And the wider world imposes new perspectives on it. Back in 1987 the fate of the Communist Party and its place in the Dutch political system seemed dramatically important; today the party has evaporated around the world and nobody cares any more. With Belgium undergoing major constitutional changes, the whole relationship to Flanders in the south is evolving new forms. And it seems less urgent than it did only a few years ago to give thought to the Dutch role in the evolution of South African apartheid.

But the point is not all this, but precisely the opposite: what has remained the same in Dutch culture through all this. The Dutch may fret constantly about where their cultural identity is in the midst of the world's convulsive change, but we as outsiders have much less trouble seeing an identity, an easily identifiable 'Dutchness' in the stamp they put on everything. It is the ferreting out of this theme throughout history and everywhere in the present that will be our main endeavor here.

By the time this book has been around another year or two, I will be able to claim a full half century of close observation of the Netherlands. I have been privileged to watch the country meeting all the challenges of practically the entire period since the Second World War, a time in which a society has undergone a series of revolutionary changes and yet remained unmistakably 'itself'.

The list of those who have contributed materially to this book in its present form has grown rather too long to present here in detail. All these have helped in one way or another in the delightful enterprise of clarifying thoughts and interpretations, some have performed the invaluable service of supplying me with concrete information, others have pointed out shortcomings in the book's ambitious but occasionally rash attempt at an overall picture. Those I have relied on most know who they are, and to them I extend my heartfelt thanks.

A book like this, trying to present an entire country 'as it is' is strictly speaking an impossible task, because any attempt to capture a many-sided modern society will begin slipping out of date the moment it appears. For those of us foolhardy enough to attempt such a venture, the struggle to remain reasonably up to date is a never-ending task. For this reason, readers are invited at all times to point out gaps, inaccuracies, and most of all, facts or interpretations that seem ready for updating. All suggestions will be welcomed and weighed seriously. Correspondence will reach me via the publisher or at the address below.

Department of Germanic Studies   W.Z.S.
Indiana University, Bloomington, IN 47405
Fax: (812) 855-8927

Table of contents

1 Approaches to the country

'When you leave the Netherlands, it disappears!' That was a remark made not long ago by someone who returned to the U.S. after having lived for years in the Netherlands, and was dismayed to see the country so quickly recede into the status of a remote place where little of importance ever seemed to be worth reporting. A minute or two in a TV news program a couple times a year gives the impression that mainly disorderly or permissive things go on there, and occasional coverage in a weekly news magazine may offer more detail but seldom has time to relate the glimpse into the country to anything else there. In 1993 the international repository Keesing's *Record of World Events* listed just 33 articles in which some newsworthy aspect of the Netherlands was the main topic, which was about the same number of entries as listed for Uzbekistan. For the average person living in a distant country, the daily news media offer very little, and one is left with a set of stereotype images some of which come from school days.

Recent comparative studies of school textbooks in both Europe and the U.S.* showed a similar picture of information. In textbooks running to hundreds of pages, the Netherlands is covered in an average 1.2 pages. What is presented tends to be sketchy, as often as not dated, and a mixture of facts—often grossly inaccurate—and stereotypes. Maps of the country often show it as part of the large mass of northwestern Europe, where it is reduced to a shapeless wedge the geographical contours of which are impossible to sense. The present-day role of windmills in water managment is often highly exaggerated, the percentage of land below sea level is vague or grossly inaccurate, and the size and shape of dikes is overdramatized. The percentage of the country assigned to tulip cultivation is wildly overestimated and at the same time its total agricultural production is presented at only a fraction of its true level. Information on cities and society tends strongly to favor the touristic.

Possibly no other country in the world is so firmly fixed in the minds of outsiders in the form of stereotype images such as the relationship to the water, the specialization in certain horticultural and agricultural products, the look of the capital city, and the general character of the people. Today the Netherlands, represented in the mind of many a foreigner by hardly more than its capital city, can boast another reputation as well: that of a center of permissiveness, where everything from drugs to crime is present in abundance.

The Dutch themselves cannot escape responsibility for the perpetuation of a certain amount of this. On the one hand is the tourist and public-relations industry which tends to reinforce the favorite images and clichés, not even shrinking from putting up a monument to the boy who performed the absurdly impossible feat of putting a finger in a dike. On the other hand is the unfortunately pervasive attitude in the Netherlands that the country, social customs and language are all private tribal matters that foreigners cannot be expected to be seriously interested in. Typically the Dutch take pride in

* Henk Meijer and Hank Aay, *Looking into each other's Mirrors*: Netherlands/United States Geography Textbook Study. Utrecht: Information and Documentation Centre for the Geography of the Netherlands / Grand Rapids: National Council for Geographic Education, 1994.

9-10

Fig. 1.1
The Dutch image
in the world?

doing the adapting to outsiders, with an implicit assumption of the lack of importance of the Netherlands and its society that goes much beyond the images already there. In addition, the Dutch abroad are apt to exaggerate faults and often make a poor presentation of their country.

In these pages we will try to present the Netherlands as the complex modern society that it is. In many ways it is a model of closely integrated interacting organizations and active planning for the future. For many centuries the Dutch have responded in their own ways to the challenges of their environment and the society that arose there. Aspects as varied as geography, the educational and political systems, the mass media, the historical background, the current assimilation of minorities, literature and so on all do interlock in the Dutch view to form a reasonably coherent culture. It will be our task to demonstrate how this all works together.

The Netherlands is a 'social experiment', a society in a constant process of adapting and of evolving new forms. But it is the underlying stability of the society that makes possible and sustains the vigorous open discussion that is at the center of it. It is one of the world's most highly urbanized societies, and one major focus of the ongoing experiment is the harmonization of progressive urbanization with the rest of the environment. Another is the adaptation of social institutions to meet the demands of this society. Possibly the Netherlands is providing the rest of the world with a glimpse at what the near future will be like, and offering one means of giving it form. The Dutch occupy one of the world's most densely populated countries, and they structure life in it by a commitment to a meticulously detailed but at the same time flexible system of interlocking organizations. The Dutch have an instinct for international receptivity that continues a long tradition. They are grafting a technological, information-based society onto old forms inherited from the past, with results that are impossible to foresee. It remains to be seen whether an environment can be managed and planned to withstand such severe pressure, and whether a society can find ways of adjusting to both social and technological change without sacrificing its identity. It will be left to the reader to decide what the rest of us might learn from the experiment. The reader is invited to join in this quest.

Herinnering aan Holland

Denkend aan Holland
zie ik brede rivieren
traag door oneindig
laagland gaan,
rijen ondenkbaar
ijle populieren
als hoge pluimen
aan de einder staan;
en in de geweldige
ruimte verzonken
de boerderijen
verspreid door het land.
boomgroepen, dorpen,
geknotte torens,
kerken en olmen
in een groots verband.
de lucht hangt er laag
en de zon wordt er langzaam
in grijze veelkleurige
dampen gesmoord.
en in alle gewesten
wordt de stem van het water
met zijn eeuwige rampen
gevreesd en gehoord.

Memory of Holland

Thinking of Holland
I see slow-moving rivers
cutting broad paths
through endless lowlands;
rows of unspeakably
delicate poplars
line the horizon
like feathers from fans;
and sunken away
in the measureless spaces
the farms lie scattered
over the land,
tree clusters, villages,
blunt stumps of towers,
churches and elms
in one grand expanse.
the sky hangs low there
and the sun's slowly smothered
in mists, grey,
multicolored and blurred,
and in every region
the voice of the water
with its endless disasters
is feared and is heard.

Hendrik Marsman

Two views of the Netherlands a half century apart

Denkend aan Holland

zie ik brede autobanen
onstuitbaar door oneindig
steenland gaan,
rijen onaantastbare
limousines
als dooie torren
langs de bermen staan;
en in de razende
ruimte verzonken
de wegenwachters
verspreid door het land,
benzinepompen, garages,
gesloopte steden,
fabrieken en hekken
in een strak verband.
de lucht hangt er laag
en de zon wordt er langzaam
in gore eentonige
dampen gesmoord.
en in alle gewesten
wordt de dreun van benzine
met zijn eeuwige stanken
gevreesd en gehoord.

Thinking of Holland

I see broad bands of highways
cutting unchecked
through endless stoneland,
rows of untouchable
shiny limousines
line all the shoulders
like dead bugs in the sand;
and sunken away
in the fast, frenzied spaces
the AAA
is spread through the land,
gas pumps, garages,
demolished cities,
factories and fences
in a rigid expanse.
the sky hangs low there
and the sun's slowly smothered
in mists, monotonous,
rank and foul-smeared,
and in every region
the roar of combustion
with its unending stenches
is heard and is feared.

English translations by Myra Scholz

'The Netherlands? Where's that? — oh yes, Holland. The Dutch. That's what you mean.' A little scene of confusion like this, turning into the light of recognition on substitution of a name, is familiar to anyone who has occasion to mention the country to a foreigner. The name 'Holland' is of wide international currency in readily recognizable forms such as *'Hollande', 'Ollandia', 'Holanda', 'Olanda', 'Hollanti'* and the like. Adjectives related to it, even if divergent in form like 'Dutch', present no problem. But many languages, especially in Europe, use in addition to this name one that is a translation of 'Lowlands' or 'Low Countries', and this takes on a wondrous proliferation of

Fig. 1.2

forms such as *'the Netherlands'*, *'Die Niederlande'*, *'Les Pays Bas'*, *'i Paesi Bassi'*, *'Nizozemí'*, *'Alankomaat'*. This name has the double disadvantage that by being plural it suggests that more than one country is being referred to. Many people are hardly aware that both names refer to the same country. 'Holland' is the informal name, in actuality the name of only one section of the country, much as 'England' often refers informally to 'The United Kingdom' or 'Great Britain'. 'The Netherlands' is the more formal name. Besides the Dutch language, only English makes a further distinction between this name and 'The Low Countries', usually intended to refer to the Netherlands and Belgium together.

The Dutch do not offer much help here, because they themselves call their country by not two but three names. The name *Holland* is used informally for the whole country, partly for international convenience and partly because a high percentage of the population lives in the historically most important region. The formal name of the country, the one normally used by residents outside the two provinces called 'Holland', is *Nederland*. But the really official name of the country, used in government documents and international organizations, is *Koninkrijk der Nederlanden* 'Kingdom of the Netherlands' — which uses a plural, while *Nederland* is singular in Dutch. The term *De Lage Landen* is used, as is 'The Low Countries', to refer to a wider cultural region without a single political identity. The historical background of this terminological profusion will appear in some of the later chapters. The name 'The Netherlands' is the one that will be used throughout this book.

Most visitors to the Netherlands today come by air, and see a neatly laid out land below. The old approach by sea, however, gives a different, and in some ways truer, feeling for the physical nature of the country. Ships entering the coastal waters must pass through one of the world's most treacherous areas of unpredictable, shifting sands, requiring pilots that are highly skilled and thoroughly familiar with the ways of the coast. Looking from on board a ship, the visitor gets the impression that the approaching land is hardly more substantial than something painted on the water. The land begins in such a tentative way that it is as if the water might swallow it up at any moment. The sea does not stop suddenly as at a wall. Huge, broad arms of it reach into the land area and merge with wide rivers, and even well inside the land area the estuaries are so broad and the coast so low that one is still uncertain whether this is really 'dry land' or not. Slightly farther inland the rivers themselves begin transforming into large canals whose uniform width and straight lines make human intervention plainly obvious. Each further step 'upstream' in this labyrinth of waterways continually subdividing into smaller ones is—excepting only the rivers—a step not up, following backwards the way water normally flows by gravity, but down to a lower level.

In these first few dozen miles of the country, inland from any part of the coast, water is seldom more than a short distance away. The fields are strips between regularly-spaced ditches filled with water, transport barges and pleasure boats move along traffic arteries, and an occasional larger ship will look from a distance as if it is traveling across land. Travelers in the Netherlands in the 17th and 18th centuries marveled at a land that some of them called 'a mixture of land and water' or 'a land that is floating in the water'. For millennia there have been people living in this delta region who were completely at home in the shifting sands and marshy land honeycombed with meandering waterways. The environment and its rhythms must have formed their ritual and mythology. The water still has something of a vital circulatory system about it, and even the most ambitious civil engineers have never proposed walling it out entirely. Let the sea continue being in intimate partnership with the land, they thought, but keep an eye on it and be ready to control its excesses. It was in this watery region that culture began and evolved here.

The country occupies such a small area that an outsider is not quite prepared for the surprising variety of landscape types. Textbooks often give the impression that all of the Netherlands is below sea level, whereas only about half of it is, and that only at high tide; only one quarter of the land area lies permanently below sea level.

Fig. 1.3

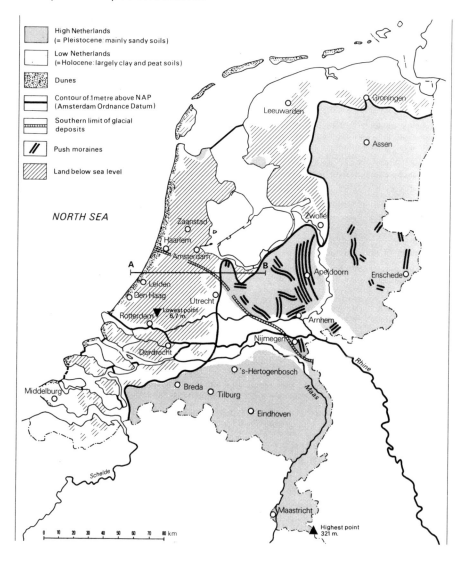

THE NETHERLANDS IN PERSPECTIVE

The 'Low Netherlands'

- The western polderland is the watery region that has served the world as the image of what 'Holland' looks like. It is an area crossed by a close network of waterways and dotted with lakes, and from the air it looks like a highly geometrical patchwork that makes many centuries of human intervention and forming plain.
- The delta and mouths of the rivers is the land that still has some of the character of the shifting marshy area that always has been part sea and part land, mainly in the southwest.
- The dunes area is the last continuous natural one that retains much of its primitive character. It consists of a strip of sandy hills all the way along the coast, ranging from about 10m (33 ft.) to 50m (165 ft.) in height, and covered with a wide variety of vegetation from grasses to dense pine forest. Although today because of population pressures it is less than a quarter of its original natural extent, it is prime recreational area, the home of a great deal of wildlife, and used for water collection and filtration.
- The low region of the broad, meandering rivers with its spacious vistas has a grandeur that reminds the Dutch of their intricate alliance with the water.

The 'High Netherlands'

- This is not just one landscape region but several distinct ones. In the far south can be found the old coast of a prehistoric sea, a limestone region sharply distinct from all the rest. Farther north it includes an extensive sandy heath area, a plateau without large waterways. In earlier times this plateau was surrounded by regions of peat, most of which has by now been cut away. In a strip along the present border with Germany there is another distinct landscape, a previously impassable marsh region that has been reclaimed by the construction of miles-long, straight drainage canals.
- The *Veluwe* consists of the hilly, heavily wooded area of glacial ridges remaining from the second-last Ice Age, a combination of forest and sandy heath that is especially rich in wildlife. The *Veluwe* includes one of the few remaining patches of untouched primitive forest in the country, and part of it today is a national park.
- The north: In a wide band along the northern coast is an area of clay that has gradually accumulated over many centuries, much of it slowly gathered from the sea by primitive means of reclamation. The area includes the *Waddenzee*, an extensive region of tidal flats that is a unique wildlife wetlands area. The wetlands region is highly prized as a primitive natural area in a country where this is in short supply.
- The *IJsselmeer* polderland is an area which is all reclaimed from the floor of the former Zuiderzee, and thus in a sense has no truly 'primitive' landscape of its own. A high percentage of this area was not lost to the water until the 13th century, and even Roman artifacts have been found here. The polderland here is stark, severely geometrical, and new-looking. The Dutch generally think of it as bleak and monotonous. Its true extent comes home when it is realized that one can take a leisurely drive there in a straight line for an hour before coming to the end of it.

It was the west that formed the 'cradle' of later civilization in the Low Countries. In this region, archeologists have discovered evidence of farms and fishing as early as 6,000 B.C. It is hard to think of any other place in the world where a 'time machine' journey back, imagining away all human intervention, would find such a totally different environment. But even without human modifications over thousands of years, it would have been quite unrecognizable: The presumed coastline of that time bears little resemblance to the one that can be traced through the last several centuries. Even in Roman times the coast had a strikingly different appearance from the one that appears in the first modern maps. Roman settlement and military occupation restricted itself mainly to the more hospitable southern region where the land was more predictable and secure. Large quantities of Roman artifacts have been found, including villas and military posts. The map of the coast in four different periods (Fig. 1.4) shows how many changes have taken place.

After about 700 B.C. the sea advanced far inland, washing away some unprotected peat areas and radically changing the shape of the environment. In 1282 a storm and a huge tidal wave broke through the dunes and greatly enlarged the inland sea, forming at the same time a wide entrance to it. The earliest form of human shaping of this environment began around 500 B.C. with the building of *terpen*, earthen mounds one to eight meters (4-25 ft.) high with an area large enough for anything from a single house or church to an entire village. These refuges from high water continued being built down to about 1000 A.D. They can be seen today mostly along the northern coast, and there are still about a thousand of them in existence. The first dikes were probably the result of the idea of building a string of terpen to form a wall, the first ones serving as levees along rivers and inlets. For centuries they were steep walls (rather close to what foreigners imagine dikes to look like) faced with wooden poles, and the whole system required constant rebuilding. These dikes evolved into the massive, mathematically designed gently-sloping defenses that are used today.

The Netherlands area taken as a whole poses a wide variety of different challenges to settlement, and requires an equal variety of responses for successful survival. People who settled in various parts of this region developed and evolved widely different types of economic activity, and this led to a rich variety of habits, rhythms of life, traditions, folklore and mythologies. As everywhere else, the old rhythms of agrarian life have been overtaken and nearly inundated by modern industrial society. Much of it, though, still finds ways of contributing today to the individual's sense of cultural identity.

In an older time, agrarian life determined the forms of villages that developed on high land, marshy land, along dikes, at dams, around fortification mounds ... and this variety of functional form is still clearly traceable. Regional particularism used to be communicated in style of dress: regional costume spoke a whole language of its own, telling about social and marital status, occupation, religion, region and even village. Very little of this survives today; disregarding those places where costumes are worn for exclusively tourist purposes, they persist only in a few relatively isolated pockets where some elements of local community life have survived. One of the

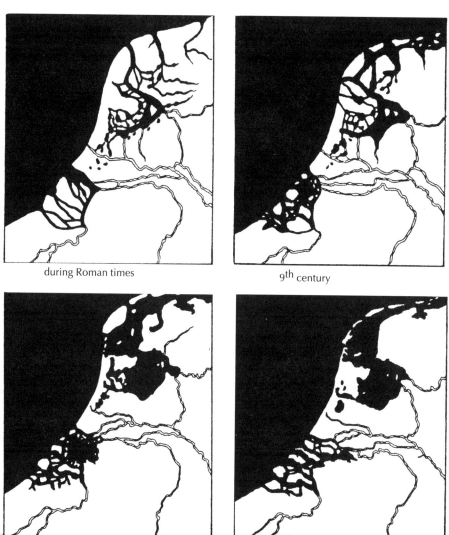

during Roman times

9th century

Fig. 1.4
The impact of the sea
during the centuries

13th century

17th century

most important ways in which regional culture was manifested was in speech, the dialects that evolved in relatively isolated communities. Today they are part of many people's consciousness of regional origin and loyalty—an identity that many cling to.

The towns that are so crucial to the development of the distinctive culture of the Netherlands began as primitive settlements in intimate cooperation with the environment. Today's important cities all owe their origins to a variety of geographical advantages. The city of Leiden, for instance, lies on a quiet northern arm of the Rhine that is hardly distinguishable from the surrounding canals (the bulk of the water of the Rhine joins the complicated network of rivers and enters the sea farther to the south). At one point in the marshy lowlands the Rhine split into two branches which rejoined a bit farther downstream. At this junction there was built, probably sometime in the

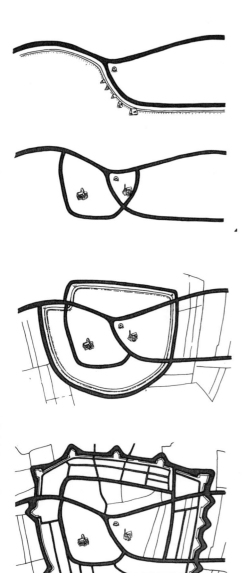

9th or 10th century but perhaps even earlier, a primitive mound to serve as observation post and fortification. By around the year 1000, a dike had been built along the river, and the first permanent settlement began along this. It still forms the main street of the modern city.

In the succeeding centuries, settlement in Leiden was built up in the area between the two branches of the river, and as the town expanded it was protected and defended by a wall and moat. These first successive expansions on to about 1300 are still easily traceable in the direction of the present streets and canals. As the town continued to expand, the streets and canals retained the direction and form of the polder drainage ditches and canals they replaced. Each stage in the long expansion of the city is thus clearly visible today, and the growth follows a logical pattern.

The moat surrounding the 17th-century fortification wall is still preserved intact. In the cities of the 'Low Netherlands' the countryside's network of waterways extends without interruption into the heart of the city.

In a physical environment in which the land lies low on the horizon and the sky dominates everywhere, meteorological conditions will inevitably assume a special significance. The climate is not a gentle, seductive one. Rainfall amounts to about 800 mm (31 inches) annually, distributed more or less evenly throughout the year. The most prominent feature of the weather is its variability and unpredictability within very short periods of time. Blaming various ills, habits, and even national character on the climate is part of Dutch folklore. The spaces in the physical environment have a large feel, the weather is always dramatic, and the world can have a grandioseness of the same kind that captivated the 17th-century painters who raised it to a form of mythology and fixed for all time our way of looking at nature in the Netherlands. The same monumental landscapes can still be seen there today.

Fig. 1.5
The stages in the settlement that became the city of Leiden.
(a) The Roman road and the mound at the junction of the arms of the Rhine; (b) The medieval town has extended toward the west and the south; (c) The town around 1500, with fortification wall; (d) The city in the 17th century, enclosed with its expanded fortifications; (e) an aerial view of the modern city.

It is impossible to list here even a small selection of the many general surveys of the Netherlands that are readily available. A few titles the reader may not come across immediately are:

Country Report: The Netherlands. London: The Economist Intelligence Unit. [Each annual series consists of four quarterly 'Reports' and one 'Country Profile'].

Dutch Crossing. A Journal of Low Countries Studies. London: Centre for Low Countries Studies, University College.

Fact Sheet. Rijswijk: Ministry of Welfare, Health and Cultural Affairs. [A series of regularly updated pamphlets on a variety of cultural matters, such as the press, broadcasting, film, public libraries, literature, the performing arts, museums, sports, health care, and general cultural policy. They may be requested free of charge from the ministry in Rijswijk.]

Holland Horizon. The Hague: Ministry of Foreign Affairs [Quarterly].

The Low Countries. Arts and Society in Flanders and the Netherlands. Rekkem (Belgium): Stichting Ons Erfdeel, 1993- (annual).

The Netherlands in Brief. The Hague: Ministry of Foreign Affairs, 1994.

The Netherlands in Focus. The Hague: Ministry of Foreign Affairs. [A series of regularly-updated booklets covering a wide variety of different aspects of the country. They may be gotten free of charge from the ministry in The Hague].

The quantity of up-to-the-minute information in English available on the Internet increases daily. Those who know, or can find out, how to use the World Wide Web will find home pages of the Netherlands Information Service and all of the major Ministries.

2 Shaping the space

The Dutch word *kunstwerk* has, from our point of view, two distinct meanings. On the one hand it refers to any 'work of art' such as painting or writing, and on the other it means anything other than the products of nature, what is made through human ingenuity. In the Netherlands, engineers use the word *kunstwerk* to refer to artifacts such as bridges, tunnels and locks. The fact that all these are referred to with the same word suggests that, although the Dutch are perfectly well able to distinguish a watercolor from a viaduct, it is not unnatural, from the Dutch point of view, to think of some manmade modifications of their environment as 'works of art'.

Eventually the inhabitants of the Lowlands were able to turn from passive protection from the water to the active enterprise of land reclamation. It was in the 17th century that this got underway on a large scale, when sharp rises in land values in the prosperous west made it economically advantageous. A start was made with the drainage of many of the lakes that had been created by the removal of peat and the incursions of the sea. The basic technique for land reclamation was as simple as it was ingenious. First a canal had to be dug around the watery or marshy area to be reclaimed and dikes built, then batteries of windmills pumped the water out of the area into the canal. One or two of these strings of mills still survive today as reminders of the past. This pumping did not of course solve the problem of excess water, because the surrounding land itself was normally below sea level and itself protected by dikes. The water, therefore, unless it could be discharged directly into a river or the sea, had to enter a complex system of waterways that carried it up by steps and eventually to the sea. It was in ways like this that a complicated water system arose, consisting of an almost infinite number of different water levels. This is the basis of today's nationwide water management system. The almost infinite variety of these constantly fluctuating water levels is

Fig. 2.1
Old polderland.
A portion of the province
of Zuid-Holland

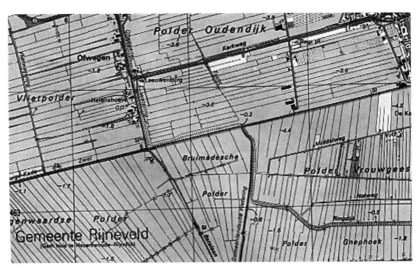

measured by means of the NAP (*Nieuw Amsterdams Peil* 'Amsterdam Ordnance Datum'). This is an agreed 'zero point', a sort of vertical Greenwich Meridian—prominently displayed in the lobby of the city hall in Amsterdam—used as the water standard throughout western Europe.

Quite early a system of rural corporations began developing, to deal with the organization and care of dikes, roads, bridges and mills. These have become known as *waterschappen*. This early example of a rurally-evolved democratic system is interesting because it was based on the principle of no taxation without representation, and a partyless system. Most of this organization is still in place today. Elections are still held independently of governmental ones, and membership is still based on landowner's franchise.

The entire western half of the Netherlands consists of a dense network of 'polders'.

A polder is a parcel of land that is protected from—and often reclaimed from—the water, where the ground water table can be regulated. The drawing shows in a simplified fashion how a typical polder operates, how water must be raised in stages to higher levels until it can be discharged. Moving all this water is seldom done today with windmills, but rather with huge electric turbines. The entire system has to be maintained on a continuous basis, and the costs of this are high. Constant dredging is necessary, from farmers' ditches to the broad transport canals, harbors, and channels from the sea. Even city canals: Amsterdam has some 80 km (50 mi.) of canals, around 335 km (210 mi.) in the whole municipal area. About 80,000 cubic meters (nearly three million cubic feet) of sludge must be cleaned out each year.

Everything that has to do with this vast undertaking of shaping water and land is ultimately under the supervision of the Ministry of *Verkeer en Waterstaat*, which might be translated 'Transport and Water Affairs'. This ministry manages the organization that does the actual work with the water, the department of *Rijkswaterstaat*, 'National Water Affairs'. It was only in the 19th century that competing local organizations came to be coordinated in a national effort.

Fig. 2.2
Schematic picture of a typical polder (just left of center), ringed by a canal in which water is stored, to be released into the river (right); this, in turn, is directly connected to the sea through the dunes (left).

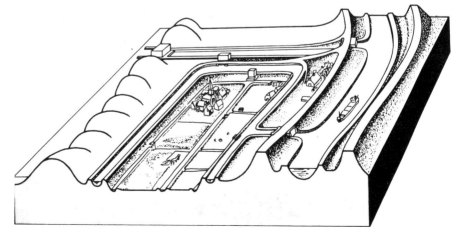

For centuries Dutch engineers have cast an eye at the huge bite out of the heart of the country called the *Zuiderzee* and conceived schemes to remain protected and at the same time gain large areas of useful land. The first thoroughly thought-out plan was proposed in 1667, but its ambition went far beyond the technological, organizational, and financial resources of the time. With the later development of technology it was possible to reclaim in 1852 the 18,000 hectares (45,000 acres) of the *Haarlemmermeer*, on part of which Amsterdam's Schiphol airport now stands. The plan finally adopted in this century for the Zuiderzee was that of Cornelis Lely, which provided for two major phases:

1. Construction of a barrier dam (the *Afsluitdijk*) across the narrowest mouth of the sea, a distance of about 30 km (20 mi); this would have the effect of converting the inland sea into a lake, which since it was fed by the IJssel River would eventually become fresh water.

2. Construction of dikes within this lake area to create five huge polders with a combined area of 165,000 ha (413,000 acres). The map shows the location and names of each of these, with the amount of land gained in each one.

The primary goal of all these polders was the gaining of additional agricultural land, and the first two, the Wieringermeer and Northeast polder, were

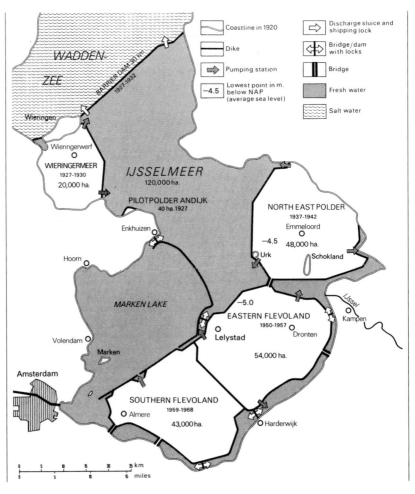

Fig. 2.3
The IJsselmeer polders

devoted almost entirely to this purpose. As time went on, planners have looked increasingly to the new land for residential and industrial purposes, the latter partly for providing employment for polder residents. The need for additional agricultural land is less pressing thanks to the rapid postwar integration of agriculture into an overall European structure. The possibility of reclaiming a final polder was discussed for many years before finally being decided against. All that now remains of that plan is a large dike running from the North Holland coast to Lelystad, which serves as a highway link and also to separate the IJsselmeer into two separate basins.

The reclamation of polders from the bottom of the IJsselmeer also resulted in the creation of a remarkable wildlife area, the *Oostvaardersplassen*, in a region between Almere and Lelystad that was originally intended for industrial use. A large area just inside the dike was somewhat lower than the rest, and after the surrounding polder was already under cultivation it remained marshy. Wetland wildlife developed here so quickly, and in such profusion, that it was set aside as a permanent wildlife preserve. It is one of the most important wetlands in western Europe.

The second of the two major shaping projects that have been altering the face of the modern Netherlands is the Delta Project. This is totally different from the IJsselmeer Project in that it involves little significant land reclamation and thus little introduction of whole new populations, but it is even more impressive in the boldness and grandeur of its design. It was not until a disastrous winter storm in 1953 flooded large areas of the southwest that it was decided to proceed immediately with an existing plan to connect the tips of all the islands with dikes, effectively reducing 800 km (500 mi) of exposure to the sea to 80 km (50 mi).

The map (Fig. 2.4) shows the extreme complexity of the area, with each section and branch of the water creating a special problem. The whole plan is conceived not as a 'wall' along the coast, but an intricate set of methods of working with the water, allowing it by stages progressively smaller access to the land. Inside, the waterways are protected by a variety of ingenious means of assuring a safe flow of water—mainly from the sea in tides and storms, but also spring floods from the rivers. This whole control process is 'alive' in its own way, it all interacts with the constant movement of the water and operates as a vast interacting mechanism.

The Delta Project is an engineering enterprise that, for sheer massiveness, is one of the boldest ever undertaken anywhere. It required, and stimulated, development of vast new areas of technology, and called for experimentation on a previously unheard-of scale. The phase of the Delta Plan that has claimed most worldwide attention is the construction of the barrier across the mouth of the *Oosterschelde* 'Eastern Scheldt'. Originally a solid dam was proposed, which would have sealed the largest of the estuaries off from the tides and created a 'stagnant' salt-water lake. But by the time the Oosterschelde dam was ready for completion, environmental concerns had grown to such strength that overwhelming protest was raised against the destruction of a complex and unique ecological zone.

So it was decided to build instead a movable barrier, which would allow the tides free flow and still provide protection from storm surges. This vast in-

Fig. 2.4
The Delta Project
(This page)

Fig. 2.5
The Oosterschelde
barrier in cross section
(Opposite page)

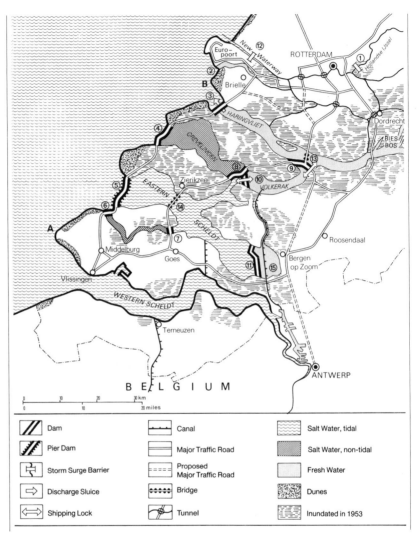

	Dam		Canal		Salt Water, tidal
	Pier Dam		Major Traffic Road		Salt Water, non-tidal
	Storm Surge Barrier		Proposed Major Traffic Road		Fresh Water
	Discharge Sluice		Bridge		Dunes
	Shipping Lock		Tunnel		Inundated in 1953

crease in complexity cost more than the whole rest of the Delta Project plus the IJsselmeer Project combined. The Eastern Scheldt estuary at the point where the barrier is constructed is 8 km (5 mi) wide, and it consists of three tidal channels each with a different rate of flow. The barrier consists of a structure of concrete, steel and stone that forms a frame for 62 huge steel gates which can be raised and lowered. The reinforced concrete piers on which these are hung are up to twelve stories high and weigh 18,000 tons apiece. The gates are each 41 m (135 ft.) wide, 5.5 m (18 ft.) thick, up to 12 m (39 ft.) high, and weigh up to 500 tons. The illustration shows, for instance in the size of the cars on the road along the top, the vastness of its scale and something of its complexity.

But the design and assembly of all this was only part of the engineering problem. Since it all had to be built on constantly shifting tidal sands of greatly differing depths, new means had to be designed to assure a firm foundation of even height. The most revolutionary aspect of the whole project was the

construction of enormous mats which had to be laid out in the tidal channels to a tolerance of only a few centimeters. The mats weigh 5600 tons each, are 36 cm (14 in.) thick, and are filled with sand and gravel. There are 750 of them, covering nearly five million square meters (over 50,000,000 sq. ft.) of sea floor. A complete factory had to be built on location to manufacture them. For the transportation and assembly of all these unprecedented structures, a whole fleet of vessels had to be designed, with strange shapes dictated by their specific functions. The Oosterschelde barrier was officially inaugurated by Queen Beatrix in October, 1986.

After a little more than thirty years, the Delta Project is as good as complete. A 22 meter (72 foot) high storm-surge barrier across the *Nieuwe Waterweg* west of Rotterdam is scheduled for completion in 1997. It has represented a national effort and shaping of the land of unprecedented proportions. Hydraulic engineering has become an important national symbol, and in the Netherlands the engineer is today's cousin, in social power and technological prestige, of the atomic physicist or the genetic engineer. It is interesting to note that the words 'Delta Project' have such luster now that they are coming into use in the language as a means of referring to any huge, all-inclusive, bold project involving any kind of engineering, even social. *Rijkswaterstaat* has been a powerful organization, but now a large part of it has been turned over to private hands.

The Delta region now consists of a wide variety of aquatic ecological communities created by the construction of dams, locks, barriers—changing the whole natural flow of the water down from the rivers and in from the sea. Thanks to the elaborate canalization of the Rhine, the entire 'Low' Netherlands forms a single, delicately balanced system of physical and ecological forces, a laboratory that is regulated on a continuous basis. A remarkable, and unanticipated, result of the Delta Project has been the appearance of several large new sandbanks off the coast, totaling 900 sq. km (348 sq. mi.) in area. Some of them have turned into stable, permanent islands and been given names. Engineers have numerous plans for reclaiming and using this land, which has attracted a wide variety of animal life, provided it can keep ahead of the natural rise in sea level. For years now, an annual average 6,000,000 cubic meters (nearly 8,000,000 cubic yards) of sand dredged from the floor of the North Sea has had to be added to the coast just to compensate for natural erosion.

A look at the map suggests that the Netherlands is indeed to a great extent a human 'work of art', a physical interacting mechanism on a scale that is not possible to find anywhere else. But many feel that the enterprise of shaping the existing Netherlands is surely as good as complete, there being relatively little that can be done to the physical environment without introducing intolerable alterations into an already delicately balanced interlocking network of uses—nearly every proposal to interfere with the existing landscape now calls forth massive opposition. In the next century, sea level is expected to rise by some 60 cm. (24 in.), which means that existing protection from the sea is inevitably going to become inadequate. This presents the country with several difficult alternatives (raising the level of the dikes, storm-surge barriers and bridges, abandoning parts of the country and making major efforts to protect the rest), all of which will be burdensomely expensive. 'Shaping the Netherlands' is an unending enterprise.

A foreign observer recently remarked 'when Dutch people speak about regional differences, which is frequently and with evident relish, they give the impression that the Netherlands is at least the size of Canada'. The shaping of the landscape and the creation of new environments, the tightly interlocking uses of the space, and the many levels of social organization to be considered in later chapters are all being carried on inside a space that is cramped indeed. To gain a sense of the true scale of it: the Netherlands occupies a total surface area of 37,360 square km (14,400 sq. mi.). It is roughly 160 km (100 mi.) average distance between the North Sea and the German border, and about 250 km (160 mi.) from the northern islands to the nearest border in the south. The distance by train from Rotterdam in the southwest to Groningen in the northeast is under 3 hours; from Amsterdam to Rotterdam, stopping at several of the most important cities, about an hour. The longest stretch, from the extreme southwest to the northeastern corner, can be driven at ordinary highway speed in about 4 hours. Put more picturesquely: Greater Paris would fit in this space just five times with hardly any room to spare, and it would only take four New Yorks to fill the Netherlands. The Dutch population stands at 15,400,000, which divided by 32,777 square km (12,655 sq. mi.) of habitable land space works out to 470 inhabitants per sq. km (1,217 per sq. mi.). The Netherlands is the most densely populated country in Europe, and after Bangladesh and Taiwan the 3rd most densely populated in the world.

What is all this detail packed into a small space? Let us take a rapid bird's-eye survey of the 12 provinces into which the country is divided, sweeping quickly over a lot of ground in order to get a sense of how truly different from each other in geography, economy and culture these regions can be.

NOORD-HOLLAND consists almost entirely of polderland in addition to the coastal dunes. The province contains one of the largest concentrations of population and industry, the capital Amsterdam and the nearby city of Haarlem. Industrial complexes include the large steel mills at the mouth of the North Sea Canal.

ZUID-HOLLAND is likewise made up mainly of the characteristic geometric water landscape of the polderland, and the province includes dunes, part of the river region in the south and the uppermost of the southwestern islands. It is the location of the lowest point in the Netherlands at 6.7 m (22 ft.) below sea level. It contains most of the balance of the population centers of the west, plus the largest center of heavy industry around Rotterdam. Together these two provinces—which until the 19th century were the single province 'Holland' from which the whole country took its informal name—have a disproportionate share of the economic weight and population density.

ZEELAND consists almost entirely of islands or former islands, now joined to each other or to the mainland. Because of its island nature it was one of the most isolated regions until the implementation of the Delta Plan provided links in the form of roads over the new dams and barriers. Within the provincial borders is also a strip of mainland, Zeeuws-Vlaanderen. The province has a concentration of heavy industry around Vlissingen in the south, and across the estuary in *Zeeuws-Vlaanderen*. Thanks to its greatly increased accessibility it has become a major recreational area.

UTRECHT lies at the geographical heart of the country, straddling the 'High' and 'Low' Netherlands. The northern part of the province contains lakes that form an important recreational area, and in the east is a range of low hills and forest. The city of Utrecht and its neighboring communities form the easternmost extension of the western urban complex.

NOORD-BRABANT lies south of most of the great rivers and mostly occupies land above sea level. It contains a varied ecology and many types of landscape. The province has a string of industrial towns that have their own special character and specialization but do not form part of the heavy-industry structure.

LIMBURG occupies the southernmost corner of the country, and at the same time is the location of its highest point at 321 m (1,053 ft.). It is an area of mainly rolling countryside with some hilly regions and limestone caves. Until fairly recently it was a prime mining region containing one of the largest coal mines in Europe. It is socially and linguistically complex, being the region where Dutch culture and dialects merge into those of the lower Rhineland. Its capital Maastricht, the Netherlands' oldest city, is rapidly growing in importance as the 'Pan-European city of tomorrow', but at the same time it is struggling to preserve its identity as it is being overwhelmed by foreigners.

GELDERLAND is the largest province, and probably the one with the greatest ecological contrasts. It consists of a fertile mixed-farming region in the east (the *Achterhoek*), a section of the country between the great rivers devoted largely to fruit orchards (the *Betuwe*), and the hilly forested area to the northeast (the *Veluwe*) that is one of the Netherlands' prime natural preserves.

OVERIJSSEL is an eastern province that lies mainly, though not entirely, in the 'High' area. In the east, along the border with Germany, is the region known as *Twente*, with a distinct landscape, farm type, and traditional local culture. The region around Hengelo and Enschede in the extreme east is one of the country's important industrial centers. Like the province of Gelderland, Overijssel has a particularly large number of aristocratic country homes that provide a reminder of a bygone culture and lend the province a certain 'aristocratic' flavor even today.

DRENTHE is a province that occupies somewhat higher ground, including a diagonal glacial ridge (the *Hondsrug*) that was occupied in prehistoric times. Previously there were extensive areas of peat; even today, with much of this gone, the province retains more than any other its mainly rural character. It is the most thinly populated of the provinces.

GRONINGEN is, like the two Hollands and Zeeland, a coastal province almost entirely in the 'Low' Netherlands. In the Dutch perception Groningen is a culturally 'remote' place, in spite of the fact that the city of Groningen was economically and politically prominent at a very early time. The province has an important industrial region and the fifth seaport of the Netherlands. The discovery of natural gas in the province has changed the relationship with the west.

FRIESLAND is geographically also a 'Low' coastal province with the most extensive area of lakes and waterways in the country—the lake area derived mainly from the removal of peat in older times. The province embraces as well the tidal *Waddenzee*, and most of the chain of islands that continue the line of the dunes in the north. Friesland is a province with a distinct regional culture and language, the one least fully 'homogenized' into a general Netherlands cultural identity.

FLEVOLAND consists entirely of land reclaimed from the bottom of the old Zuider Zee. The land area consists of the Northeast Polder attached to Overijssel, Eastern Flevoland and Southern Flevoland. The sense of 'pioneer' on land that has not simply been claimed and settled but created, still seems to be a dominant one in the new province (it became a full-fledged province in 1986), a place to make a fresh start. In addition to this, three major new cities have been created out of nothing, offering a chance for urban design according to an overall plan arising from the land itself.

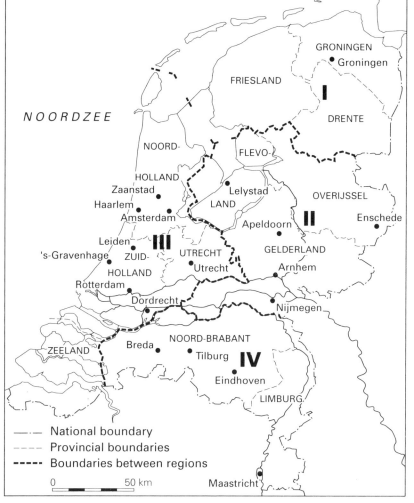

Fig. 2.6
The four economic-cultural regions.
I. THE NORTH, largely agrarian, consists of Friesland, Groningen and Drenthe.
II. THE EAST consists of Overijssel, Gelderland and the new province of Flevoland.
III. THE WEST consists of Noord-Holland, Zuid-Holland and Utrecht, with the major western urban cluster, the economic and industrial heart of the country. The Southwest includes only the province of Zeeland. Its former special identity preserved in distinctive dress, dialect and folklore has largely given way to an identity largely coinciding with the area of the Delta Project.
IV. THE SOUTH consists of Noord-Brabant and Limburg. The great rivers form the most prominent cultural boundary of the country, dividing it in Dutch consciousness into everything *beneden* ('below') *de Moerdijk* [the wide river mouth south of Rotterdam] from all that is 'above' it. Region IV is predominantly Catholic and its traditions and accent are distinctly different.

The title of this chapter is 'Shaping the space', but it could well have been something more catchy like 'The great jigsaw puzzle'. The fact is that agriculture, industry, urbanization, recreation and wildlife fit each other so neatly and are all so tightly interlocking that when we survey them we have to marvel at the stability of the whole that somehow still manages to preserve an openness to constant change. We will look at each carefully fitted piece in turn.

The map shows the geographical distribution of agriculture and horticulture. Of the total land area, 60% is used agriculturally, some 25% of this for crops and 32% pasture. The map also shows the much smaller (3.5%) but even more intensively exploited horticultural regions. Foremost among these are the flower and bulb districts along the dunes and in the province of Noord-Holland. The number of visitors to the Netherlands who come for the express purpose of experiencing untamed nature is no doubt small, but each year in April and May the world beats a path there to marvel at the spectacle

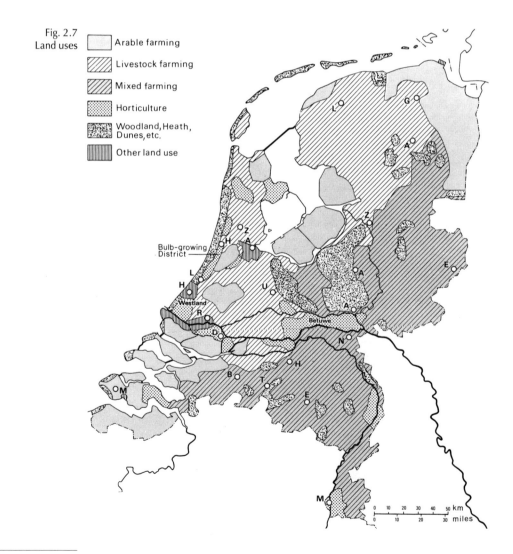

Fig. 2.7
Land uses

Arable farming

Livestock farming

Mixed farming

Horticulture

Woodland, Heath, Dunes, etc.

Other land use

ably intense colors neatly arranged in a severely geometric Mondrian-like design. The other horticultural activities are the orchard district between the rivers and the *Westland*, an extensive concentration of greenhouse culture. This relatively tiny area devoted to horticulture contributes some 25% of the Netherlands' total agricultural production.

The geographical aspect of industry is a complex one. Industry is concentrated primarily around the port areas of Rotterdam and Amsterdam, with a number of other major industrialized regions around the country. The development of industry in the Netherlands has always profited from the country's favorable central location and accessibility. In addition to these, the highly developed infrastructure has favored industrial development over the whole country. At the mouth of the North Sea Canal (*IJmond*) is the heart of the heavy-metals industry. Rotterdam is the center of the petroleum refining and processing, and chemical industries. A major industrial center lies in the eastern part of the Netherlands near the German border. With the decline in importance of textile manufacture, a region that once specialized heavily in weaving has been rescued by diversification from economic disaster. Another industrial region is located in the east of the province of Groningen and around the port of Delfzijl.

Natural gas deposits, one of the largest fields in the world, were discovered in 1959 in the province of Groningen. Since then a distribution grid has been laid over the whole country, natural gas is being exported, and income from natural gas has been an important factor in the highly-developed social-welfare program. Though the Netherlands does exploit its allotted share of the North Sea continental shelf for petroleum, nearly all the oil processed in the refineries in the Rotterdam area is imported.

The Netherlands has two operating nuclear power plants accounting for only 1.4% of the country's total energy output. Although sweeping increases in this have been proposed, public opposition to further nuclear development makes their future anything but clear.

The agricultural map shows the way urbanization fits into this tightly interlocking picture. Built-up areas, plus roads and waterways, occupy some 19% of the total area of the Netherlands. These are heavily clustered in the west, where they put constant pressure on agriculture and the environment.

The final piece in this geographical mosaic is the distribution of wildlife and recreational areas in the dunes, lakes and forests. Since there is no space for extensive natural areas, those that do exist are carefully managed and intensively used. The total forest, heath and dune area of the Netherlands amounts to a mere 13% of the total—forests occupying just 8% of the total land area. The country has only a little over 700,000 acres of forest land, and up to a fifth of this has suffered to some extent from the effects of acid rain—some of this is industrial, but another portion is traceable to the country's extremely intensive livestock population. This suggests the sobering thought that any effort to increase the Netherlands' competitive edge is increasingly likely to come at the expense of courting environmental collapse. The Waddenzee, the tidewater area between the Frisian Islands and the mainland in the north, and the Eastern Scheldt in the southwest are, together with the *Oostvaardersplassen* already mentioned, the main wildlife areas.

The chain of dunes stretching along the whole coast is an extensive natural area as well as an important source of water purification, but here recreational pressures are also at their most extreme. The seaside resorts are very heavily used in the summer by foreign tourists, especially from Germany.

Recreational areas are scattered around in greater abundance in the east than in the west—the hills in south Limburg, various places in the east, and water regions in Friesland and Zeeland; the large reclamation projects in the IJsselmeer have created many new recreational possibilities. Sailing, motorboats and windsurfing are enjoying an ever-increasing popularity in the Netherlands. To an outsider, one of the most remarkable aspects of the geographical distribution of natural areas is the care that is given to each small natural possibility—natural areas are nowhere very far away, and no extensive part of the country is allowed to turn exclusively industrial, residential or even agricultural.

But along with this, the preservation of the fragile, threatened natural environment is probably the Netherlands' major challenge of the '90s, intensified beyond what most countries are required to face. After the growing national worry about the Netherlands being full to bursting, the second national debate at the present time, rapidly coming more to the front of public discussion, is based on growing doubts about whether the environment can in fact stand the economic pressure brought to bear on it. During the last several years there has been a massive and intensive effort to keep environmental issues in full public discussion, and considerable far-sighted environmental legislation has already been enacted.

So it is not too great an exaggeration to claim that the Dutch live in one of the world's most wondrous full-scale jigsaw puzzles. The majority that lives in the western polderland, where most visitors gather their impressions of the country, are surrounded by a thoroughly designed landscape marked off in canals, dikes and all those other artifacts called *kunstwerken*, which at the beginning of this chapter we saw can also mean 'works of art'.

Observers throughout the centuries have reported sensing a peculiarly elegant balance of nature and the built environment. As we look today at the innumerable old prints that meticulously recorded a town and its surrounding countryside, we are indeed struck by the remarkable extent to which villages, fortified towns and cities appear to grow organically out of the landscape itself. In both their origins and their later successive expansions, these urban developments give plain evidence of an uninterrupted intricate interaction with the environment, which in the western landscapes means with water. The landscape of the Netherlands is an integrated design, the elements of its form continued to the edge of the sea in the monumental present-day 'works of art' that relate land and water.

Atlas van Nederland. The Hague: Staatsuitgeverij, 1985-1990. [A set of twenty 24-page books in large format, covering (Dutch-only text) all aspects of geography in its widest sense].

Compact Geography of the Netherlands. Utrecht: Information and Documentation Centre for the Geography of the Netherlands, 1994. [A thorough, lavishly illustrated 56-page survey of all geographical aspects of the Netherlands, including population distribution, the cities, physical planning, and the environment. It is available from the IDG or from Dutch consulates and embassies.]
The IDG also publishes a biennial English-language *Bulletin* which contains lead articles and updated bibliographical information on a variety of special geographical topics. In alternate years the Center publishes the IDG *Newsletter*.

*The Delta Project. Preserving the Environment and Securing Zeeland against Floodin*g. The Hague: Ministry of Transport and Public Works, 1989.

Van Duin, R., and F. Kwaad (eds.), *The Pocket Guide to the Zuyder Zee Project*. Lelystad: Rijksdienst IJsselmeerpolders, 1990.

Facts and Figures. Highlights of Dutch Agriculture, Nature Management and Fisheries. The Hague: Ministry of Agriculture, Nature Management and Fisheries (published annually).

Lambert, Audrey M., *The Making of the Dutch Landscape: An Historical Geography of the Netherlands*. London: Academic Press, 2nd ed. 1985.

De Smidt, Marc, and Egbert Wever, *An Industrial Geography of the Netherlands: An International Perspective*. London/New York: Routledge, 1990.

Van de Ven, G.P. (ed.), *Man-Made Lowlands. History of Water Management and Land Reclamation in the Netherlands*. Utrecht: Matrijs, 2nd ed. 1994.

3   The closely interlocking systems

The 'jigsaw puzzle' metaphor, tempting as it may have been, breaks down at this point and needs to be abandoned. We need to introduce some new dimensions and look at the interacting of a number of systems that are 'overlaid' on each other, as we might say, at many levels. Surveying these will lead us into how the Dutch are planning their space for the decades to come.

After the national and provincial, the municipality as an administrative unit is not third in importance, as its relative size would seem to imply, but second to—and in some ways coordinate with—the national level. The country is divided into some 650 municipalities; the general map of the Netherlands shows the seventeen largest cities. Today there is a trend toward decentralization and regionalization, these economic 'regions' standing between the municipal and the provincial level. Such joining together of municipalities for the furthering of regional economic issues has as yet no final official status, though plans are far advanced that will form them into administrative units independent of—and probably eventually replacing—the provinces. Some day the entire country may be organized into a number of 'regions' instead of the provinces, whose borders were often decided by conquests in a forgotten past. The first of these new 'city provinces' might be that of Rotterdam and its surrounding economic region, carved out of the existing province of Zuid-Holland.

This urban network is securely knit by many overlaid systems of interacting infrastructure networks: waterways, roads, railroads, air traffic, communications. The waterway system is interconnected with the water transport system that spans western Europe, in which it occupies a central location. The network carries 17% of inland goods, 22% when counted as ton per kilometer (l990). Since the greatest proportion of the traffic goes across the border, its share in international traffic is even higher. The importance and density of this network, which is the traditional backbone of freight transport in the country, has meant that any road or rail construction can be done only at extremely high cost. And yet both these systems interweave everywhere with the water network, the canal systems.

The highway system now carries about 60% of the commercial transport in the Netherlands. The Dutch began their modern history 400 to 500 years ago as commercial carriers, and in the European context they retain this lead in the truck traffic of today. Commercial traffic, however, is not the most heavy user of the highway network. Private car registrations have multiplied so rapidly that only the most determined planning has been able to keep up with them. Before the Second World War there were a mere 100,000 automobiles, now there are 6,000,000 registrations and about 7,500,000 are expected by the year 2000—by which time according to a government estimate fully 15% of the Netherlands will have been paved over! Just between 1986 and 1989, use of private automobiles on main roads grew by no less than

20%. Schools in the three large regions into which the country is divided take their summer vacations at staggered times in order to avoid overloading of the transportation and recreation systems. Finally, in addition to the motor-road network there is a system of bicycle roads and paths that is over 19,000 km (12,000 mi.) long—about 12,000 km (7,500 mi.) of this outside urban areas. There are 16,000,000 bicycles in use in the Netherlands, which means that they outnumber inhabitants of the country.

Whereas in the last forty years or so attention has been heavily on the highway system, emphasis—in public discussion but also in the budget—is now shifting to rail transportation and other forms of public transport. The management of the national railway system is now in private hands. The total length of the rail net is 2798 km (1737 mi.). The entire domestic railroad timetable repeats every hour, and a considerable part of it every half hour. In 1990 the railroad moved over twenty million tons of freight, three quarters of it across the border. An additional network, not shown on the map, is urban and interurban transportation. A single standard ticket available in train stations, post offices, tourist offices and the like is used on all streetcars and buses throughout the country.

Even without this growth, increasingly hopeless traffic jams have led to the 'Rail 21' plan scheduled to become a reality in the year 2005. Already the strong emphasis given to the railroads is visible in centrally-located, highly visible station complexes in Leiden, Almere and Lelystad. And the network is being expanded in a European direction as well. In 1996 the extension toward the north of the originally French TGV line will be completed; these high-speed trains will be traveling at full speed north to Amsterdam by 2003. If the distance between Rotterdam and Amsterdam is to be covered in the projected half hour (it now takes 1 hour), the TGV will require its own roadbed. This is still highly controversial because it will probably mean sacrificing some of the relatively unurbanized 'Green Heart' in the western area, to be discussed in the next chapter. There has even been a proposal to run the train through a tunnel under most of this area. An eastern, freight-only line, the Betuwe Line, linking Rotterdam to Germany, is scheduled to be ready about the same time but has become even more fiercely controversial than the high-speed line because of its disruption of pastoral living condi-

Fig. 3.1
Motor vehicle density in seven industrial countries: number of vehicles per square kilometer.
The numbers of vehicles per square mile are: The Netherlands 332, Belgium 218, Germany 186, United Kingdom 153, Japan 122, France 73 and the United States 31.
Since this chart was made, the density has risen: As of 1994 the Netherlands has 145 per sq. km. (375 per sq. mi.). In the next century this will rise to 200 per sq. km. (520 per sq. mi.).

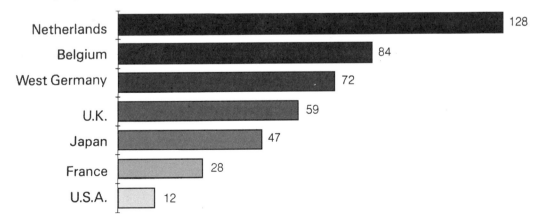

Netherlands	128
Belgium	84
West Germany	72
U.K.	59
Japan	47
France	28
U.S.A.	12

Fig. 3.2
The Netherlands'
railway system

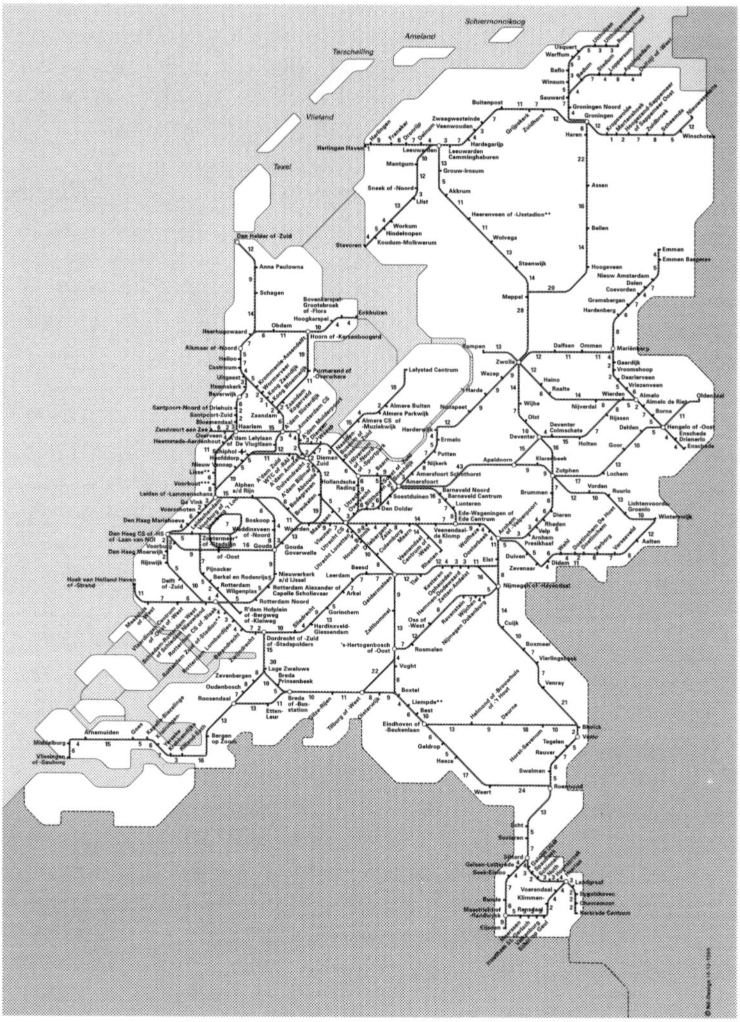

tions all along its route. Both will probably run through tunnels for part of their routes. After 2000, the High Speed Train is also to run across the country to Germany.

Domestic air traffic is relatively insignificant because of the small size of the country. Internationally the Netherlands depends heavily on air traffic, among other things for the transport of large quantities of highly perishable goods such as cut flowers. Schiphol international airport near Amsterdam (so named because it occupies a polder that until the 19th century was a harbor for ships) in 1994 handled over 23,000,000 passengers and over 800,000 tons of air freight in almost 300,000 flights. *KLM (Koninklijke Luchtvaart Maatschappij)* is a company that began in 1920, and as are all major national airlines, it is a not unimportant 'face' of the country abroad. Plans for the year 2000 have the airport handling 30,000,000 passengers and one million tons of freight per year, and development into a European distribution center equal to Rotterdam's role in water traffic. The new integrated Europe is being served by five main airline terminals, and Schiphol has every intention of being one of them. Competition for business is extremely intense, and Schiphol does not hesitate to exploit the fact that it is regularly voted the best-run airport in Europe.

The communications aspect of the infrastructure can be dealt with in passing —they are densely organized, but not fundamentally different from systems elsewhere in Europe. The Post and Telegraph service, which in most countries remains in government hands, has recently been largely turned over to private contractors for daily management, while remaining a public company. It is yet another example of the current trend all through the public sector toward privatization. This privatized PTT, now called *Koninklijke PTT Nederland*, consists of the postal system itself and the telephone system, now PTT Telecommunications. Besides the telephone system this now includes teletext and new computer services, part of the enormous expansion of communications currently being undertaken. The Netherlands claims to have been the first to offer 'electronic money' to the general public on the Internet, where is has the world's second-highest density of usage.

There are two coordinate savings systems, the *postgiro* run by the PTT and *bankgiro* by banks. The largest of the banks, ABN-Amro, is 18th in the world, and 6th in Europe. Payment traffic is highly efficient, much of it moving by way of the giro system and 'Euro-checks' which represent a very low cost to the user. This has meant that up until now relatively little use has been made of ordinary check systems or the credit card, but the latter is coming to be more and more accepted.

There is one popular image of Dutch society that, unlike most of them, comes reasonably close to real facts: the role the Dutch have played and are still playing in the physical creation of their own land. But while this may be dramatic enough, water management and land reclamation is only one feature of the total management of the space. The Netherlands is facing and attempting to solve problems now that more and more will be worldwide problems. It is the pressure of large-scale social, economic and technological change that has evoked the society's response of evolving a highly-developed system of discussion, compromise and implementation, an incorporation of change into the most basic attitudes in decision-making. They have, in other words, learned to view their space not as an object but as a process.

Agriculture in the past was fragmented and subject only to local control. Because of local traditions of land inheritance, many holdings became so small as to be unworkable, and by the end of the 19th century this had become critical. Reallotment and rationalization of the whole agricultural picture was originally the main reason for centralized policy-making. In the past thirty years there have been many changes that directly affect physical planning: the size of holdings has increased but agricultural land has been lost to development and highways; greenhouse horticulture has expanded its area, evolved a complex structure and now employs a complete artificial climate electronically regulated by computer. Specialization has greatly increased in all phases, heralding the end of traditional mixed farming. As elsewhere, agriculture is rapidly becoming a large-scale and expensive undertaking. But it makes a major contribution to the economy.

The Netherlands became a leader in the '50s in the new petrochemical industry, helped in no small way by the advantage of the central location of the port of Rotterdam. Its development into an industrial center, with an ambitious seaport expansion, was pursued vigorously in the '50s and '60s. In the '70s reversals in the industry led to needed diversification. In light of all this, physical planning for industrial development has become more sophisticated as regional policy has had to be integrated with overall planning and with the national picture.

After agriculture and industry, the third—and most significant—aspect of change has been rapid population expansion and the resulting pressure from housing, infrastructure and recreation. One reason for even greater pressure on previously unbuilt-up areas was the high level of migration away from the cities in the '60s—reversing a previous trend. Construction of shopping centers, office buildings and streets lowered the average occupancy rate in center cities, and city population fell sharply. The resulting suburbanization predictably brought a great increase in commuting. Because of the high costs of building, houses in the Netherlands have always been small. Expectations have slowly risen, and housing construction has steadily tended to provide for a higher average amount of space. But the space-saving large apartment buildings of the '60s and early '70s have not found favor, and housing has returned to the 'neighborhood' style. A chronic housing shortage, aggravated by destruction of some 10% of all housing during the Second World War, is added to by rapid population growth and the rising demand for 1- and 2-person housing.

Some environmental issues in recent years have been highly publicized and occasioned vigorous debate. The number of seals in the Waddenzee was found to have dropped drastically, some wetlands along the northern coast were claimed for a military reservation, an entire hill in the province of Limburg was excavated for marl for the cement industry (to get some sense of the impact of what may seem like a trivial loss, remember the country does not have all that many hills to throw away!), and the Delta Project engineers planned to seal off the wide *Oosterschelde* estuary and thereby destroy the tidewater ecology. The last of these resulted in the construction of the enormously expensive storm-surge barrier described in the previous chapter. But response to all these has been on individual initiative, in the form of instance-by-instance organized protest and public action. The total problem is far more pervasive than this and is now being dealt with in the form of a national environmental plan.

Inland waters suffer from the pollution of the rivers, particularly the Rhine and to an only slightly lesser extent the Meuse. The location of the Netherlands at the outlet of what is often called the 'sewer of Europe' creates gigantic problems in provision of drinking water. It is true, though, that thanks to firm international agreements the purity of the Rhine has been slowly improving. The fresh-water reservoirs created as part of the Delta Project are part of the solution; the dunes are also a heavily used resource in water purification. Air pollution is much less easy to localize than are other types. One main source is the industrial area in the vicinity of Rotterdam, aggravated by the fact that the prevailing winds are from the west or southwest. The other region of strongest air pollution is the extreme southwest, the source of which lies in Germany's Ruhr industrial area and thus outside the direct control of planners in the Netherlands.

There is no empty territory to expand into and no significant gains in land reclamation can be expected; an expanding population has reduced the options per person until the only possible response is an ever more intensive use of the space available. The practical limits to growth into agricultural and natural areas are by now also fully in view. It hardly comes as a surprise that the phrase 'the Netherlands is full!' is spoken with more and more conviction in public discussion. But as we will see in the chapters to follow, this simple phrase masks some troubling social questions.

Physical planning is defined in the Netherlands as 'the best conceivable adjustment of space and society to each other', and the whole planning process is viewed as 'an instrument for giving everyone a voice'. On the surface this looks like a remarkable example of something that is often claimed about the Netherlands, that democratic traditions have evolved out of the obligation to cooperate imposed by the land itself. As we will see, the process does not work quite this smoothly.

The first physical-planning milestone was the Housing Act of 1901, which among other things provided for a strict segregation of residential and rural, specifically prohibiting the building of houses scattered about the landscape. This has given the Netherlands the clean-cut look of a sharp separation between urbanized and pure countryside that is still one of its striking features today. The present phase of the national physical-planning enterprise was stimulated by the reconstruction and growing prosperity after World War II. The first of a series of Reports on Physical Planning appeared in 1960, and it was occupied mainly with planning for the western urbanized-industrial region. The department set up to deal with all these problems was—and still is—the *Rijksplanologische Dienst*, the 'National Physical Planning Agency'.

We can get a great deal of insight from comparing these successive Reports, especially from the way they have of revealing both changes in economic conditions and in society's attitudes. The Reports are always well publicized and public discussion is encouraged. There is a variety of national organizations concerned with physical planning, one of the most important of which is the *Raad van Advies voor de Ruimtelijke Ordening* (Advisory Council for Physical Planning), an independent advisory body of about forty members.

The Second Report, issued in 1966, was far more ambitious and for the first time took a close look at the balance of needs in the entire country. It operated on the assumption of a population of 20,000,000 by the year 2000, an estimate that has since been revised downward by some 25%. The solution to urbanization was seen in 'clustered decentralization'. This involved moving large numbers of a growing population away from the urban centers and spreading growth fairly evenly around the country, with particular emphasis on the more thinly-populated north.

The evolution of the whole planning process is perhaps its most interesting aspect to us. Most significant is the shift from what is called 'end-state' to 'process' planning. Planning has continually modified to adapt to changing social needs, and moreover it has evolved in a society which has a long-standing traditional reluctance to leave its affairs uncritically in the hands of central administrations. This traditional 'consensus culture', the inner workings of which is the theme of a good deal of this book, requires a large—and often unwieldy—amount of consultation, discussion and subsequent adjustment. It is time-consuming and therefore expensive, often contentious, and the resulting compromise is often satisfactory to no one.

The Third Report on physical planning was issued between 1973 and 1984. The previous plan for distributing population in concentrated smaller centers all around the country was abandoned, and attention turned toward intensive development of housing and infrastructure in the already urbanized western cities. The concept of the 'compact city' had been launched. These cities were to be strictly segregated by undeveloped buffer zones, to prevent the 'ribbon' development that has happened in many places in the world. Population spillover from these cities was to be gradually guided outward into designated 'growth towns' and 'growth centers'.

The Fourth Report made its first appearance in 1988. It was subtitled 'En route to 2015', though some predicted that change would come so rapidly that this document too would be obsolete before the year 2000. The Fourth Report entered quite a different world from that of its predecessor, and many of its proposals for the future were radical in a different way. Its appearance was attended by a great deal of publicity in the form of articles, broadcasts, conferences and even a video version distributed nationally. This Report, like its predecessors, was intended not to impose any conformity but to attract public attention as a step in building consensus. Physical planning in the Netherlands proceeds by consultation and negotiation.

It was without a doubt the prospect of greatly intensified competition in the new, economically integrated Europe that made for the Report's conspicuously strong emphasis on assuring the reinforcement of the country's international economic position. The reader of the Report watches a parade of bold new proposals made necessary—the public is assured—by the hard competition of the immediate future. The map (Fig. 3.3) shows the new designation of thirteen urban 'nodes', locations that are in the best competitive position to develop farther into high-quality residence and business centers. Their number has tended to grow as ever more municipalities protest being left out of the competition. The 'mainports' (the English word is used) of Rotterdam and Amsterdam are scheduled to undergo massive development, and both cities are to attract large new residential and work areas clustered around them. This will inevitably mean sacrifice of some of the sacrosanct green areas surrounding them.

Traffic plans were also radical, as planners proposed strict separation of commercial from other traffic. This was made necessary by the clash between the current daily traffic jams and the need to assure the free flow of business traffic, especially around the distribution centers of Amsterdam and Rotterdam. Taking some of the burden off the highway system will entail an effort to improve mass transportation unprecedented in scale, though the total capacity of the road network will nevertheless have to be increased by

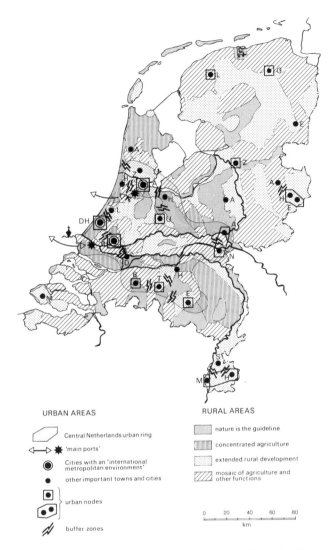

URBAN AREAS

⬡ Central Netherlands urban ring

◁—▷ ✳ 'main ports'

◉ Cities with an 'international metropolitan environment'

• other important towns and cities

⬡[•] urban nodes
⬡[• •]

⚡ buffer zones

RURAL AREAS

▦ nature is the guideline

▥ concentrated agriculture

▦ extended rural development

▨ mosaic of agriculture and other functions

0   20   40   60   80
km.

the year 2010, by as much as 40%. Upgrading of rail transport will involve large-scale expansion. All this will bring with it the sacrifice of still more space and the acceptance of still more congestion and pollution. A later version of the Fourth Report in 1990 shifted emphasis even more heavily to public transportation.

Possibly the most radical proposal of the Fourth Report was the use of space beyond just the western distribution centers. Where traditionally the green area enclosed by the large western cities (Amsterdam, The Hague, Rotterdam, Utrecht) has been considered the vital 'lung' of the most heavily urbanized area, this green, relatively undeveloped area whose main function will be agriculture plus recreation has been expanded until it comprises a strip through the entire middle of the country, from the western coast all the way to the German border. On the map it appears clearly, ringed by urban centers. Officially this looks like the final abandonment of the 'west' vs. 'rest' concept, though changing people's habits of thought will no doubt take quite a bit longer.

Most importantly in the eyes of some, the Fourth Report established for the first time a clear relationship between physical planning and environmental management, reflecting a greatly increased public awareness. In fact, in 1989 the government had changed and the minister responsible for environmental concerns was from the Social Democratic Party, one that stood for even tougher environmental measures. The result was 'Fourth Report Extra', which proposed even stricter regulations, for instance those on parking in favor of public transportation.

The Netherlands, at the mouth of three large rivers, is particularly vulnerable to pollution. Today an awareness of environmental concerns reaches well beyond the ministry of 'Housing, Physical Planning and Environmental Policy' into more and more aspects of the domains of other ministries, and thus of other aspects of society. The government's *Nationaal milieubeleidsplan* ('National Environmental Policy Plan') still holds a unique place in the world as the first laying down of the outlines of a permanently sustainable society into the foreseeable future. What is of interest to us in all this is not so much the physical details as the serious attempts to get and keep public involvement in the ongoing discussion.

The Netherlands is, as mentioned above, the first country to find itself faced with all the strains of an expanding economy and technology, and to meet head-on all the intolerable strains being placed on the whole environment. More and more the Dutch public is asking whether all this economic competition, dictated partly by outside economic conditions (for instance the highway network, which is used more and more for international traffic), is really worth the sacrifices in quality of life that the Dutch are being asked to make.

FURTHER READING

Atlas van Nederland (Ch. 2) [Especially vol. 11 'Poort van Europa', vol. 12 'Infrastructuur' and vol. 19 'Stadsinrichting'].

Environmental Issues in the Netherlands Today. Special theme issue of *Dutch Crossing: A Journal of Low Countries Studies,* No. 50 (winter 1993). London: Centre for Low Countries Studies, University College.

Faludi, Andreas and Arnold van der Valk, *Rule and Order: Dutch Planning Doctrine in the Twentieth Century.* The GeoJournal Library, vol. 28. Dordrecht: Kluwer, 1994.

Groen, Maurits (ed.), *To Choose or to Lose: National Environmental Policy Plan.* The Hague: SDU, 1989.

Langeweg, F., *Concern for Tomorrow: A National Environmental Survey 1985-2010.* Bilthoven: RIVM, 1989.

On the Road to 2015. Comprehensive Summary of the Fourth Report on Physical Planning in the Netherlands. The Hague: Ministry of Housing, Physical Planning and the Environment, 1988. See also the same Ministry's Comprehensive Summary of the Fourth Report (EXTRA) on Physical Planning in the Netherlands. 1991.

4 The Randstad

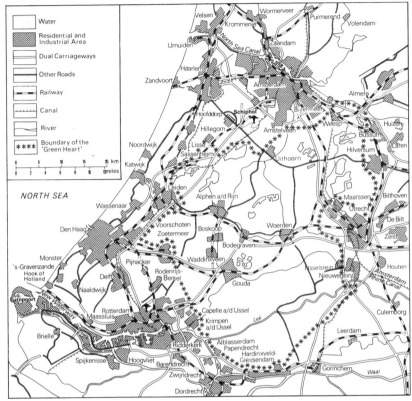

Legend:
- Water
- Residential and Industrial Area
- Dual Carriageways
- Other Roads
- Railway
- Canal
- River
- **** Boundary of the 'Green Heart'

0 5 10 15 20 km
0 2 4 6 8 10 miles

NORTH SEA

Fig. 4.1
The Randstad

The name *Randstad* means 'city along the edge', but rather than adopt one of the current English translations of it we will simply use the Dutch name. It is a string of cities—eight of the 21 municipalities of over 100,000 population —forming a crescent-shaped region around a more or less open center. This urbanized region spreads over parts of three provinces and lies in its entirety in the 'Low' Netherlands. Its relatively unurbanized 'hollow center' gives the Randstad a radically different appearance from any other large metropolis. It is called the 'Green Heart', a brilliantly-conceived metaphor that is crucial to all Randstad planning. There are two inviolable components in the planning of the Randstad region: one is distinct separation of the major urban centers by 'green' functions (the 'buffer zones' indicated by the jagged lines on the map), whether these be agriculture, recreation or natural preserves. The other is permanent maintenance (albeit in the face of constant nibbling-away) of a relatively lightly developed heartland. But because of the conspicuously favorable location of green-heart cities such as Gouda, restriction of urbanization has proved extremely difficult in practice. The increasing decentralization of planning has only added to this difficulty. The functional and spatial distinctness of each of the component cities is without a doubt the most significant aspect of the Randstad concept.

The Randstad today includes a high percentage of the prominent social-cultural institutions, including the government and industrial centers, six universities, and headquarters of the mass media, railroads and meteorological services. From the frame of reference of the Randstad, all the rest of the country is apt to be thought of as the 'provinces', and its inhabitants tend to feel attachment to the usual metropolitan life style. It is the center of Dutch history, culture, economic activity and planning, and it is home to some 44% of the total population in 18% of the land, an area with a diameter of at most 74 km (about 47 miles). Its name, however, is strictly an informal one: it has no official status and does not correspond to any administrative entity. Even though the Randstad is the world's 28th metropolis, it is possible to find only individual city maps, but never one of the 'Randstad metropolitan area'.

The dotted line on the Randstad map (Fig. 4.1) shows the approximate natural division into a 'northern wing' and a 'southern wing'. The northern Randstad wing is dominated by Amsterdam, with its satellite industrial centers of Zaanstad and IJmuiden. This northern half is the center of the heavy-metals industry, and of flower production and distribution. It also includes the radio-TV center of Hilversum and the city of Utrecht. A cluster of distinct, semi-autonomous urban centers with a clear 'division of labor' very much like this was a notable feature of Amsterdam and its neighbors at least as early as the 17th century. The Amsterdam area being the most heavily urbanized conglomerate in the country, it is naturally one of the prime focal points for national physical planning efforts. The new city of Almere, and to a lesser extent Lelystad, has been planned because of the inevitability of Flevoland's southern region figuring in the city's population spillover.

The southern Randstad wing is dominated, at least economically, by Rotterdam and its ports area stretching all the way to the coast, the center of the petrochemical and chemical industries. As already noted, there is increasing evolution of a reorganization of the country by economic regions where mutual cooperation is already strong. The first one of these to be given official status will be the *Rijnmond* region, the cluster of economically interdependent communities in the region around Rotterdam. The proposal has long been to give it provincial authority, directly under the national government. Though the inhabitants of the city have clearly expressed their opposition to having their city reorganized into more manageable-sized municipalities, the evolution toward some form of *stadsprovincie* ('city province') is pro bably inescapable.

At the heart of policy is the refusal to allow the development of a single megalopolis— or even two of them—in favor of a delicately-balanced system of coordinate units. As a major metropolitan area this fact alone makes the Randstad unique in the world. As we saw, it plays a crucial role in planning for economic development and competition on a world scale in the immediate future. There are forces operating in the opposite direction, however. Not only is the Randstad as a whole central to planning, with the two cities Amsterdam and Rotterdam to become 'mainports' in a new European world in which *Randstad Wereldstad* functions, as a unit, as distribution center. But business interests are overtaking even these bold visions. In the sharp competition among world cities for commercial prominence, the Randstad is viewed—and pushed—more and more as a single region, treating competition among the urban centers that make it up as an anachronism. The Dutch are only beginning to adjust to this abrupt enlargement in scale.

The numerous social functions of the Randstad are all in a dynamic, if often uneasy, tension with each other that is viewed as a permanent, ongoing harmony. It can be seen as an experiment in orderly transition from a natural environment into a totally planned one. If this is in some ways a disquieting look at the future for more and more of the world, at least the Dutch seem to be helping the rest of us look at it squarely.

The Randstad is a dense structure of a number of cities of various sizes, but the real focal points amount to only four. Let us take a closer look at each of these in turn.

UTRECHT The city is one of the oldest in the Netherlands. It began as a Roman town, one of a string of settlements on the highway along the Lower Rhine at the northern edge of the empire. It played a crucial role in the Christianization of the Low Countries as early as the seventh century. During the late Middle Ages the city and its surrounding region (more or less corresponding to the present province of Utrecht) were church lands administered by the archbishop. Today the province is still referred to informally as the *Sticht*, which really means 'bishopric'. The city's location on the busy river and its central geographical position made it an important trade center. During the centuries, its attractive location between a watery, lake area to the west and ranges of wooded hills to the east made it a residential center as well. The city developed a conservative, gracious life style that is still part of its reputation.

Fig. 4.2
The edge of the old section of Utrecht dominated by Hoog Catharijne

Today Utrecht finds itself 'out on the edge' of the Randstad but nevertheless very much part of the heart of the country's commercial life. The city is the national headquarters of the *Nederlandse Spoorwegen* (the railway system), and the NS has been indirectly or even directly responsible for a significant share of the city's current economic development. The city's location at the focal point of rail and highway networks has stimulated development of a wide variety of commercial enterprises, most important of which is probably the *Jaarbeurs*, called 'annual fair' but in reality in operation throughout the year for exhibitions, trade fairs and an endless variety of conferences. The *Koninklijke Jaarbeurs*, located next to the rail terminal, is a conference center that hosts around 25,000 meetings per year (that works out to a new one each hour during a 12-hour day!). The center claims 9th place internationally for conferences.

It was the railroad administration that conceived and brought into reality a major expansion of this, a diversified commercial center housed in a modern complex that is connected—all indoors—with both Jaarbeurs and railroad terminal. *Hoog Catharijne* is a labyrinthine mall with theaters, shops, and spaces for exhibitions, conferences, offices and even residences. Pedestrian traffic is all segregated from vehicular traffic, and rail, bus and parking are all within a few minutes' walk. It claims about twenty million visitors annually. But the use of rail travel is growing so rapidly and will continue to grow in the future (by the turn of the century, the railroad expects to be handling three times the number of passengers it now has), that much of all this will have to be rebuilt and expanded. Because of the heavy emphasis on public transportation in the future, this expansion is being vigorously pursued as the area is seen as an ideal office location.

The old center of Utrecht, gathered around the focal point of the *Domtoren* (cathedral tower), is only 10 minutes by foot. The planning and design problems in forming a transition between an old center city with its densely-packed small buildings and winding narrow streets, and a gleaming multistory commercial center were considerable, and not everyone will agree that it has been managed successfully. The Dutch refer to this process by which the old mixed-function urban centers are transformed into massive, exclusively commercial concentrations as *cityvorming*, using the borrowed word 'city' for a phenomenon felt to be imported from abroad.

THE HAGUE In the 13th century one of the counts of Holland laid out a hunting preserve and residence on some higher land at the edge of the dunes, a function that is still preserved in the official name *'s-Gravenhage*, although this is coming to sound more and more old-fashioned and the city almost always goes by the more informal name *Den Haag*. Around this residence there developed a full-fledged if still modest court, visible in today's *Ridderzaal* (Knights' Hall) in the center of the parliament complex. The Hague thus has the unusual distinction of being a rare conspicuous reminder of the landed aristocracy, a class that never played a dominant role in the Netherlands. One of the city's proudest possessions is the small gem known as the world-famous Mauritshuis museum. This 17th-century house standing right in the heart of the present-day metropolitan center still serenely offers, with its perfect harmony of building, atmosphere and paintings, a concise overview of

Fig. 4.3
The Hague,
Parliament buildings

life in that spot when The Hague was in its heyday in the 'Golden Age' and the residence of rulers and aristocrats. For a combination of reasons, this 'aristocratic' flavor has lingered in the city until the present day, in the form of a hard-to-define quiet elegance, graciousness and reserve. The city is still primarily a residential one, and its inhabitants are generally thought of a smugly bourgeois and a bit condescending.

Sometimes called 'the desk of the Netherlands', it has traditionally been a city of civil servants, with particularly strong ties to the East Indies. Even though the original East Indies Company was founded and run in Amsterdam, upper-level officials from the later colonies settled in The Hague, creating a whole sub-culture of 'better' families. This society was preserved for all time in the works of the novelist Louis Couperus. But the city was not only the home of those with aristocratic pretensions. It received large-scale migration from the Indies, creating whole 'Indies' neighborhoods, and it became the home of a wide variety of philosophically radical but politically and socially conservative groups, mostly living in genteel poverty.

If asked to define 'capital city', most of us—and most dictionaries—will tend to say something like 'the seat of the government and/or the official residence of the head of state'. By both these criteria, The Hague should be the capital of the Netherlands, but nevertheless it is not. In the Dutch scheme of things, the presence of parliament, most of the foreign embassies, and the official palace of the royal family are merely the city's assigned function in the whole, while Amsterdam is assigned the role of 'capital', apparently for no more compelling reason than that the constitution states 'the investiture of the king shall take place in Amsterdam'. The rapid development of governmental and business functions has completely transformed both the society and the face of The Hague. The old, somewhat quaint Hague society has been pushed aside by an influx of technocrats and managers and the large population of mostly white-collar workers that comes with them.

Fig. 4.4
The modern city of
Rotterdam

Cityvorming has invaded and revolutionized the architectural design of The Hague more brutally than any other city in the Netherlands. A new central railroad station, the new stark-white Royal Library, a cluster of large Ministries buildings, the headquarters of the postal banking service and a series of other large office buildings have all created a glass-and-concrete city in which no effort has been made to provide a transition from the older sections of town or integrate new and old. Part of this is because The Hague has only a fraction of the land available to other Randstad cities, and thus has practically no space to expand into. An artificial island in the form of a 42 sq.km. (16 sq.mi) strip along the coast is being planned.

ROTTERDAM The city is at the mouths of the Rhine and Meuse rivers, and forms an entry to a vast rail, highway and waterway network stretching across Europe. A circle with a 500-km (311 mi.) radius drawn around it encompasses a population—and therefore potential market—of 160 million, and a 1000-km (621 mi.) circle some 300 million. Rotterdam began its existence in the 13th century as a dam on a little stream called the Rotte, and over the centuries developed steadily as a fishing and trading port and later manufacturing and shipbuilding center. In May 1940 it was firebombed by the Germans and the whole central city was almost completely destroyed. At the end of the war, much of the harbor area was destroyed by the retreating German army. Plans for reconstruction were begun immediately and developed all during the war years, though construction did not begin until the end of the war. Right at the start, the decision was made not to try to rebuild the old, crowded port city but to replan it completely along modern, spacious lines. Today Rotterdam is a city of wide, straight streets and boulevards, though this deliberate break with the past made it difficult for some prewar inhabitants to resume life in the city after its reconstruction.

Modern Rotterdam was designed around the deliberate though not rigid idea of clear separation of functions: business and administrative, shipping, residence, entertainment. As more and more new neighborhoods were constructed where old ones had been, attention in the area of the *Oude Haven* (Old Harbor) returned to an older concept of a compact, multi-function city. This area is one of Rotterdam's showplaces, a deliberately crowded, intimate, jumbled neighborhood along old lines, with something of a 'Mediterranean' look. Walking around there is an experience of being in an old, dense city with lively geometrical forms all around and above. This is nowhere more strikingly suggested than in the geometrically playful 'pile dwellings' built right up to the water's edge.

It was the port area of Rotterdam that received first priority for development, and it followed the lines of an ambitious and optimistic plan that was designed to capture and hold first place in Europe. Since the 19th century, when the port was in the heart of the city, with the development of more and more petrochemical industries and the necessity for handling increasingly larger ships, the port area has moved steadily westward, a development that culminated in the construction of the Europort, on a reclaimed and filled-in area at the mouth of the river jutting out into the sea.

Fig. 4.5
The development
of the *Oude Haven*

Statistics for Rotterdam-Europort are an exercise in large numbers, which one quotes only with some hesitation because they are so rapidly superseded. The port is now handling about 300,000,000 tons of cargo a year, making it still the world's busiest port. More than 180,000 inland waterway vessels and 32,000 seagoing vessels annually call at Rotterdam. Ships are unloaded and sent on their way in an average of 15 hours. It is the world's fourth container terminal, with well over a million being handled each year. Managing all this requires endless maintenance, mainly in the form of dredging, enough scooped up each year to fill seven supertankers. The dangerous, treacherously shifting offshore sands require a team of highly trained pilots, 300 of them just for Rotterdam. The 'Traffic Center Hook' is the nerve center for all the shipping lanes, a modern computerized traffic-control system that is on a level of sophistication of those at large airports.

Rotterdam is a working city, highly conscious of its debt and responsibility to its vast hinterland of Europe. There is a saying 'When you buy a shirt in Rotterdam, it comes with the sleeves already rolled up'. Its inhabitants tend to be impatient with the past, pragmatic and businesslike. It has somewhat of a 'blue-collar' reputation, but culturally goes well beyond this by building on its avant-garde image. It is by all accounts the architectural showcase of the country, and hosts an increasing number of cultural festivals of a wide variety of types. This robustness and cultural ambition make for an ongoing, intense rivalry between Rotterdam and Amsterdam, extending all the way down to regular fights between supporters of the two cities' nationally-famous soccer teams. The cartoon shows eloquently the resentment Rotterdammers are apt to feel about the arrogance of Amsterdam.

Fig. 4.6
In what should be a duet, Rotterdam is apt to find itself upstaged by Amsterdam

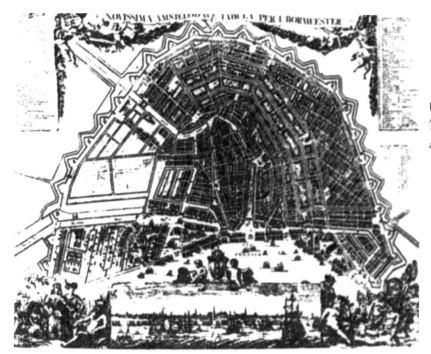

Fig. 4.7
Amsterdam in the
17th century, with North
at the bottom

AMSTERDAM The city is the capital and the country's cultural center. A recent 'literary tour guide' listing places mentioned in literary works, the setting of a story or poem or the home of a writer or poet, devoted 84 pages of fine print to Amsterdam, far more than any other place. The city has provided material for Dutch writers from at least the 16th century, and it is thoroughly rooted in the Dutch imagination—literary or otherwise. Amsterdam's ethnic and cultural subdivisions are a part of the cultural fabric of the Netherlands itself; even those who spend their lives in distant parts of the country are aware of at least some of the city's inner geography and how it came to be that way.

In the 16th century a large, busy fortified city grew up around a dam built sometime in the Middle Ages across the Amstel river flowing through watery lowlands and emptying into the *IJ*, itself an arm of the sea. It was during the 17th century, in the period when Amsterdam was the commercial capital of the world, that the famous concentric-canal system was laid out, the concept that for all time fixed the 'look' of the city and gave it its international recognizability. The spacious elegance of these new neighborhoods—spacious at least compared to the crowded older districts—shows the mark of their ownership by an increasingly affluent population. It was in this period that Amsterdam built, as its city hall, the magnificent building that today is the Royal Palace on the Dam.

Amsterdammers tend to be conscious of the city's cultural centrality. As are the inhabitants of other large cosmopolitan cities such as London, Paris, Berlin or New York, they are apt to be seen as cynical, pushy, vital, irreverent, unorthodox, quick with a smart answer. It is the city's role to be a progressive, even radical cutting edge however uncomfortable that may be. Amsterdam is, and always has been, the principal home of radical movements. It is formally the capital of a monarchy but houses many decidedly republican sentiments; it is more than just a historical accident that the constitutional monarchy's day-to-day operations are mostly in The Hague.

Municipal politics operates mostly to the left of center. Though dominated by a large, progressive party it is still an unpredictable patchwork of a few conservative and many radical movements. Politics in the Netherlands works at all levels according to the multi-party system, which means that a large number of small parties are apt to be represented in the Municipal Council. The radical tradition of Amsterdam frequently descends to the frivolous. More than any other city, Amsterdam is in a permanent fermentation process that is forced to try ever new ways to meet the needs of a constantly changing population. Watching a city beset by crime and drug problems, losing its bargaining position on the international stage and sinking further into pessimism in the '80s, many citizens began to feel that the famous leftish democratization and permissiveness of Amsterdam had gone a bit too far, and there has been a noticeable reaction against this.

As in other cities, there has been a drop in urban population, which now stands at around 700,000. The mass exodus of a prosperous, young, middle-class population has drained the tax base, and the city's average income is below the national average. The families migrated out have been to a great extent replaced by the older and retired living on pensions, welfare recipients, and the new growing ethnic minorities.

The slang name of Amsterdam is *Mokum.* It is the Yiddish form of a Hebrew word meaning 'place', and it is only one of a large number of enrichments of the Dutch colloquial vocabulary contributed by Amsterdam's Jewish population. Jews first immigrated to the city in the 16th century, and quickly contributed their financial expertise to its prosperity; Rembrandt captured some of the personalities in this secure community. The Jewish component in Amsterdam's folklore, its ways and its special brand of humor is widely recognized while still being difficult to pin down exactly. An important aspect of the past of the city has recently been enshrined in the extensive Jewish Historical Museum, using a cluster of synagogues unused by today's Jewish population decimated in the Second World War.

Amsterdam has always drawn its prosperity from the sea (as the orientation of the 17th-century map suggests), and even today it has not lost this link. It was a world map-making center in the 17th century. Since the closing off of the old entrance to the Zuyder Zee by the Barrier Dam in 1932, entry to the city's harbor has been via a canal dug westward across the land to the coast.

But the city's function as world port has long since been eclipsed by Rotterdam, and its commercial function has developed in other areas. It is well aware that, in order to maintain any position of prestige or even credibility as a metropolitan center in the competitive Europe of the '90s, it must develop even newer strengths. It competes with several cities in other countries in hoping to become the 'Gateway to Europe' partly by being an indispensable center for the distribution of goods— a function centered on Schiphol Airport—and for telecommunications.

The massive economic and residential development throughout the greater-Amsterdam area has inevitably led to the joining of all these communities

into an administrative 'region' of the type mentioned in connection with Rotterdam. It is called *Regionaal Orgaan Amsterdam* or more commonly ROA (Amsterdam Regional Authority). As such it is poised to become, along with 14 surrounding municipalities, a new 'city province'. This enlargement in scale has obvious advantages for physical planning, managing the environment, and for all types of infrastructural construction. At the same time and on another level, Amsterdam has been moving in precisely the opposite direction. It has been experimenting with the system of 16 semi-autonomous *deelraden* (sub-councils) as a means of decentralizing some of its functions. Within the newly-constituted region, these are destined to take on more and more functions of independent municipalities. So we might be forgiven for asking 'Where does all this leave the identity of Amsterdam itself?' In a recent referendum the inhabitants of the city soundly rejected the idea of this reorganization of their city, so the next steps are anything but clear.

Adapting an old, densely-built city to the needs of modern commerce has been a major challenge. The city of mainly 2- to 6-story houses crisscrossed by canals plus the inhabitants' determination to preserve the city's character adds up to something like a planner's nightmare. But the *cityvorming* that has made such inroads in the old centers of Utrecht and The Hague is still being successfully resisted in Amsterdam.

The reputation of the city abroad is a blend of charm, international-mindedness and relaxed tolerance. It faithfully reflects Dutch society as a whole in the care for its inner city, the ingenious use of cramped spaces, the liking for particular styles of housing, the generally urban style of habit and attitude, the disdain for show of authority, the pragmatic businesslike attitudes of its entrepreneurs, and the international outlook. For better or worse it is the world's window on the Netherlands, often the only basis for generalizations about the country.

Fig. 4.8
The city of Amsterdam

Baaij, Hans (et al., ed.), *Rotterdam 650 jaar. Vijftig jaar wederopbouw*. Utrecht: Veen, 1990.

Hall, Peter, *The World Cities*. New York: St. Martin's, 3rd ed. 1984.

Lodder, P., *The Port of Rotterdam in Figures*. Rotterdam: Chamber of Commerce and Industry [Annual publication].

Minshull, G.N., 'Randstad Holland: The Ring City', in *The New Europe into the 1990s*. London: Hodder and Stoughton, 1990.

Roegholt, Richter, *A Concise History of Amsterdam*. Amsterdam: Gemeente Amsterdam, 4th ed. 1992.

Stoutenbeek, Jan and Paul Vigevano, *A Guide to Jewish Amsterdam*. Weesp: De Haan, 1985.

Weightman, Christine B., *A Short History of The Hague*. The Hague: Kruseman, 3rd ed. 1991.

5 The commercial picture

The map of Amsterdam in the preceding chapter (Fig. 4.7) shows the same attitude of most maps of that time: in the foreground is the sea, the land arises from it and blooms because of it, and the hinterland fades quickly from view in the background. Through most of its life, the Netherlands has faced the sea and turned its back to its neighbors on the European continent. In the seventeenth century the shrewd observer Pieter de la Court wrote that since Holland's trade interests were so plainly based on sea trade, and since small-ness was so obviously in its favor, it made sense to dig a canal all around the west—thus shrinking while other nations were vigorously expanding—to complete and symbolize this isolation from surrounding countries.

The Dutch carrying and transshipment trade that once brought the coun-try—especially the city-state Amsterdam—unparalleled prosperity by sea has, with the coming of the EC, turned the Netherlands firmly toward the Eu-ropean continent. This activity is still one of the country's economic corner-stones, just one example of which is the transshipping and refining activity around Rotterdam. It is this traditional carrying function that is being ambi-tiously expanded now by means of a radically upgraded infrastructure, plus the envisioned 'mainports', to enable the Netherlands to become the distri-bution center of Europe. The promotion of Amsterdam as 'gateway' to Eu-rope is already readily apparent in advertising, for instance by KLM.

Exports account for some 60% of the total Dutch agricultural, processing and manufacturing activity. About 20% of the total agrarian export picture is accounted for by horticulture: fruits and vegetables (to a great extent cultivat-ed in greenhouses) on the one hand, and all ornamentals, including cut flow-ers, on the other. Some 60% of the world's cut flowers are traded (though not necessarily grown) in the Netherlands, a figure that is slowly decreasing. It is

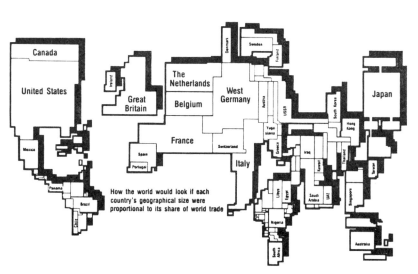

How the world would look if each country's geographical size were proportional to its share of world trade

Fig. 5.1
Looked at differently, a small country can loom quite large. In 1995 the Netherlands' world ranking in exports was seventh place.

amusing to note, in passing, that the Netherlands' export of flower bulbs recently reached over 6.5 billion within a single year, or enough to give one to each inhabitant of the planet.

The extent to which the Netherlands relies on agricultural production for its export strength is, given the tiny size of this intensely urbanized area, astonishing to say the least. Some agricultural products are exported as such, but a significant share of it is channeled into the highly-developed food-processing industry. The many millions of cattle, pigs and poultry are the raw material for the meat-processing sector, and the pasturelands form the basis for the dairy industry. In all these areas, the Netherlands is listed at or near the top of world suppliers. But the environmental cost of all this agricultural intensity is very high, and more and more people are claiming it is excessively so. The greenhouse consumption of energy with its resulting pollution is high, and the overproduction of manure has reached crisis proportions—to which might be added the fact that at any given time some five million acres in third-world countries are devoted to production of feed for Dutch cattle.

The large and diverse Dutch food-processing sector also forms a link between agriculture and industry. It was the margarine company that had developed out of the processing of oils and fats that in 1930 merged with Lever Brothers to form *Unilever,* today one of the large multinational corporations. The coffee, tea, chocolate and tobacco-processing industry all operate exclusively with imported raw materials, and all—including the relatively minor but important beer and *jenever* industries—have played their roles via a circuitous route in the development of the Netherlands' world position in the chemical area. The salt deposits in the east, one of the country's few natural resources, were the original basis for one of the chemical companies that eventually joined to form the present chemical giant *Akzo.*

The list of the dozen or so largest corporations in the Netherlands varies somewhat from year to year as companies change places in the sequence, but a good average picture is:

ROYAL DUTCH SHELL GROUP World supplier of oil and of petroleum products; energy supplier

UNILEVER Foods, detergents and other products; the company maintains a low-profile image, hidden behind a variety of brand names

ABN-AMRO, ING AND RABO Banking and financial services

POLYGRAM, WOLTERS-KLUWER AND ELSEVIER Publishing, the latter two including scholarly and professional journals

AEGON Insurance

HEINEKEN Brewery products

AKZO GROUP Chemicals and synthetic fibers, pharmaceuticals, industrial coatings, consumer food products

AHOLD A supermarket chain operated under the old name of Albert Heijn

PHILIPS Consumer electronics and industrial electronic equipment

KLM Royal Dutch Airlines

HOOGOVENS Steel and other metals

Though some of these companies operate mainly within the country, most are multinational corporations, making the Netherlands a country with notably strong multinational specialization. Three of these corporations belong to the largest in the world, only the U.S. being home to a greater number. In

Fig. 5.2
Part of the
Philips conglomerate
in Eindhoven

fact it is common for Dutch companies to find themselves operating all over the world, for instance engineers and contractors for the construction of harbors, dredging, and land reclamation projects. Publishing companies have joined the business trend toward internationalization, and they rely increasingly on an overseas market. They specialize in trade journals and magazines for a wide variety of professions. As they create this information network, they help take the concept of publishing into new areas. The Netherlands' international orientation places both its economic future and its national identity in vulnerable positions.

With the possible exception of KLM and Heineken, probably only the Philips Corporation carries its identity as a Dutch company with it all over the world. It is the one large corporation that has its roots firmly in the Netherlands and is not the result of international mergers; as such it is symbolically important as a national enterprise. In fact the company is so thoroughly entwined in the country's entire industrial base that it is occasionally said 'when Philips sneezes, the Netherlands catches cold'. It began in 1891 as a small light-bulb manufacturer in Eindhoven in Noord-Brabant, which is still its home. Even though management has long since passed out of the hands of the Philips family itself, it remains a company with a 'personality'. This traditionally included fostering a strong identification with and loyalty to the company and a certain mild protective paternalism toward workers, habits which are being steadily diluted in the present-day world.

Philips is made up of a group of companies called 'national organizations' in some sixty countries, with around 250,000 employees worldwide. In addition to these companies, Philips participates in a constantly-shifting pattern of joint ventures with other corporations. It is a diversified electronics company consisting of nine 'product divisions', whose four main fields of activity are lighting, consumer electronics, electronic components and professional systems. It dominates the first of these, by far its most lucrative branch, and in the second has the distinction of being the European leader and the principal competitor of the Japanese, recently challenging their monopoly in the digital audio market. It is one of the world's manufacturers of personal computers. The videocassette recorder, the digital compact cassette and the compact disc were all innovated by Philips, and at present it is investing in high-definition TV and in liquid-crystal technology for airline entertainment systems, and in music and video software. The most recent addition of a new product division has been the organization of 'Philips Media', a coordination of efforts in these areas plus software, all seen as areas where the 'action' of the future will be.

The company is strongly committed to the expanding European communications infrastructure. As have many other companies, they have moved into the opening eastern European market.

Participation in a variety of European technological organizations and programs notwithstanding, it remains a Dutch company, and some of the disastrous market slide in the last few years—by no means all ventures have been successful—has been attributed to a historically-evolved structure that was slipping into obsolescence. Philips' international form was based on a 'federal' idea, allowing a high degree of local autonomy that was the pride of the company. But it was modeled on home-country habits which required long discussions to avoid conflict, and often had overly long lines of communication. At present the company is just emerging from an agonizing process of streamlining and retrenchment to hold its own as one of the last western bastions in consumer electronics.

Although Philips' outlay for research and development is inevitably quite high (along with the four other large corporations Shell, Unilever, Akzo and DSM it accounts for 28% of the country's total expenditure in this area), the Netherlands as a whole lags well behind the OESO average in R&D spending—a little over half that of Switzerland, for instance. This is partly offset by the Netherlands' relative strength in service industries, where this expense is not a factor.

Not all companies carry on their own research in advanced technological areas. An example is the development of biotechnology, in which the Netherlands hopes to occupy a leading role into the '90s. Several of the established chemical and antibiotics industries are strongly committed to this, relying on research being done at the universities in Leiden and Delft. A related example is the seed industry, where the research being done on plant technology in the Agricultural University in Wageningen is regularly made available to companies. The country is a leader in seed technology, holding about 70% of the market abroad. But many in the business community complain that the links to universities are still too weak, resulting in considerable pressures on the universities to produce applicable research in a meaningful program. In fact the question might be asked whether the Netherlands is properly positioned for the industrial strength that will be required in coming decades. Industries of the future are said to be not agriculture and processing but electronics, where Philips has to be heavily relied on, biotechnology where the country has a chance to compete, and telecommunications where the initiative is practically all abroad.

Running a business in the Netherlands means contending with a number of different kinds of difficulties. First among these is one already mentioned, a small domestic market. This means dependance on a high percentage of trade from abroad, and international economic factors which by their nature are highly unpredictable and in any case not within ready control. For a long time Dutch business was handicapped by a lack of the business schools that are a prominent feature in other industrialized countries, but in recent years much of this has been remedied. The largest business school in the country is now the Rotterdam School of Management of the Erasmus Universiteit in Rotterdam. It offers an MBA degree in 'general management' in both Dutch and English, and is in the early stages of a doctoral program in business. But the American-style 'MBA', though it is offered by now in some twenty institutions, is not part of the Dutch higher-education system and its controls.

The national government plays a significant role in business. The government's role in business consists partially in attempting to hold down wage demands to protect the country's international competitive position. A high degree of price control is in government hands, giving the economy a unique flavor on the international scene. In international business the Dutch find themselves in a favorable position in their overall stability, with a well-educated labor force, highly developed transportation and communications systems, and tax laws that are attractive abroad.

On the other hand, the Philips story as recounted just above is a prime example of what is meant when Dutch business is called too 'domestic' in its outlook. It unconsciously follows a national ethic in being hesistant to stand out and risk seeming eccentric, and Dutch businessmen are part of a social pattern that demands endless deliberations groping for consensus. As we will see a bit later on, they consistently call themselves, usually not without a sigh, a 'consensus culture' or a 'deliberation culture'. The decision-making links within Dutch industry and business operate along traditional and socially-accepted—indeed to a great extent unconscious—lines. These probably continue some forms evolved in the 17th century, and one can fairly speak of a Dutch business 'style'.

This consultation is found at all levels, and its formalization fits into a very Dutch social pattern. By law, any company employing at least 35 people is required to have an employees' council called the *ondernemingsraad*. This is a committee elected by employees, and it has the power to mediate with management about day-to-day personnel matters and to offer advice about internal management of the company. But these councils are not unions, which have their own negotiating functions (such as contracts) and do not replace them.

Dutch workers are a little under 30% unionized, a figure which after a long period of increase up to 40% is now declining again. The *Federatie Nederlandse Vakbeweging* (Netherlands Trade Union Federation) has just under a million members. It is a coordinating organization of trade-union councils which themselves coordinate individual unions. The FNV operates alongside the smaller *Christelijk Nationaal Vakverbond* (Protestant Trade Union Alliance), and a still smaller one.

On the employers' side are two large organizations, the *Verbond van Nederlandse Ondernemingen* (Alliance of Netherlands Companies) and the

Nederlands Christelijk Werkgeversverbond (Netherlands Protestant Employ-ers' Alliance), plus two smaller ones. The *Stichting van de Arbeid* (Labor Foundation) coordinates the organizations of employees and employers and keeps watch on labor and wage conditions.

Employer relations with workers—whether via unions or not—tend to be considerably better than in most other western industrialized countries. Labor and management have traditionally been not in adversary but more or less cooperative roles. In the period before the war and for a generation after it, industrial relations were smooth, under a union leadership that showed flexibility and intelligent planning for recovery. Polarization did not become prominent until the 1970's, when the gap between expectations and rewards had become too large, and economic recession caused painful readjust-ments. Though mass unemployment may be occasioned by the failure of a company, mass layoffs are unheard of. This, among other things, makes it ex-tremely difficult to adjust the labor force to the changing demands of indus-try.

Bargaining between labor and management is done along lines legally es-tablished by the agreements known as the *Collectieve Arbeids Overeen-komst* (Collective Labor Agreement). Individual contracts must meet at least its standards, and negotiations decide what level beyond an existing CAO is to be reached. About 700 of these are concluded each year, the most important one being that negotiated by the metal workers, the largest single labor group. This CAO traditionally sets the tone for the rest. These contracts con-cern mainly wages and benefits, and here there is a further factor that greatly lessens the adversary distance between bargaining partners. What has to be negotiated is only that portion of unemployment insurance, medical bene-fits, retirement and the like that go beyond the basic package that is provided for everyone by far-reaching social-welfare legislation.

FURTHER READING

Publications in booklet and pamphlet form on all the topics in this chapter are avail-able at all times from embassies and consulates, and from the relevant ministries, especially those of Agriculture, Nature Management and Fisheries and of Economic Affairs. Current information also appears regularly in the newsletters and magazines published by a wide variety of trade agencies. Note also the *London Economist*'s an-nual 'Country Report' (chapter 1).

Economic and Social History in the Netherlands. Amsterdam [Annual].

Economic Survey of the Netherlands. Paris: OECD [Biennial].

Lawrence, Peter, *Management in the Netherlands.* London: Oxford University, 1991.

Van Zanden, J.L., and R.T. Griffiths, *Economische geschiedenis van Nederland in de twintigste eeuw.*

Utrecht: Spectrum, 1990 [This can be supplemented by Griffiths' somewhat older *The Economy and Politics of the Netherlands since 1945.* The Hague: Martinus Nijhoff, 1980].

6 Planning a society

Fig. 6.1
The 'welfare state' runs on '*f*', the guilder, and this contraption is topped by parliament. The rest of the attitude expressed by this cartoon speaks for itself.

In careful Dutch society 'planning' is one of the central cultural institutions. The earnestness and thoroughness of physical and environmental planning is at least paralleled by economic and social planning. But here we need to be alert to a possible conflict: many societies today are thoroughly planned, but isn't this kind of control often at odds with what we think of a truly democratic system, with all its untidiness and unpredictability? This brings us to the interesting question how—and even whether—Dutch society manages a tightly-controlled welfare state while at the same time safeguarding the processes of a free, democratic system.

Both economic and social planning flow naturally from the two well-entrenched Dutch habits of careful organization and preparation, and of consultation at many levels. Economic planning involves first of all the *Sociaal Economische Raad* (Social Economic Council). Back in the era of postwar recovery, the *SER* was based on the idea of labor and management cooperating by keeping demands low in order to maintain a competitive position. The *SER* consists of 45 members representing both employers and workers. Historically, the *SER* was the cornerstone of a delicately balanced framework of postwar industrial relations.

Along with the *SER* come three other institutions, the *Nederlandsche Bank*, the central bank that controls economic policy, the *Stichting van de Arbeid* (the Labor Foundation mentioned in the preceding chapter), and the *Centraal Planbureau* (Central Planning Bureau). The *CPB* is a deliberate attempt to depoliticize economic and social planning and create a social institution that could not be monopolized by a single interest group. Along with the *SER*, it owes its existence to the idealism and vision of its world-famous founder and first director, the economist Jan Tinbergen. Tinbergen's strong strain of morality and conscience in combining economic science with the solution of social problems has, as we will see in a later chapter, carried this moral aspect of Dutch ways far beyond the narrow borders of his country.

The CPB now aids the government in the preparation of the budget, prepares reports for ministries and has close relations with many organizations and corporations. It is a sort of 'think tank' whose primary concern is attempting the frustrating task of peering into the future. Forecasts made by the CPB are given immediate coverage by the press and influence parliamentary debate. Another cog in this planning system is the much older *Centraal Bureau voor de Statistiek* (Central Bureau for Statistics).

Social planning, the fourth part of the planning picture in the Netherlands, is the concern of the *Sociaal en Cultureel Planbureau* (Social and Cultural Planning Bureau), one of the branches of the Ministry of Culture. Like the CPB, the Bureau's name is somewhat misleading: it too does not 'plan' in the strict sense of the term, but its task is to provide constantly up-to-date information in the area of culture and social welfare, to help in suggesting policy guidelines, and to act as information center. Both these bureaus can only trust each year that their descriptions are paid attention to. Which they normally are, because they are high-prestige institutions and thoroughly integrated parts of the Dutch deliberation system.

Social Services as % of GNP (April 1988)	
Netherlands	32.8
Belgium	30.2
Denmark	29.3
Germany	28.1
France	27.2
Italy	24.7
U.Kingdom	23.5
Ireland	22.0
Spain	17.7
Portugal	17.0

Progressive thinking along social-welfare lines was already a conspicuous tradition in the Netherlands in the 17th century, but it was only in the period from the 1930's until the sixties that a complex, liberal social-welfare system was legislated into place. The key piece of legislation that is still in force today was the *Algemene Bijstandswet* (General Assistance Act) of 1963. The enactment of social welfare legislation was the result of a powerful social-emancipation movement that involved a high degree of competition among primarily religious groups, of which the Catholic was the strongest. Here once again, Dutch social patterns reassert themselves. 'Competition' has never been understood as securing benefits at the expense of any other group, but assuring equal treatment for all—down to the most minute detail. Social welfare today is still administered by the central government but implemented and distributed—in addition to local authorities—by private organizations of a wide variety of types. It is these private groups, intertwined

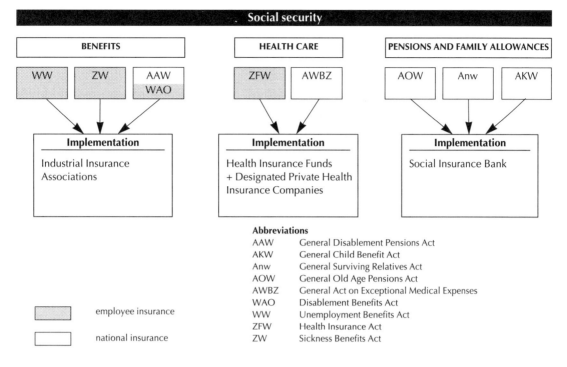

Social security

BENEFITS	HEALTH CARE	PENSIONS AND FAMILY ALLOWANCES

BENEFITS: WW | ZW | AAW WAO

HEALTH CARE: ZFW | AWBZ

PENSIONS AND FAMILY ALLOWANCES: AOW | Anw | AKW

Implementation

Industrial Insurance Associations

Implementation

Health Insurance Funds + Designated Private Health Insurance Companies

Implementation

Social Insurance Bank

Abbreviations

AAW	General Disablement Pensions Act
AKW	General Child Benefit Act
Anw	General Surviving Relatives Act
AOW	General Old Age Pensions Act
AWBZ	General Act on Exceptional Medical Expenses
WAO	Disablement Benefits Act
WW	Unemployment Benefits Act
ZFW	Health Insurance Act
ZW	Sickness Benefits Act

employee insurance

national insurance

with state agencies, that give the Netherlands welfare system a unique aspect. As of the beginning of the '90s, social services amounted to over 30% of total GNP.

Fig. 6.2
The general structure of social welfare legislation

The chart shows the rather intimidating-looking structure of the whole social-welfare system. 'Social welfare', as we have been calling it, is a slightly less misleading translation than the chart's 'social security', which in the U.S. implies only retirement benefits. We do not need to know in detail how this whole machinery works, is order to get a sense of what sorts of things are covered and for whom. In other words, we are looking for no more than a little taste of its 'personality' as a social institution.

The system is based on a primary distinction between employee benefits of several types, and social benefits applying to the population as a whole. All benefits of both types fall in the category of social insurance, whether disability, medical, retirement or some other, and they are intended to serve only as a minimum.

The other side of social welfare legislation, not shown on the chart, is the *Algemene Bijstandswet* (General Assistance Act) mentioned above, under which everyone over age 18 can claim minimum benefits. Not surprisingly, this is the most expensive and by far the most controversial segment of the total system, one that has produced public impressions of inadequacy, instability and temptations for abuse. The whole system has grown into such complexity that few people are able to sense its overall structure. More significant than this, however, is the brute fact that the economy is increasingly unable to support a liberal public-welfare system on this scale. Not only have enemployment and disability benefits increased (the Dutch have the world's highest claim rate here), but the number of citizens in the higher age categories has as well, and throughout this system the rules became increasingly liberal. But in recent years eligibility requirements have been tightened throughout the system, benefit periods have been trimmed, and 'takeup rates' drastically lessened.

Because of the necessity brought by EU integration moves to make the system approximately equal to those of other European countries, the system is on the verge of drastic overhauling. As this is being written, only the first steps are being taken toward facing the economic problem squarely. The *Ziektewet* (zw on the chart, fig. 6.2) has just been turned over to private companies, an important first step out of social welfare. Labor unions, among other groups, are not inclined to accept decreased benefits. The result so far, aside from the reforms just mentioned, has been that the problem is shifted via numerous small cutbacks onto the various implementing organizations.

The national debate about the future of the welfare state is the third great issue the Dutch cast a troubled eye at as they contemplate their future. The other two we have already noted: questions about the effects of a continuously expanding economy on the environment and the 'the Netherlands is full' idea. Part of the discussion in the chapters to come will be trying to get a picture of the interaction of these three national issues, as well as how they relate to other issues in public discussion.

There should be something particularly satisfying in talking about housing. It is the one area where all three kinds of planning—physical, economic and social—join and overlap. The Ministry responsible for housing matters, the *Ministerie van Volkshuisvesting, Ruimtelijke Ordening en Milieubeheer* (usually referred to as VROM) places 'housing' before 'physical planning' and 'environment'. There has been a steadily increasing demand ever since the war (when 10% of all housing was destroyed), fueled not only by a growing population but by rising expectations. The average shortage nationwide remains at about 36,000 (33,000 of them in the Randstad). And this stubborn shortage not only persists but grows: by the year 2000 it might have topped 100,000.

It has been estimated that, all told, over 50% of all housing construction is subsidized—in some communities much more—a figure that is quite high by foreign standards. Public authorities supply 80% of land coming into development, which has the fortunate result for planners that it cuts out most land speculation. The risk of inequity and speculation in a situation of severe shortage and extreme space limitations forced the imposition of not only strict land-use restrictions but far-reaching regulation of the market. The majority of housing units are built in what is known as the 'free sector', financed by private enterprise and by 'building associations' that provide capital.

Ideas about and tastes in mass-housing design have changed many times over the years, and the styles of successive eras are clearly visible in nearly all Dutch cities. The late 19th century built housing in the form of closely-packed rows in streets without trees or gardens. Some early 20th-century housing emphasized a 'total look' that sometimes gave a sculptured shape to the exteriors of housing complexes. Housing built in the '20s and '30s continued the row idea but allowed for a garden in front, creating the closely-packed but individual and neatly cared-for look of residential neighborhoods throughout the country. Early postwar housing saw the first large apartment blocks, which evolved in ever larger forms through the '60s and '70s. Since then, mass housing has returned to the more intimate scale and style that remains the favorite.

Planners projected in 1965 that by the year 2000 the country would have to accommodate a population of about 21,000,000. For a combination of reasons, demographic trends proved to be different: fertility rates dropped, a trend toward earlier marriage was reversed, and the population increase did not materialize. Some forecasts now show a population of 'only' 16,000,000 by 2000, and possibly a drop in population following that. Immigrant minorities, which thanks to continued heavy immigration and a higher birth rate have accounted for an increasingly higher percentage of the total population, are expected by 2000 to be following overall Dutch demographic trends.

Residence (1986)   *in percentages*   A few social statistics

Total number: 5,488,000

one- family house	apartment	central heating
68.3	31.7	66.1

Households (1988)

single-person household	single-parent family	number in household
29.3	12.1	2.53

Place of residence (1988)

rural	urbanized rural	urban (cities over 100.000)
11.0	38.0	51.0

Occupations(1988)

	% of total work force	men	women
industry, trades, transportation	24.4	35.2	5.9
specialists (arts, medical, engineering, education)	23.8	22.3	26.2
office workers	17.8	12.2	27.5
service (restaurant, police en fire, maintenance)	12.2	5.6	23.4
commercial (merchants, salespersons)	11.2	10.4	12.6
agriculture, fisheries	5.1	6.2	3.1
managerial, administration	4.0	5.6	1.2
military	1.6	2.5	0.0

Possession of durable goods (1989)		*in percentages*
refrigerator	98	
color television	94	
washer	89	
automobile	64	
deep-freeze	49	
home computer	19	
dishwasher	10	
microwave oven	12 (in 1992 this last had reached 22%)	

Household moves (1988)		*in percentages*
within the municipality	7.3	
within the province	1.65	
outside the province	2.35	
total	11.3	

Religious affiliation (1990)		*in percentages*
roman catholic	32	
protestant	25	
other	5	
none	38	

Means of transportation per individual (1988)		*in kilometers*
automobile	8,378 (5,205 mi)	
public transportation	1,258 (844 mi)	
bicycle	0,784 (487 mi)	

Change on an ever more massive scale is something all modern societies must find their own solution to, but is becomes particularly absorbing to see how a country that is already 'full' confronts its own problems. Automobile registrations will have increased to about 7½ million by the year 2000. The provision of roads and of drinking water for an increased population in a more polluted environment will be major problems to be dealt with in a cramped space that is already fully used. A large region, at least northwest-ern Europe, will have to be subjected to an integrated planning program. Two-thirds of all Dutch households will consist of one or two persons, and there can be expected to be more emphasis on pursuing one's own aims and going one's individual way. It might be added here that in the responsiveness of social services to these trends toward the individual, the Netherlands is still lagging behind the rest of Europe.

The Netherlands' drug policy is also part of the society's approach to difficult problems through its government. What has widely been seen as 'permis-siveness' toward drugs has actually been a conscious attempt to treat various types of drugs socially and retain control of them, rather than banning them outright and, as other countries have done, declaring 'war' on them and driving them underground out of reach. 'Soft' drugs are sold openly to keep them off the criminal market; selling 'hard' drugs is strictly illegal though addiction is treated as a health problem rather than as a criminal one. It remains to be seen whether greatly increased European pressure toward stricter measures and across-the-board banning will result in modification of this notably flexible system.

The difficult issues surrounding euthanasia have also been the subject, in recent years, of public debate in the press and parliament. The Netherlands is still the only country discreetly experimenting with active euthanasia. Though it is technically still illegal, the courts have in fact drawn up a set of conditions that, when all are strictly adhered to, can serve to protect doctors from prosecution.

FURTHER READING

Couwenberg, S.W. (ed.), *Op de grens van twee eeuwen. Positie en perspectief van Nederland in het zicht van het jaar 2000*. Kampen: Kok/Agora, 1989.

Dupuis, H.M., 'Euthanasia in the Netherlands. Facts and moral arguments.' *The Low Countries*, 1994-5.

Fact Sheet [The series described in chapter 1].

'A Short Survey of Social Security'. *Info*. The Hague: Ministry of Social Affairs and Employment.

Social and Cultural Report. The Hague: Government Publishing Office [published biennially].

Social Security in the Netherlands. Deventer/Boston: Kluwer Law and Taxation Publications, 1990.

Statistical Yearbook of the Netherlands. The Hague: Central Bureau for Statistics [Annual. The Bureau also publishes a *Monthly Bulletin*].

7 Education

A society's educational system is uniquely revealing: it follows the lines of the society's most deeply held cultural values, and at the same time it has the task of preparing succeeding generations for entry into that society. The Dutch educational system has several features which set it apart from other countries and at the same time tend to illuminate some aspects of the society we are examining.

The whole system is administered centrally by the Ministry of Education and Science, and all schools are required to comply with the same structure, standards, and examinations. Though the Dutch 'multiple-track' system can seem bafflingly complex to an outsider, the drawing (Fig. 7.1) shows graphically how the route through it works in practice and what choices there are at each stage along the route.

Each type of school is represented here as a separate building, its number of stories (or, in the instance of the *Basisschool* 'elementary school', windows) standing for the number of years it includes. This is important to keep track of, as are the little walkways at some stories leading from one building to another, which indicate the possibilities of transferring between types of school. The pictures at the right give a general impression of the types of occupations likely to follow from each level and type of schooling. A little farther along there will be more to say about this correlation.

Compulsory schooling begins at age 5, though today most children begin before this with the *Crèche* 'nursery school'. A total of ten years of schooling on a daily basis is compulsory, from age 16 on two days per week, and from 17 one day. These latter obligations can be fulfilled by the two-year *Vormingscentrum* 'Education center' or *Streekschool* 'regional school', which appear on the right side of the drawing with the title 'Partial education'.

The eight-year *Basisschool* 'Primary school' is the only one within the compulsory system that is identical for all. In 1993 the *Basisvorming*, 'fundamental education', was introduced in all types of secondary education. All schools have the obligation to teach the same 15 subjects in the first two years. After these two years, children have the possibility—depending on their results—to choose one of the various types of secondary education. About a third of all children at this point enter LBO, *Lager Beroepsonderwijs* 'Lower Vocational Education'—the percentage of children of immigrant minorities somewhat higher than that of Dutch children. LBO consists of a further three years' education and feeds into the next higher group of occupations (Fig. 7.1), mainly trades.

After the *Basisvorming*—the two years of fundamental education—there are three other possible choices, each of which leads to a higher level. The *MAVO, Middelbaar Algemeen Voortgezet Onderwijs*, accounts for three additional years of secondary education. Here national examinations must be taken in six subjects, which are chosen with an eye to the occupational area

Schema van het Nederlandse onderwijssysteem vanaf 1 augustus 1997

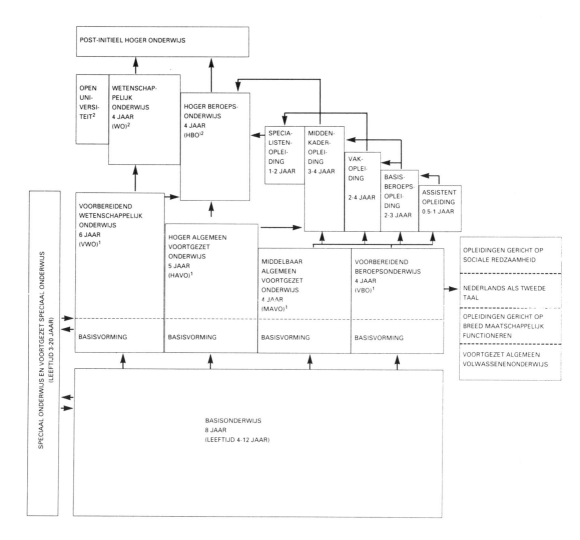

POST-INITIEEL HOGER ONDERWIJS

| OPEN UNI-VERSI-TEIT[2] | WETENSCHAP-PELIJK ONDERWIJS 4 JAAR (WO)[2] |

HOGER BEROEPS-ONDERWIJS 4 JAAR (HBO)[12]

SPECIA-LISTEN-OPLEI-DING 1-2 JAAR

MIDDEN-KADER-OPLEI-DING 3-4 JAAR

VAK-OPLEI-DING 2-4 JAAR

BASIS-BEROEPS-OPLEI-DING 2-3 JAAR

ASSISTENT OPLEIDING 0.5-1 JAAR

VOORBEREIDEND WETENSCHAPPELIJK ONDERWIJS 6 JAAR (VWO)[1]

HOGER ALGEMEEN VOORTGEZET ONDERWIJS 5 JAAR (HAVO)[1]

MIDDELBAAR ALGEMEEN VOORTGEZET ONDERWIJS 4 JAAR (MAVO)[1]

VOORBEREIDEND BEROEPSONDERWIJS 4 JAAR (VBO)[1]

OPLEIDINGEN GERICHT OP SOCIALE REDZAAMHEID

NEDERLANDS ALS TWEEDE TAAL

OPLEIDINGEN GERICHT OP BREED MAATSCHAPPELIJK FUNCTIONEREN

VOORTGEZET ALGEMEEN VOLWASSENENONDERWIJS

BASISVORMING · BASISVORMING · BASISVORMING · BASISVORMING

SPECIAAL ONDERWIJS EN VOORTGEZET SPECIAAL ONDERWIJS (LEEFTIJD 3-20 JAAR)

BASISONDERWIJS 8 JAAR (LEEFTIJD 4-12 JAAR)

supposedly being worked toward. This is generally thought of as preparatory to the *MBO*-colleges, schools for *Middelbaar Beroeps Onderwijs*, for an additional two to five years of specialized vocational training for fields such as agriculture and horticulture, small business administration, and various administrative and technical occupations. After the *MAVO* exams the option is open to shift to the *HAVO*, which is a year longer and leads to a higher form of vocational training. But since a shift loses a year, the result is two extra years of school.

Fig. 7.1
The educational system.

The *HAVO* is *Hoger Algemeen Voortgezet Onderwijs*, accounting for a total of five years of secondary education. Here too, the standard exam requirement is for a packet of six, to be chosen by the individual, who has to make some guess about general occupational specialization. In most instances this type of school leads to the *hogescholen*, schools for *Hoger Beroeps Onderwijs* *(HBO)*, which are vocational schools, offering education in a wide variety of technical fields, but also the arts and teacher training. The *hogescholen* train for skilled occupations; the course of study is four years.

The *VWO* is *Voorbereidend Wetenschappelijk Onderwijs*, offering a total of six years and requiring seven examination fields. The *VWO* is divided into two types, either of which gives a diploma that leads to university education. Some 60% of those in *VWO* go on to higher education. The *Gymnasium* requires at least one classical language and the *Atheneum* does not, but otherwise they are similar. Schools called *Lyceum* combine these two in the first year. Many of the schools in these different tracks seldom exist independently but are part of a consolidation known as a *Scholengemeenschap* 'School community', where a single building and administration will typically include *MAVO*, *HAVO* and *Gymnasium/Atheneum*. This type of organization makes transferring between types relatively convenient.

This system has a high degree of flexibility in allowing shifts from one 'track' to another, replacing an older one which required a choice at a very early age and then separate channels which could be bridged only with difficulty and loss of years. In the present system the choice is in effect postponed until the age of 15 or 16. But all these school levels should be thought of as grade levels and numbers of years rather than as ages, because of the strict application of the passing-grade rules: if the average drops too low, the weak subject is repeated. The result of these rules is that some leave a particular type of school one or two years older than others.

One of the prime purposes of the *Basisvorming* (and prior reorganizations of the school system) is the gradual elimination of a social class system that kept options narrow and limited. The 15 subjects are obligatory for all schools and the definite choice for one of the secondary school types is postponed until the third year of secondary education. Whether the *Basisvorming* actually leads to better possibilities and choices remains to be seen. Society remains stratified, even if not in the rigid way it was two generations ago. Children of different families enter the system with different types of expectations and family pressure, and a vision of a type of occupation inevitably leads to a choice—the *LBO*, for example. The present system, for all its flexibility and opportunity, still allows for the perpetuation within families and groups of the population of an 'unskilled' or 'semi-skilled' or 'elite' way of thinking. Vocational training in its elaborate specialized diploma system still shows some of the form of the ancient guild and apprenticeship tradition.

At the uppermost level, an ambition in the direction of the *Atheneum* on the part of a working-class child would often be greeted with suspicion as a 'betrayal' of one's own people. The *Gymnasium* with its classical-language requirement is the modern survivor, and modest perpetuator, of a very old system of education for the sons of a privileged class, one which in the time-honored tradition focused on classical languages and literatures.

At the elementary and secondary level there are special schools of various types, the *speciaal onderwijs*, for those with learning disabilities for whatever cause. Part-time and adult education are possible from primary through university training. For all those both children and adults who are slowed by insufficient knowledge of the language, an educational effort which has shown a vast increase in recent years is the teaching of Dutch as a second language. It is now possible for adults to get an official diploma `Dutch as a second language' at two different levels. Newly arrived immigrant adults are obliged—if they depend for their income on the state—to participate in *inburgeringsprogramma*, a settle-in program, that consists of Dutch language lessons and a course `orientation in Dutch society'.

The schematic drawing we have been referring to attempts to represent the basic structure of the educational system in the Netherlands by suggesting three dimensions. But this is only its organizational structure as it appears to those working their way through the system from entrance to exit. This whole system has another major distinction running, as it were, 'perpendicular' to it: the distinction between 'general' or 'public' education and what is called 'particular' education. This involves sometimes duplicate, and in essence competing school administrations running parallel systems all following the same centralized requirements.

In the Netherlands, freedom to provide education is an established social right. In principle, any group wanting to found and run a school can constitute a legal corporation and, provided the requirements and standards are met, can claim the right to full funding by the government. Such schools are called *Bijzonder* 'particular', and in spite of the name they account for approximately two-thirds of all education in the Netherlands. The breakdown of subsidized schools is

Public:		33%
Particular:	Catholic	30
	Protestant	27
	Neutral	5
	All others	5

At the elementary level, 63% of all children attend a protestant school. In addition to these are some 'private' schools that meet the education requirements but are not subsidized.

The 'particular' schools owe their origin to the emancipation movements in the churches, and the great majority of them are still religious schools, at least in name. They are run by large, well-entrenched organizations that exercise a constant vigilance over their educational territory. In other words, very extensive use has been made of the opportunity to found 'particular' schools with government financing, and the whole system today is locked into a network of parallel school boards that has proved very difficult to

Fig. 7.2
The school listings
for a typical
medium-sized town.

OPENBARE TRADITIONELE VERNIEU-WINGSSCHOLEN
De Bothoven (Freinetbasisschool), Reudinkstraat 15, 7511 ZG, tel. 4303235.
Dir.: J.H. Minnegal.
Lonneker, (werken volgens Daltonprincipe), Dorpsstraat 104, 7524 CK, tel. 4355993.
Dir.: B. Boswinkel.
De Wielerbaan, Montessoribasisschool, Batshoek 5, 7546 LC, tel. 4768761.
Dir.: mevr. M.H. Wansink-Gilles.
Het Zeggelt, Montessoribasisschool, Dr. Benthemstraat 14, 7514 CM, tel. 4358682
Dep.: Multatulistraat 14, 7514 CZ, tel. 4358581.
Dir.: mevr. E.J. Smit.

BIJZONDER BASISONDERWIJS (KATHOLIEK)
Alfonsusschool, Past. Geertmanstraat 10, 7535 BZ, tel. 4314249.
Dir.: G.J. Grooters.
De Regenboog, Het Stroink 60, 7542 GT, tel. 4766477.
Dir.: J.G.P. Hommels.
Godfried Bomansschool, Veldhoflanden 92, 7542 LX, tel. 4771751.
Dir.: A.M. Bosz.
Bonifatiusschool, Zaanstraat 10, 7523 HC, tel. 4354871.
Dep.: dr. A.H.J. Copperstraat 30, 7523 EN, tel. 4357332.
Dir.: J.A.M. Vermeulen.
St. Gerardusschool, Past. Meyerstraat 5, 7532 AJ, tel. 4611667.
Dep.: Past. Meyerstraat 3, 7532 AJ, tel. 4611667.
Dir.: J.H.B.G. Koenders.
De Kubus, Drebbelstraat 15, 7533 WV, tel. 4306037.
Dir.: L.H. Driessen.
Weth. A.F. van de Heydenschool, Ravenhorsthoek 38, 7546 EA, tel. 4774654.
Dep.: Runenberghoek 3, 7546 EG, tel. 4763474.
Dir.: G.J.M. Bottenberg.
St. Janschool, Haaksbergerstraat 255, 7545 GH, tel. 4314301.
Dir.: A.M.C. Zwerink.
Paus Johannesschool, Floraparkstraat 155, 7531 XG, tel. 4353811.
Dep.: Saffierstraat 30.
Dir.: H.J. Sprakel.
De Windroos, Zunabrink 10, 7544 DR, tel. 4762082.
Dep.: Het Leunenberg 570, 7544 JM, tel. 4761416.
Dir.: mevr. E.T. Lurvink-Nijkamp.
St. Liduinaschool, Scholten Reimerstraat 8, 7524 CS, tel. 4352447.

Dir.: B. Olde Dubbelink.
Paulusschool, Regulusstraat 8, 7521 DX, tel. 4350763.
Dir.: P.L. Besselink.
De Triangel, M. Hobbemastraat 37, 7545 CJ, tel. 4313986.
Dir.: J.F. Haasink.
De Troubadour, Sonatestraat 44a, 7534 XC, tel. 4611691.
Dir.: H.J.F. Snijders.
Willibrordschool, Rijnstraat 15, 7523 GD, tel. 4355351.
Dir.: J.J. Vermeer.

BIJZONDER BASISONDERWIJS (PROTESTANT-CHRISTELIJK)
Koningin Beatrix, Tomatenstraat 27, 7545 WP, tel. 4319701.
Dir.: J. Nijemeisland.
Prins Bernhard, J.P. Coenstraat 9, 7541 BP, tel. 4310005.
Dir.: J. Zuydgeest.
Anna van Buren, IJstraat 30, 7523 HK, tel. 4355334.
Dep.: G.J. van Heekstraat 173, 7521 EC, tel. 4359376.
Dir.: mevr. C.H. Hogebrink.
De Dillenburg, Ouverturestraat 68, 7534 CP, tel. 4611776.
Dir.: B. Menkveld.
Prins Floris, Vastertlanden 169, 7542 LR, tel. 4764661.
Dep.: het Stroink 112, 7542 GT, tel. 4770946.
Dir.: H. Peters.
Marnix, De Posten 145, 7544 LR, tel. 4763709.
Dep.: De Posten 153, 7544 LR, tel. 4763709.
Dir.: W. Wilts-Verbeek.
Prins Maurits, Geessinkbrink 1, 7544 CW, tel. 4763165.
Dir.: J.N. Noordman.
Oranje-Nassau, Staringstraat 15, 7514 DE, tel. 4358616.
Dir.: R. Slok.
Prins Willem, Veldkampplantsoen 9, 7513 ZD, tel. 4317090.
Dir.: A. ten Bouwhuis-Veldhuizen.
Prins Willem Alexander, Ravenhorsthoek 34, 7546 EA, tel. 4774729.
Dir.: E. Koppen-Beimers.

BIJZONDER BASISONDERWIJS (GEREFORMEERD)
De Bron, Haaksbergerstraat 416, 7545 GA, tel. 4323489.
Dir.: A.C. van Ooijen.
De Fontein, Elshofplein 7, 7531 ZD, tel. 4357932.
Dir.: L. Sollie.

BIJZONDER BASISONDERWIJS (NEUTRAAL)
ESV, Enschedese Schoolvereniging, Tichelweg 7, 7523 AL, tel. 4357787.
Dir.: J.W. Vodégel.
Vrije School, Dr. Benthemstraat 54, 7514 CM, tel. 4354654.
Dir.: mevr. E. Steinmeijer-van Ooyen.
Interzuilaire opvangklas, Javastraat 6, 7512 ZJ, tel. 4354654.
Dir.: L.C.M. Geilenkirchen.

BIJZONDER BASISONDERWIJS (ISLAMITISCH)
Al-Ummah, Javastraat 6, 7512 ZJ, tel. 4319935.
Dir.: J.E.L. Maduro.

OPENBAAR SPECIAAL EN VOORTGEZET SPECIAAL ONDERWIJS
De Ark (so-lom), Madoerastraat 4, 7512 DL, tel. 4316164.
Dir.: G.H.A. Wiggers.
Het Sloepje (iobk), het Bijvank 250, 7544 DB, tel. 4775826.
Dir.: mevr. A. Rotting.
De Huifkar (so en vso-zmlk), Keppelerdijk 2, 7535 PE, tel. 4312148.
Dep.:Meeuwenstraat 160, 7523 XZ, tel. 4332240.
Dir.: J.J. v. Zorge.
De Klipper (vso-lom), het Bijvank 270, 7504 RC, tel. 4766652.
Dir.: W.M. de Vette.
Het Schip (vso- zmok), Groot Bruninkstraat 9, 7544 RN, tel. 4773300.
Dep.: Blekerstraat 105, 7513 DT, tel. 4321403.
Dir.: G. Dijkhuizen.
De Tender (so-mlk), Poolmansweg 245, 7545 LR, tel. 4318848.
Dir.: H. Zwarteveen.
De Werkhaven (so-lom), Meeuwenstraat 4, 7523 XV, tel. 4333762.
Dir.: A.N. Schulenberg.
De Wissel (vso-mlk), Weth. Nijhuisstraat 70, 7545 NK, tel. 4317347.
Dir.: H. Akkerman.

BIJZONDER SPECIAAL EN VOORTGEZET SPECIAAL ONDERWIJS
Dr. Ariënsschool, rk (so-mlk) Park de Kotten 320, 7522 EN, tel. 4356795.
Dir.: H.B.A. Ticheler.
Titus Brandsmaschool, rk (vso-mlk), Mekkelholtspad 4, 7523 DC, tel. 4339126
Dir.: F.P.M.J. Coehorst.

break into or modify. One prime perpetuator of the system is the legal requirement that all schools, run by whatever group, must be treated with meticulous equality. This has the consequence that whatever new financial gain one makes must automatically be granted to all—even if they have not specifically requested it.

While these 'particular' schools—in particular the religious schools—were originally intended to serve mainly a specific segment of the population, they are not exclusive and in practice there is considerable crossing of 'lines'. Many otherwise strongly religiously-oriented families send their children to public school if they think it offers better education, but the opposite happens even more commonly. Recent surveys have shown that denominational schools enjoy a higher reputation than public schools, both protestant and Catholic *Atheneums* and HAVO's showing a significantly higher rate of continuation into university; the protestant schools averaged a higher percentage of choices of mathematics as an exam subject, and a higher rate of those awarded the diploma.

Apparently these schools are being used by large numbers of families not otherwise connected with the religious denomination. Still, the enrollment in these denominational schools has been slowly decreasing in recent years to the advantage of 'neutral', non-denominational schools. Another thing that has been happening, a considerably less fortunate one, is the tendency of these schools, both denominational and neutral, to reflect a new social class system. In the school systems in the western cities, public schools show a far higher percentage of attendance by the children of ethnic minorities while 'neutral particular' (= private) schools have a disproportionately high percentage of white children. There are protestant and Catholic schools in the west attended largely by Moslem children.

Even though the central government has the final say in deciding basic standards such as teacher training, teacher/class ratios and examinations, the necessity of dealing with so many well-entrenched special interests at every turn greatly restricts its maneuverability, and even its assigned role, in educational issues and policy. What might look like anarchy, however, is turned into a reasonably smoothly-working system by the deeply-engrained habit in the Netherlands of accommodation and compromise.

The first university in the Netherlands was Leiden, founded in 1575 on the initiative of Prince William of Orange. It was followed by the universities of Groningen in 1614 and Utrecht in 1636. These are universities run by the State; Amsterdam's Municipal University was founded in 1632. Two other universities were founded in the 17th century that have since disappeared again: Franeker in Friesland and Harderwijk in Gelderland—where the old 'academy' building can still be seen today. Though all these are far from being the oldest in Europe, during the 17th and 18th centuries they developed a distinguished reputation as centers of learning. It was to this group of universities, under the leadership of Leiden, that both scholars and students migrated from all over Europe because they were the homes of the new scientific method based on the philosophy of Descartes. For a long period they were the battleground on which the debate over the new Cartesian system of inquiry was carried on.

In the 'old' academic style of organization that evolved during this 17th century and lasted until after World War II, the university consisted of a number of relatively autonomous professors. Each of these had staked out an area of specialization and ruled over a small empire of staff and students. Universities were fully supported by the state, which however did not interfere in organization or curriculum. University study was for a small elite, who customarily took advantage of the relatively lax rules for progression through to completion of education. The university was seen not primarily as a training ground for specific professional requirements but more as a place to sharpen the wits and develop the personality into the *homo universalis*, the man of universal breadth and learning. A group of about a dozen *stellingen* 'theses' today still form the last page of all dissertations written at Dutch universities, and they propose points of view on a wide variety of topics the writer is willing to defend in public. They are the last modern survival of this much older ideal of learning.

Today there are thirteen universities in the Netherlands. These are divided, first of all, into 'universities' and *technische universiteiten* or 'universities of technology'. Secondly there is a distinction, at least theoretical, between state and private institutions. Erasmus University was founded in 1973 from an amalgamation of the School of Economics and the School of Medicine in Rotterdam, and the newest university, Limburg, was opened in Maastricht in 1976. The first of the privately-run universities was the *Vrije Universiteit*

'Free University' in Amsterdam, founded in 1880 by the orthodox-Calvinist protestant church. Today it is dependent on state support and the church influence on administration is minimal. The Catholic University of Nijmegen was founded in 1923 as a means of expanding educational opportunities for Catholic Students, though over the years it has lost more and more of its specifically Catholic character. Recently the trend has been to emphasize the religious component even at the expense of smaller numbers of students. The Catholic University in Tilburg, now called the Catholic University of Brabant, was founded in 1927 as a university of business and economics.

The universities in the Netherlands

STATE	PRIVATE
Erasmus (Rotterdam)	Amsterdam (Municipal)
Leiden	Amsterdam, Free (Orthodox Reformed)
Groningen	Nijmegen (Roman Catholic)
Utrecht	Brabant (Tilburg; Roman Catholic)
Open university (Heerlen)	

UNIVERSITIES OF TECHNOLOGY
Delft
Eindhoven
Twente (Enschede)
Wageningen

The universities of Technology are Delft (1905), Wageningen (1918)—an agricultural university and probably the best known of all of them abroad, Eindhoven (1957) and Twente in Enschede (1964). All these institutions, whether privately run or not, are fully financed by the state. Universities of course supplement their budgets by undertaking research for government institutions and private companies. Next to these thirteen there is the 'Open University', offering university education on a non-resident, 'extension' basis.

With the founding of new universities to meet increasingly specific needs, and especially after the *technische universiteiten* were instituted, the whole higher-education concept became increasingly 'rationalized' and oriented toward specific professional and career goals. This meant gradually growing pressure on the old-style elite institutions which had become relatively self-serving and inaccessible to the rest of society. But the gradual evolution that was taking place in the first half of the 20th century was apparently not rapid enough. The social upheavals of the '60s that affected all western countries did not allow time for gradual development but swept away a good bit of the old system—in all institutions, including the presumably more modern technologically-oriented ones—and substituted a 'democratic' system that is still a predominant feature.

The revolts and radical confrontations of the '60s led to a thorough reorganization of the universities in the '70s as well as a firmer government role. Today research is done by closely supervised teams, the whole path through university toward a degree has been spelled out in strict requirements, and the professor's former all-powerful role has been deemphasized. In 1982 a basic study of four years was instituted, successful completion of which gives the right to use the title *doctorandus* 'candidate'. About 40% of students then go on to more specialized study. Students have long since ceased to be an elite group, and the numbers of those going on into higher education match figures in other countries—provided we count other non-university higher-education institutions, to be discussed in a moment.

Now that the confrontational style of the '60s and '70s has become a fading memory, universities are more and more expected to 'repay their debt to society' by showing closer connections with it. Ties with the business community are increasing rapidly and universities are subtly (and many would take exception to that word 'subtly') becoming more market-driven. One new element in the picture has been the strong competition between universities that until now have been accustomed to being comfortable parts of the same system. All universities place advertisements in an effort to attract good students.

But these 13 universities, preparing students for independent work in an academic or professional setting, are only half the higher-education picture. A roughly equal number of students get professional education at the 80 *hogescholen*, many of which we could call 'polytechnic colleges' (rather than 'high schools'; it is precisely to avoid this misunderstanding abroad that they are more and more tending to style themselves 'universities' but without joining the ranks of the above 13). The universities and the *hogescholen* used to be two separate worlds, but in recent years they have been coming closer together and now complement each other. Moving from one side of higher-education to the other can now be accomplished relatively readily.

FURTHER READING

The Dutch Education System. Zoetermeer: Ministry of Education and Science, 1988.

The Institutes of Technology in the Netherlands. Zoetermeer: Ministry of Education and Science [Annual].

Stannard, Jessica and Robert Warmenhoven, *Higher Education in the Netherlands.* The Hague: NUFFIC, n.d.

Newsletter. Zoetermeer, Ministry of Education and Science [Each 2-4 page issue is devoted to one topic in Dutch education; published irregularly].

8 The Dutch language

The little word 'the' in the title of this chapter implies that we are about to talk about something as clearly delimited as 'THE Dutch government', but its tone of confidence is a bit misplaced. Though 'the Standard Language' has just as real an existence as a cultural institution as the government does, those who use it as their everyday means of communication are seldom aware of how much is going on all the time in 'the language' or where the boundaries of 'standardness' are. There is wide disagreement about who, if anyone, has any right to prescribe any standard at all for the country. The fact that the Dutch language is used throughout the country is merely based on tradition; it has never been declared the 'official' language of the country. The 'standard language' of education and the mass media is in actuality a general ideal to be aimed at, and the simplicity implied in its name covers a much more diffuse and unwieldy reality.

Where English speakers—including Americans—will occasionally invoke the ideal of the best usage with the phrase 'the King's English', the Dutch even more often speak of ABN, a form of the language supposedly in use throughout the country by all social classes. But although most people call the language by these initials, the term they represent, *Algemeen Beschaafd Nederlands*, is itself rapidly becoming obsolete because the word *beschaafd* 'polite' or 'civilized' carries a paternalistic implication that is out of step with present-day attitudes. Some speak of *Algemeen Nederlands*, the first word meaning 'general'. The term *Standaardnederlands* is perhaps more popular, but in fact no universally accepted term for the standard language has ever evolved. The term *Nederlands* for the language is more or less what we mean by 'Dutch'. However diffuse and hard to define, the standard language is a powerful instrument for national cultural consciousness, and it plays a role in the much larger question of national identity.

Every language that is used as a means of everyday communication has many types of social variation within it. The Dutch language reflects stylistic variation in a striking way in the sharp distinction that is made between 'spoken language' and 'written language'. The first, called *spreektaal*, refers to the style, types of sentence construction, and especially vocabulary in general use in all informal situations: casual conversation, family letter writing, newsletters of modest pretensions, and so on. Written language, called *schrijftaal*, occupies a different social niche and is ultimately inherited from the social manners of the 17th century. Formal documents, bureaucratic pronouncements, newspapers and many types of public speaking beyond the most ordinary are apt to fall readily into a distinctly different, more 'elegant' style. This uses many words not part of everyday speech and has its own more elaborate types of sentence construction.

For most of its history down to the present century, the special written-language style was a useful means by which any individual could demonstrate an elegant, well-bred command of good manners. In the present age in which less importance is attached to one's public image, the written style

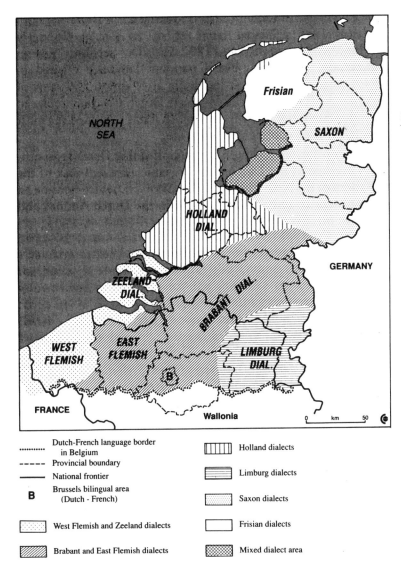

Fig. 8.1
The Dutch dialects

··········	Dutch-French language border in Belgium	⊞	Holland dialects
- - - - -	Provincial boundary	⊟	Limburg dialects
———	National frontier	▒	Saxon dialects
B	Brussels bilingual area (Dutch - French)	☐	Frisian dialects
⣿	West Flemish and Zeeland dialects	▨	Mixed dialect area
⫽	Brabant and East Flemish dialects		

has been edging steadily closer to the ordinary spoken style, though the gap is still noticeable. Many Dutch writers are fond of exploiting the distinction between spoken and written styles for various effects. Playing with the language is a favorite sport among the educated, and central to this is the pun. Display ads in the newspaper and in public places such as train plaforms are as often as not based on some word play—whether the intent is commercial or public service.

Some years ago, there was a popular radio series called *Wie brengt me thuis?* (Can you tell where I come from?). Each program featured someone talking for a few minutes, whereupon listeners were invited to venture, on the basis of accent, rhythm and intonation, a guess as to what region, city—or, if possible, the section of the city—the speaker came from. Whether challenged by a program or not, Dutch speakers when listening to each other are sharply aware of the many little differences in speech that betray region of origin, and it is part of the social game of placing the other person that goes on all the time. Standardization can never be complete, and the differences that arise when speakers are separated geographically have their own social communicative value.

Any language is always slowly but steadily changing, and if speakers are spread out in groups in the countryside and out of communication with each other for long enough periods of time, what was first a subtly different accent will eventually evolve into a sharply distinct form of the language, a 'dialect'. It was just this that happened in the Netherlands over many centuries, as it did in all European countries. Along with other regional agrarian traditions such as folklore and dress, these apparently innumerable local dialects form a dense network that covers the country. Many of them, though, differ from each other only slightly, so that it is possible to group them into a small number of major regions.

In spite of the homogenizing effects of modern communications, dialect speech still survives in the Netherlands, in some regions naturally more strongly than in others. Some of the accent that allows speakers to place each other geographically is there because that person has carried over some habits from the dialect speech of 'home'. Linguists have for many years looked at the overwhelming pressure exerted by the standard language and predicted the disappearance of all the local dialects except perhaps a few remnants in remote areas. But present-day consciousness of 'roots' and pride in regional origin may be reversing this trend. Investigators have noted the rise of what they call 'regiolects', forms of speech common to a large region. Strong identification with locality has not yet been centralized out of existence in the Netherlands, where there are few truly 'remote' areas. Speakers apparently continue to need these complex social signals of local group solidarity.

If the forms of speech of distinct communities are isolated from each other for even longer periods of time, say one or two thousand years instead of a few hundred, 'dialect' variations of a recognizable form of speech will continue to diverge until they are distinct, often mutually unintelligible languages. There is no sharp line between the 'dialect' and the 'language' stage of differences between any two given forms of speech. This divergence process is always socially complicated, with some neighboring speech communities 'splitting off' and become isolated sooner than others, and as a result becoming more divergent. Since there are usually no historical records of changing speech over such long periods of time, we can only look at the end result and guess at how the various divergences must have taken place.

This diagram presents a short list of words in each of the four languages most closely related to Dutch: Frisian, English and German. Each of these four language names refers to a 'standard' language that serves as a general means of communication but is itself in ultimate origin a local dialect. If we look at the lists starting at the bottom, it appears that in some respects English and Frisian have some similarities not shared by Dutch and German (an *ee*-like vowel in many words where the latter have an *aa*- or *oo*-like one; no *-n-* in some common words where the latter have one; a *ch*-like sound where the

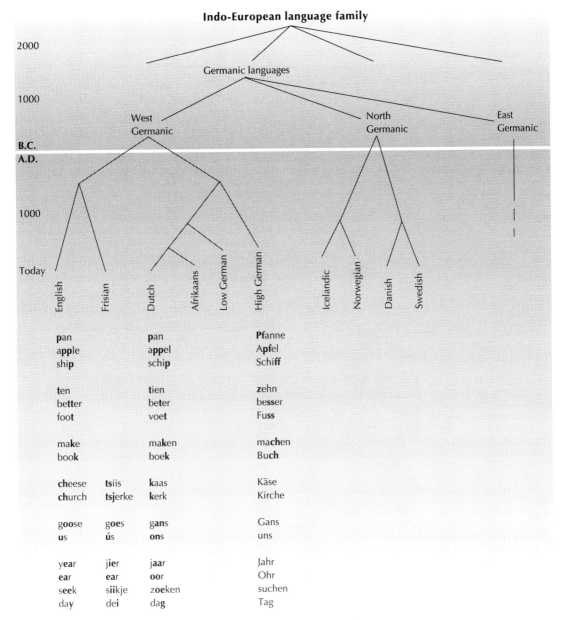

Indo-European language family

			English	Frisian	Dutch	Afrikaans	Low German	High German	Icelandic	Norwegian	Danish	Swedish

English	Frisian	Dutch	High German
pan		pan	Pfanne
apple		appel	Apfel
ship		schip	Schiff
ten		tien	zehn
better		beter	besser
foot		voet	Fuss
make		maken	machen
book		boek	Buch
cheese	tsiis	kaas	Käse
church	tsjerke	kerk	Kirche
goose	goes	gans	Gans
us	ús	ons	uns
year	jier	jaar	Jahr
ear	ear	oor	Ohr
seek	siikje	zoeken	suchen
day	dei	dag	Tag

latter have *k-*, for instance). But, moving up further, it appears that in a great many ways English and Dutch have things in common that differentiate them from German. These differences involve not just a half-dozen or so words but run consistently all through the vocabularies of the languages in question.

By means of this type of comparisons, and skipping over all the intervening detail, linguists justify a 'family tree' of language relationships, which we see constructed above the lists of words. The terminology varies somewhat, but 'West Germanic' is the traditional term used to refer to the grouping of four we have been considering. These family relationships are based on changes and divergences that have been going on for many centuries, and they show that the similarities between Dutch and English on the one hand, and Dutch and German on the other, have a very long history. An English speaker who gains some familiarity with the Dutch language will occasionally notice these two-way similarities and be heard to claim that it is a 'mixture of English and German', as if a language were a capricious concoction made up recently. This unfortunate impression of 'mixture' is only reinforced by another fact of modern life that has no connection with the above linguistic relationships: in recent decades Dutch— as well as German—has borrowed considerable numbers of English words.

If we were to continue with such lists of words (actually much longer than the few samples here) from apparently related but even more dissimilar languages, we would see that the Scandinavian languages have a close similarity among themselves. But they must have gone their own way geographically at an even earlier period in time, and they form what is called a 'North Germanic' branch of the Germanic family. Continuing on beyond this becomes much more difficult because the divergences have become so extreme over long periods of time, but it can be done. Such comparisons show the relationship of the Germanic family of languages to the Romance, Slavic and a number of other groups in the 'Indo-European' language family.

The route from local dialect to national standard language is different in each country in which this development has taken place. Most often it is the

Fig. 8.2
Dutch in its geographical relationship to Low German and High German

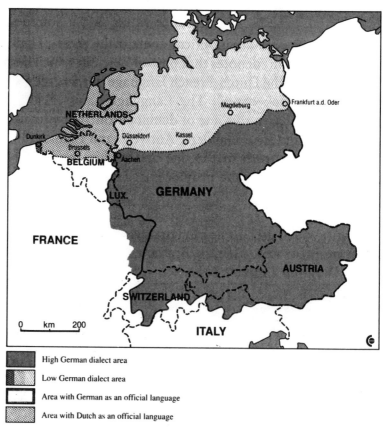

High German dialect area

Low German dialect area

Area with German as an official language

Area with Dutch as an official language

speech of a culturally dominant city that spreads its influence across the country: the French standard language is essentially the dialect of Paris, standard British English is the language of London and its environs. So it is not difficult to anticipate that the evolution of a standard language in the Netherlands might be closely involved with the cultural and commercial dominance of Amsterdam from the end of the 16th century on. The city's role as the capital of first a republic and then a monarchy created the prestige that led to the widespread imitation of its language.

By the late 1580's, over 400 years ago, Amsterdam was the commercial center of a small group of provinces that were succeeding in freeing themselves politically from foreign domination. The city was rapidly establishing itself as the economic and cultural capital of the European world. Antwerp and other cities to the south were not so fortunate, and large numbers of political refugees migrated northward and settled in Amsterdam and its satellite cities. The speech and the written style that evolved in the following decades were mainly that of Amsterdam but with a strong admixture of influences from the south. But the eventual standard language was the 'dialect of Amsterdam' only with the understanding that the 16th- and 17th-century city was just as much a mosaic of immigrants from everywhere as it is today. An equally powerful former of standard usage was the *Statenvertaling*, the government-commissioned translation of the Bible that was completed in 1637 and has had a strong influence ever since.

By around 1550 books began to be written investigating and describing the sounds of the language and describing its grammar; there were numerous guides to 'correct' pronunciation and spelling from the 16th century on, and dictionaries quickly reached the level of extensive coverage of all that could be gathered about 'the' language and all its dialect forms.

The title of the recent *Algemene Nederlandse Spraakkunst* contains, as its third word, the one meaning 'grammar', a word which was invented in the confident 17th century in an effort to 'purify' the language of foreign elements. Though all the European languages have had 'puristic' movements (and many countries around the world still regularly attempt to 'purify' their language), Dutch may be unique in the number of 17th-century purisms that have found common acceptance. The mathematician Simon Stevin—who among other achievements invented the decimal system—made up many terms that are still in use (*middellijn* 'diameter', *driehoek* 'triangle', *breuk* 'fraction'). School subjects are still referred to with the native terminology popularized in the 17th century (*wiskunde* 'mathematics', *natuurkunde* 'physics', *aardrijkskunde* 'geography' and a great many more). The entire present-day grammatical terminology prefers the native terms to the international ones nearly all other languages use:

onderwerp	subject	*meervoud*	plural
voorwerp	object	*klinker*	vowel
werkwoord	verb	*medeklinker*	consonant
bijwoord	adverb	*lettergreep*	syllable
enkelvoud	singular	*telwoord*	numeral

and so on.

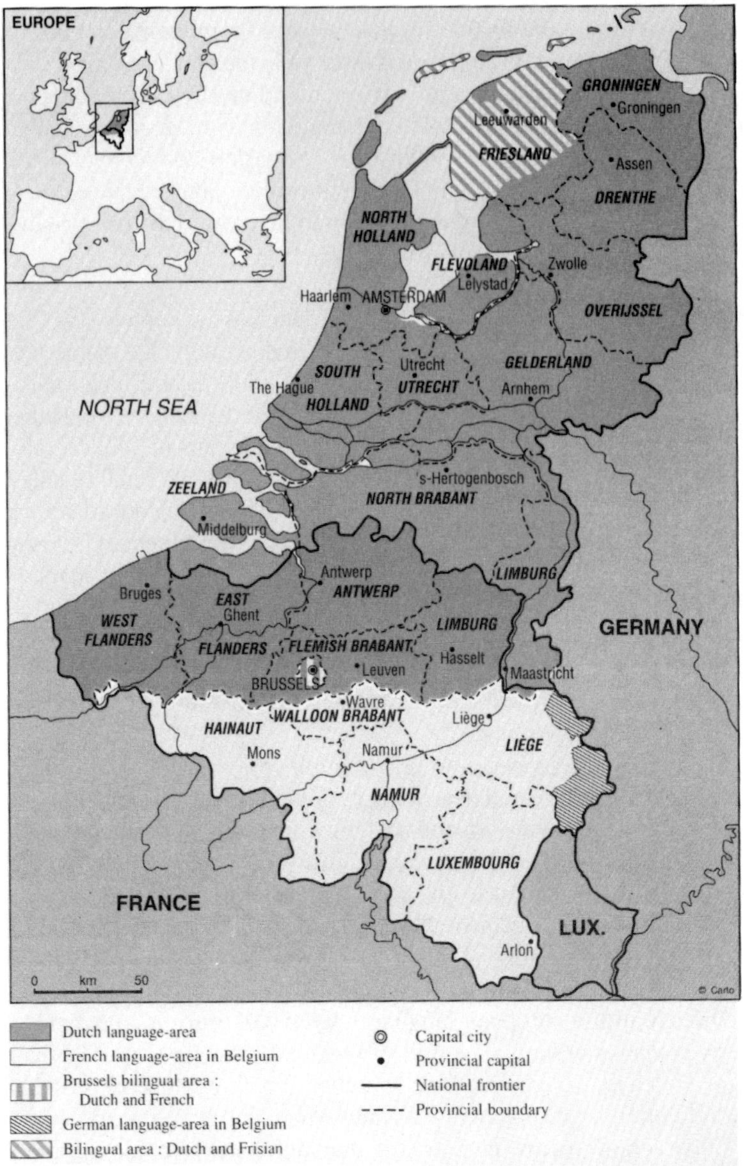

Fig. 8.3
The total Dutch-speaking area, including Flemish Belgium. The shaded area in the north is Frisian.

Dutch language-area	
French language-area in Belgium	
Brussels bilingual area : Dutch and French	
German language-area in Belgium	
Bilingual area : Dutch and Frisian	

◎ Capital city
• Provincial capital
—— National frontier
---- Provincial boundary

The stimulus for inventing so many new terms was that this literary language, developing in the commercially successful cities, was coming to replace Latin as a means of writing history, philosophy, and the sciences. In addition to this, the language was the vehicle of a many-sided literature—poetry, drama, essays, letters, stories—continuing a literary tradition that extends back into the Middle Ages.

All these developments, whether commercial, literary or linguistic, we see taking place in a cultural region that includes the present-day Netherlands and Belgium together. In fact, the earliest autonomous urban culture, and with it the first stimulus to write literature in a language that was more than just a local dialect, developed in the southern cities, what is now Belgium. A glance at the maps (Fig. 8.1 and 8.2) shows that they make no linguistic distinction between what lies north or south of the present-day national border. It was not until political separation took place toward the end of the 16th century that the 'Dutch' language with its already long cultural history came to be identified more narrowly with Amsterdam and the northern cities.

All this has some important consequences for the question of what the language is called. The term used in many of the preceding chapters was 'Dutch', along with mention of the native term *Nederlands*. This is accurate enough, though at the same time both terms conceal some vexing terminological difficulties, to say nothing of common misunderstandings. Today the same standard language is used by the 15 million speakers in the Netherlands and over 6 million in northern Belgium. Notwithstanding the name *Nederland* for only the first of these two countries, the official name of the language is *Nederlands*. Some people often do refer to the language as *Hollands,* which reflects its historical place in the 17th century and after, but this term contains the same provincialism as *Holland* for the country, and like it is more and more being replaced in ordinary usage by *Nederland* and *Nederlands*. This acceptance of a single name for the common standard language marks a conscious return to the cultural unity of an earlier time.

Both the adjective *Nederlands* and its English equivalent 'Dutch' share a certain awkwardness: when speaking of geography, social customs, folklore, politics and the like they both refer to *Nederland,* or the Netherlands, the conspicuous exception being the language. The extension of the meaning of 'Dutch' to refer equally to the standard language of northern Belgium is not yet old enough to have become habitual, though there is no reason why it should not cover the language of both cultural regions in this way. Americans, after all, speak and write 'English' and Austrians 'German'. This leaves the term *Vlaams* and its English equivalent 'Flemish' to refer, in present-day usage, to all that is unique to this southern cultural region: dialects, folklore, attitudes, but precisely *not* to the language.

Some non-standard, dialect forms of speech used by settlers in South Africa have since developed into the standard language called *Afrikaans.* In spite of a number of differences that have arisen during three centuries of separation, Dutch and Afrikaans speakers are able to converse with little difficulty, and Afrikaans spoken in a Dutch TV program is usually not subtitled, as all languages other than Dutch are. But the Dutch are not able to hear Afrikaans—a widely-spoken language of political importance and with a distinguished literary tradition of its own—as a separate but equal language. It has a slightly comical sound to the Dutch ear, as if it were still a rural dialect without urban polish, and references to it tend to have a condescending tone.

This would hardly be worth mentioning if it were not for the fact that the Dutch find themselves on the receiving end of a very similar attitude from the Germans. Both Dutch and German have an equally long historical development, many similarities in their cultural histories, and both have had extensive literature written in them for many centuries. Both the lists of words above and the map suggest the close genetic relationship of the language, and at the same time the distinctiveness of each. It is precisely this close relationship that is part of the problem. A German once remarked that Germans could respect the Dutch language more if only it were less closely related. Dutch is linguistically similar to the dialects spoken in the north of Germany ('Low' German dialects have words like *appel, maken* which closely resemble the Dutch words), and to the ear of someone accustomed to the 'High German' standard language *(Apfel, machen)*, Dutch has a slightly comical sound. Literary tradition or political and economic importance affect this attitude just as little as they affect the Dutch feeling about Afrikaans.

The Dutch have equally strong attitudes about German, but they are considerably more complicated. Germany is, and always has been, the large and at times overbearing neighbor to the east. Within the memory of many still alive it was a military occupier, and many attitudes from wartime occupation have been passed on to younger generations. The postwar relations between the Netherlands and Germany are also complex, and they have had many ups and downs (see Ch. 18). At a more fundamental level, the Dutch are well aware of German condescension toward their language and culture. The result of all this is that the German language—an even more 'close relative' than English—enjoys practically no real prestige among Dutch speakers. Many are quite ready to speak and write it as a matter of practical politics and business, but nobody wants to be taken for a German, and one some-times gets the impression that a certain level of incompetence in the language is flaunted. It is interesting to note that, in texts in the common four languages Dutch-English-French-German, they are almost invariably arranged so that Dutch and German do not stand next to each other: English or French is usually in between, and often both. Almost no Dutch people are consciously aware of this habit.

NEDERLANDS/FRANÇAIS
There is also an English/German edition
Es gibt auch eine Englisch/Deutsche Ausgabe

ENGLISH/DEUTSCH
Er is ook een Nederlands/Franse editie
Il y a aussi une edition hollandaise/française

The Dutch have some other attitudes about their language that are even more revealing to us as outside observers. From early childhood, all Dutch speakers grow up with the realization that the whole world beyond the little circle of their borders does not speak Dutch and is not going to learn to, so therefore—the reasoning continues—we are the ones who must do the accommodating. Apparently this attitude, or something like it, has a long history. In 1780 John Adams wrote home from the Netherlands 'The Dutch language is spoken by none but themselves. Therefore they converse with nobody and nobody converses with them.'*

The result is that the Dutch get an intensive exposure to foreign languages, and achievements in this area are a matter of national pride. Foreigners often feel that the Dutch take this to absurd lengths, as when in a TV documentary shown abroad a Dutch doctor and his patient are shown carrying on a confi-

---

* Barbara Tuchman, The First Salute. New York: Knopf, 1988, p. 24.

The Frisian language

Frisian is spoken and understood today as a first language by about 500,000 people, and it is read and written by somewhat smaller numbers. Nearly all of them are in the province of Friesland. The illustrations (p. 79) show how in genetic relationship, the language stands between Dutch and English. It is a distinct, related language and not a dialect of Dutch. On the infrequent occasions when Frisian is spoken on Dutch TV, subtitling needs to be provided.

The struggle of the Frisian-speaking population to win the right to begin schooling in their language and to have it used in the courts in the province has been similar to that of other minority-language speakers in Europe. In Friesland, there is a strong national pride in the language and its long literary tradition, and the language is seen as an important element in the preservation of a cultural identity. Its fostering is to a great extent in the hands of the 'Frisian Academy' in Leeuwarden, the provincial capital. There are Dutch-Frisian grammars and dictionaries, and now a grammar in English (not the first one).

Use of the language is vigorously promoted, and any opportunity to expand its use in administrative circles is exploited. Its place as official language in governmental organizations has been secured. Frisian-language radio is in existence as well as a few hours a week of Frisian TV programming. But although it is still gaining in popularity, it remains a minority language under constant pressure from the majority one.

dential conversation about the possibility of dying ... in heavily accented English.

But perhaps surprisingly, there really are limits: In 1990 the Minister of Education off-handedly but seriously proposed that eventually all the universities—becoming increasingly internationalized—switch to English as their language of instruction. The ensuing storm of protest made the news for weeks after, and the minister deemed is prudent to beat a hasty retreat. A less apparent consequence of these same circumstances, however, is that in those instances where a foreign visitor does learn the language, especially if he learns it well, the response is invariably a curious 'What did you learn Dutch for?' or an even more astonished 'Why would anyone go to the trouble to learn Dutch?' That the Dutch are not really without pride in their language comes to the surface, though, as they view permanent residents: they tend to be affronted when those participating in the society and welfare system are not able to handle the language at a reasonable level.

At the moment the Dutch are vigorously debating what might be in store for their language in the new integrated Europe, inevitably dominated by the 'large' languages. The fact that the Dutch language is already inundated with English words is admittedly not a result of this, but still it is anything but a hopeful sign. A few Dutch have resigned themselves to seeing their language reduced to the status of a quaint local dialect and ultimately disappearing altogether. The similarites in the often despairing public debate about the threat to the Dutch language to the anxious prognoses about the Dutch environment recently produced the wry remark *Het Nederlands wordt niet afgeschaft, alleen het Nederlandse landschap wordt afgeschaft* 'The Dutch language won't be abolished, it's only the Dutch landscape that will be abolished.'

Others at the opposite end of the spectrum argue that the language spoken by 21,000,000 people (after all, far from one of the smallest of languages, and one once carried around the world), and offering them rich cultural resources, should take its rightful place alongside its neighbors. But, it is often pointed out, thinking of the language being used at all on the international stage will require some sweeping changes in attitude.

FURTHER READING

Brachin, P., *The Dutch language: A Survey*. London: Thornes/Leiden: Brill, 1985.

Donaldson, Bruce C., *Dutch: A Linguistic History of Holland and Belgium*. Leiden: Martinus Nijhoff, 1983.

Fasol, P. (ed.), *De toekomst van het Nederlands in de Europese Unie*. The Hague: Nederlandse Taalunie, 1994.

Mahmood, Cynthia, *Frisian and Free: Study of an Ethnic Minority of the Netherlands*. Prospect Heights, Ill.: Waveland, 1989.

Vandeputte, O., *Dutch: The Language of Twenty Million Dutch and Flemish People*. Rekkem: Stichting Ons Erfdeel, 1993.

Wester, Jet, *Gaat het Nederlands teloor? Drie essays*. Houten: De Haan, 1989 [In the following year the debate was continued with: Diemer, W., *Gaat het Nederlands teloor? Een vierde visie*. Assen: Servo, 1990].

9 Constitutional monarchy

The monarchy in the Netherlands has a simple, readily recognized symbol in the color orange, used on any ceremonial occasions when 'nationhood' is invoked. It is a reflection of their family name Oranje Nassau, the family being indirect descendents of the 16th-century Prince William 'the Silent', regarded as the founder of the country. *Koninginnedag* (April 30) is a national 'official' celebration of the Queen's birthday displaying solidarity with the monarchy, but it is also a holiday filled with various traditional festivities. The holiday is a cultural ritual in being an extension of the family birthday celebration. Just as the person celebrating a birthday is expected to entertain, this is the day on which the monarch honors deserving subjects by graciously bestowing various medals in what is popularly known as the *lintjesregen* 'ribbon rain' (referring to the ribbon associated with the medal).

But the most important annual ceremonial reminder of the function of the monarchy is *Prinsjesdag*, the third Tuesday in September. In a colorful but solemn procession, the king or queen rides to the parliament buildings for the official opening ceremony attended by the members of both Upper and Lower Chambers. The monarch delivers the *Troonrede*, a speech written together with the governing cabinet that assesses the present and coming year. It is broadcast live and published in the dailies, and extensively commented on in the mass media.

These ceremonies are reminders of the delicate balance of monarch and government within the constitutional system. But at the more obvious level, their importance is simply the visibility of the monarchy. The two special

Fig. 9.1
Prinsjesdag. The queen arrives at the parliament building

days are the peaks, but there are birthdays of other members of the royal family throughout the year, and their names and pictures appear regularly in the press, most often in ceremonial functions. But in the Netherlands, the royal family is anything but the 'public property' its equivalent in England is. The Dutch royal family understands the need to be seen, but at the same time expects privacy from the inquisitive eye of the public. The family maintains a reserve which is an accepted aspect of social life in the Netherlands.

Queen Wilhelmina, who ruled 1898-1948, was a truly 'royal' figure who was able to maintain an old-style monarchical relationship with her subjects. Much of her personal prestige as a sort of national 'mother' image was due to the moral leadership she was able to provide from exile during the war. Juliana, queen from 1948-1980, developed a relationship that was different from her mother's, a decidedly more common touch and a good level of communication. And yet she maintained a reserve that preserved some of the lingering 19th-century mystique of monarchy. The crises that developed during her reign (her involvement with a faith healer on behalf of her youngest daughter, the marriage of her daughter Irene to a pretender to the Spanish throne and Irene's subsequent renunciation of her own succession rights, her consort Prince Bernhard's involvement in a questionable enterprise) all had their painful aspects stemming from a lack of prompt public forthrightness, but in all these instances the public identified with her human side and showed overwhelming support.

Beatrix, whose investiture took place in 1980 (there is no 'coronation' in the Netherlands), carries on the traditional reserve, with a touch of royal flavor that sets her apart but avoids any show of grandeur that would not be accepted in egalitarian Dutch society. She makes no attempt to rely on the steadily vanishing mystique of royalty itself, and treats her function as a profession among others. Both the queen and her husband Prince Claus take their designated roles seriously, even with a mild perfectionism, and their professional conscientiousness helps create a high level of esteem for the monarchy and enables it to continue its evolution into the modern world. There is no obvious or natural commensurability of a hereditary monarchy with a modern democratic system, which means that ruling and governing are continual matters of flexible adaptation. The Dutch constitution does not spell out the power or authority of the monarch, leaving each one with the burden of constructing his or her own personal credibility.

European monarchies have had to evolve from the old institutions of power they once were into the instutions of confidence that are required by modern times. Those that were not able to do this have been swept away by history. The Dutch monarchy can be abolished at any time by an act of parliament, but it remains firmly established because the strength of the consent that supports it has been proved repeatedly. The Dutch people are not monarchists at heart (as for instance the British are) but republicans. It is only the high regard for the house of Oranje Nassau and its role in Dutch history that perpetuates the monarchy. There can be little doubt that if the family were to die out, a republican form of government would be proclaimed immediately. This should not disguise the fact that the monarchy as a highly visible institution and symbol of power also serves a 'lightning-rod' function. Although the names of various members of the royal family are regularly invoked in association with various discontents of society, two examples involving Beatrix will serve best to illustrate this role. In 1966 the wedding of Princess Beatrix and Prince Claus was held not in The Hague, the official residence of the royal family, but in Amsterdam, a city of traditionally republican sentiments which at the time was full of a highly charged, anti-authoritarian political atmosphere. On top of the general social unrest of the '60s came widespread public frustration with the postwar course of relations with Germany, and the world saw a dignified ceremony surrounded by rock-throwing, provocative banners, tear gas and smoke bombs. The investiture of Queen Beatrix in Amsterdam in 1980 was a similar scene, coming into the middle of tense confrontations focused on housing problems. In both these instances the royal family could have remained austerely 'above' politics, but they allowed themselves to be used as scapegoats.

In the Netherlands, a country in which society has traditionally been fragmented into divided and competing interests, an important symbolic unity linking all this is of particularly crucial importance. The monarchy not only provides this symbol but plays a similarly delicate role in the political process. During the period in which a new administration is being formed, it is the queen who represents continuity—an institution that will always be there in spite of the coming and going of political leaders and parties. In fact the last remaining area where the king or queen has any real power to intervene in the political process is in the formation of coalition cabinets (which as we will see all of them are). He or she directs the choice of the political leader responsible for carrying out this formation. It is an unwritten rule of thumb that the more disunity the politicians show, the more maneuvering room the monarch has to intervene.

Besides the ceremonial opening of parliament and the role in the formation of new governments, the king or queen presides over the Council of State, an advisory body that must be consulted on all draft legislation and international agreements, maintains contacts with the governors of provinces and mayors of cities as well as ambassadors abroad, and signs all laws and amendments, which become official by 'royal proclamation' (though in practice a cabinet minister must always countersign, and the law's effect is solely the responsibility of the administration). The monarch also receives the heads of diplomatic missions, represents the state abroad, awards national honors, raises citizens to the nobility, grants clemency to the condemned, and puts his or her image on coins.

The Dutch constitution is the oldest in Europe, and the second oldest in the world after the U.S. The meaning of the term 'constitutional monarchy' in the Netherlands is that the role of the monarch in the governmental process is clearly delimited. The central provision of the constitution is that the responsibility for governing the country rests with the Council of Ministers (the 'cabinet') on behalf of parliament, a responsibility which includes all actions of the royal family. So not surprisingly the cabinet has to decide how much of the family is to be included in the definition of 'royal family', and what the exact line of succession to the throne is to be.

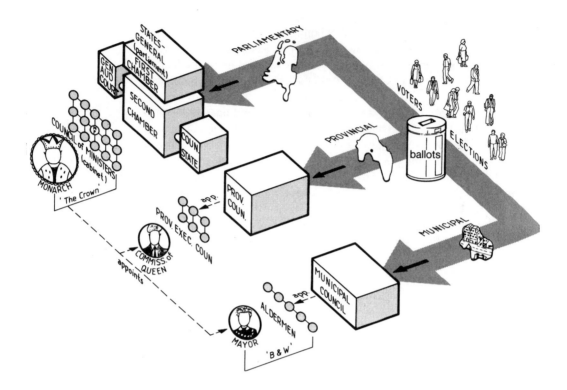

Fig. 9.2
The relationship of the national, provincial and municipal levels of administration

The governing of the country is constitutionally in the hands of the 'Crown', which means not the monarchy itself but the monarch plus the Council of Ministers together. But constitutional authority goes one step farther. Over a century and a half ago it was the popularly-elected Lower Chamber of parliament, not the ministers themselves, that won far-reaching and liberal rights from an autocratic monarch. The constitution provides that all actions of the Crown must be consented to, in turn, by parliament. The ongoing process of this review and consent—plainly the key to the whole democratic system—is spelled out below in rather simplified form. When there is wide disagreement on a major issue and support is withdrawn, the cabinet minister involved must resign. If the cabinet as a whole chooses to support him, it then resigns as a body and new elections must be held. Only the monarch remains untouched in this process.

The perspective diagram (Fig. 9.2) is an attempt to represent schematically the entire governmental system in the Netherlands. Let us take a rapid 'walk' through it, with comments along the way. Governing is the responsibility of the Crown, at the left. It is carried on in the name of, and with the cooperation of, three institutions called *Hoge Colleges van de Staat* 'Supreme Assemblies of the State', standing next to each other at the top. The *Raad van State* 'Council of State' is the senior advisory body to the Crown, the functions of which were mentioned just above. Its history goes back to 1531 when Emperor Charles V established an advisory council for his government in Brussels. The *Algemene Rekenkamer* 'General Chamber of Audit' has an even longer history, going back to the auditing courts instituted by the Dukes of Burgundy in the late Middle Ages. Though its membership and functions are regulated by parliament, the Chamber enjoys maximum independence and high prestige. Among its functions are checking and post-auditing, and reviewing policy effectiveness. Members of both these Supreme Assemblies stand outside politics and are appointed for life, which lends them both prestige and objectivity.

These two are overshadowed by the one in the center, the *Staten-Generaal* 'States General', the official name that goes back to the period when each of the autonomous provinces had its own representative assembly called 'states' and sent delegates to a 'general' coordinating one. Its everyday name is 'parliament'. Today it is a two-chamber representative assembly. The upper or 'first' serves the function of discussion and review of legislation. Its 75 members are elected not by popular vote but by the popularly-elected Provincial Assemblies. The lower or 'second' chamber with 150 members is at the heart of the whole system, the directly-elected representative assembly where ultimate power lies. But the power can be traced on back, by way of national elections, to the citizenry standing behind the whole process.

On the provincial level of government the system looks very similar. The equivalent of the Crown is the executive body formed by the Queen (or King)'s Commissioner, appointed by the Crown, and the Provincial Executive Council appointed by the Provincial Council, the popular representative assembly. This body also elects the members of the upper chamber.

Starting at the 'front' of the diagram once more at the municipal level, the equivalent of the Crown is the body formed by the mayor, also appointed by the Crown, and the 'aldermen' appointed by the popularly-elected Municipal Council. The executive body is officially *College van Burgemeester en Wethouders*, usually referred to as *B en W* for short. Elections at each of these three levels, the national, provincial and municipal, are held independently of each other, and under normal circumstances voting in the entire country is done on the same day.

One of the most striking features of this governmental system as a whole is the parallel way in which representative and executive power is organized on all three levels. In each case—municipal, provincial and national—a small executive body governs in the name of, and must have the consent of, an elected assembly. Each is headed by a chief executive not derived from the assembly itself: appointed at the municipal and provincial levels, hereditary at the national level. In other words, the 'Crown' serves as the model for all three. A closer look, however, shows a small but crucial difference. At the municipal and provincial levels the members of the executive council are selected from the representative assembly and remain members of it (the dotted line), whereas at the national level there is no such direct relationship. The absence of a dotted line here is actually the key to the way constitutional government works in the Netherlands.

Look again at the large diagram, but this time pay attention only to the 'Second Chamber' and the 'Cabinet'. The next illustration (Fig. 9.3) looks at the picture in this way, but it has also introduced some shadings that were omitted from the simplified overall diagram: the 'colors' of the different political parties. The interaction of well-defined political parties, with their various

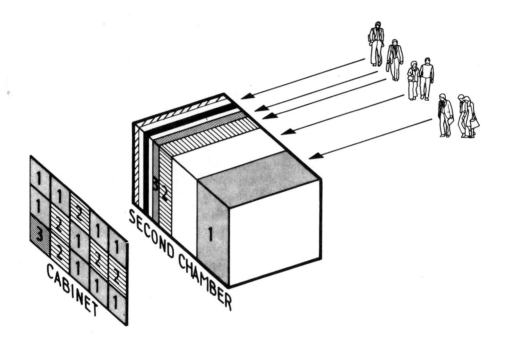

Fig. 9.3
A schematic representation
of the relation between the
parties in the lower
chamber and a coalition
cabinet. The latter reflects
some proportions
of the former.

programs and agendas, is central to the operation of all these governmental bodies at whatever level.

The 'Cabinet' is the council of ministers, the heads of the 15 or 16 ministries (the number is not fixed by law, and ministerial functions are frequently reorganized and recombined). It always consists of two or more parties which are given the power to govern after they have worked out a comprehensive enough agreement to cooperate, called the *regeerakkoord*. This is the foundation of the government's policies. The term 'government' is usually used in English to translate the Dutch word *regering*. But since this refers only to the cabinet in power at any one time, it more accurately matches the word 'administration'. The 'government' that runs all other everyday affairs is called *overheid*. The administration stays in power as long as it retains the support of parliament, but for no longer than four years. If this support is lost in midterm—the fate of more than half of all cabinets—new elections must be held.

It is in the Cabinet, which means in the staffs of the ministries, that nearly all legislation is generated. Bills are first discussed and agreed to by the cabinet, then ultimately go to parliament for discussion, amendment and approval. If a version of a bill acceptable to all concerned emerges from this process, it is signed by the monarch, countersigned by the minister most directly involved, and becomes law by *Koninklijk Besluit* 'Royal Proclamation'. The leadership of the cabinet through all this process is in the hands of its chairman, the *Minister-president* or Prime Minister. In the Netherlands this post has traditionally been a low-profile one of only modest power and prestige; the prime minister, for instance, does not control foreign policy as his colleagues do in many other countries, but must rely on the Foreign Minister to do this and thus share power with him and other ministers. Some prime ministers have, thanks to high personal achievement, managed to attain national prominence, and there is a noticeable tendency in the most recent times for the office to attract increasing prestige and glamour.

It remains to be seen whether the prime-minister post will continue to evolve into that of powerful chief executive that is a true counterpart—as the Dutch Prime Minister would like it to be—of the powerful prime ministers of the other EU countries he meets and works with regularly. Many are afraid the Dutch voice in organizations like the European Council will get progressively weaker if the prime minister's role is not strengthened. Not too many years ago, when a prime minister on a visit to the US yielded to understandable temptation and adopted a tone of authority that began to sound presidential, he had to endure considerable criticism in the press back home for this inflation of his expected role.

The cabinet acts, when it is functioning most smoothly, as a close-knit team which ideally must rise above the narrowest of political interests in compromising and getting a job done. Though, as the illustration shows, it has some of the same 'colors' as parliament does, it does not act as a party-by-party executive arm of parliament but in fact stands in a certain adversarial relationship to it. It is in the lower chamber of parliament that partisan politics finds its real arena. While partisan politics are hardly unknown in the cabinet and parliament regularly rises to the level of teamwork responsibility, a certain tension is built into the established relation between administrators and representatives. This brings both advantages and disadvantages.

On almost any day of reasonable weather, especially when it is especially pleasant, a visitor to the *Binnenhof* in The Hague, the square enclosed by the parliament buildings, sees not so much legislative earnestness or security guards as the atmosphere of a fair. People may be relaxing and enjoying refreshment, there may be small demonstrations, or the whole square may be full of protestors. It has been called a market square for ideas, feelings and demands, a sort of exchange where political views and demands are traded. Administrators are traditionally brought into constant direct contact with the issues they are expected to do something about. It is only fairly recently that the very volume of demonstrations has blunted their effectiveness, representatives paying less and less attention to any but the most forceful.

Each party's number of seats in parliament depends on the percentage of the total vote. A mere 0.67% of the total national vote is sufficient to elect one member of parliament, and there are always a certain number of single-member party delegations. By the nature of things, the parties with the largest consti-

The Ministries

Algemene Zaken
General Affairs;
the prime minister's office

Binnenlandse Zaken
Domestic Affairs

Buitenlandse Zaken
Foreign Affairs

Economische Zaken
Economic Affairs

Financiën
Finances

Sociale Zaken en Werkgelegenheid
Social Affairs and Employment

Defensie
Defense

Justitie
Justice

Onderwijs, Cultuur en Wetenschappen
Education, Culture and Sciences

Verkeer en Waterstaat
Transport and Public Works

Landbouw, Natuurbeheer en Visserij
Agriculture, Nature Management and Fisheries

Volkshuisvesting, Ruimtelijke Ordening en Milieubeheer
Housing, Physical Planning and Environment)

Volksgezondheid, Welzijn en Sport
Health, Welfare and Sports

Ontwikkelingssamenwerking
Development Cooperation

tuencies must maintain a broad, compromising stance on most issues, but the many smaller parties see their role as defending and promoting narrowly-defined, specific interests in competition with all the rest.

Each party in parliament (or in the Provincial or Municipal Councils) forms a *fractie*, a party delegation that assigns legislative specialties and assures coordinated action. Only some of the parties in the lower chamber have counterparts in the cabinet, and in fact the largest party may not necessarily be participating in it at all. It is usually anticipated that the party votes in parliament will support the counterparts in the cabinet, but this is not invariably so. The two or three parties in the cabinet may derive voting support, especially on minor issues, from any combination of the parties in parliament.

The hall where the lower chamber of parliament meets (Fig. 9.4) includes a *regeringstafel*, the 'administration table' where the minister or ministers whose bill is under debate sit and are submitted to questioning; on highly important issues, most of the cabinet may be present at the table. In the exercise of its rights, the lower chamber supervises and to some extent controls the actions of the administration, though it is expected not to interfere with the implementation of policy.

A particularly vivid example of the working of this system came a few years ago on the issue of reorganizing media legislation to take account of

Fig. 9.4
The Lower Chamber
of parliament in session

cable television. The central issue involved was whether the many new possibilities offered by cable TV were to be kept within fairly tight control by the current, non-commercial system or whether they should be allowed to follow the lead of a free market—in other words, on a commercial basis. The two partners in the cabinet were on opposite sides of this issue. The ultimate compromise, which pleased none because it made too many concessions for some and not enough for others, was patched together by securing votes from other parties in parliament which were not in the cabinet. If this had not succeeded, the government would have collapsed for lack of ability to find parliamentary support for a major piece of legislation.

The governmental system in the Netherlands is organized without built-in checks and balances among the branches. Its operation is based entirely on unwritten agreements assuring a basically democratic procedure, one that works along the lines of compromise and consensus. There is no majority rule in the strictest sense, but power is shared in coalitions that must be painstakingly assembled. The executive functions do not dominate the legislative, but stand in a delicately poised balance. The system is based not on majority or plurality but on proportionality, which makes for considerable clumsiness in decision-making but safeguards the interests of the minority.

There is an abundance of criticism of this system. In contrast to a two-party system in which a single party can draw the full heat of public discontent and be swept out of office, the Dutch system results in a 'faceless' form of representative government that is bland, and in attempting to please everyone often pleases no one. There are never any banners 'Time for a change!' or 'Throw the rogues out!'. But the governmental system itself is seldom regarded as merely a necessary evil. The voting public in the Netherlands expects government to assume a greater measure of regulatory responsibility than would by acceptable in some countries, and political discourse revolves around considerations of responsibility for maintaining a fully egalitarian and humanitarian government. Even in the heat of an election campaign, parties rarely preach bold individualism or liberation from government interference.

FURTHER READING

Andeweg, Rudy B. and Galen A. Irwin, *Dutch Government and Politics*. London: Macmillan, 1993.

The Constitution of the Kingdom of the Netherlands. The Hague: Ministry of Home Affairs, 1983.

Van Deth, J.W., and P.A. Schuszler (eds.), *Nederlandse staatkunde. Een elementaire inleiding*. Muiderberg: Coutinho, 1990.

Parliament in the Netherlands. The Hague: Government Publishing Office, 1982.

Toornvliet, H.A.H., *De staatsinrichting*. Utrecht: Spectrum, 2nd ed. 1987.

10   The political system

Fig. 10.1
A billboard for election
campaign posters

Let us imagine we arrive in the Netherlands from abroad and find a campaign for parliamentary elections in full swing. If we are thinking about other things and are not particularly politically-minded besides, it might in fact take a little time before we even noticed that much of anything was going on. Election campaigns in the Netherlands follow a national tradition that has little appetite for show, and even today with the resources of modern publicity and advertising, they are carried on in a tone that is decidedly low-key.

But ironically, elections in the Netherlands seem to have achieved a certain notoriety abroad for their apparent chaotic complexity. For instance, Alvin Toffler in his popular *The Third Wave* speaks of 'the Dutch free-for-all with two dozen parties'. At intersections, shopping centers, parks—and in Amsterdam on some of the bridges—there are temporary large wooden signboards erected, and assigned spaces for campaign posters. These signs are plastered, usually in a rather disorderly way involving a lot of overlapping, with a colorful profusion of posters, most of them featuring a large number, initials and a logo, and usually all three.

Parties are marketing not personalities but a slate of candidates and a specific program that takes account of a fairly specific constituency. Large parties must appeal to a wider variety of voters, but even they have a relatively focused group of voters in mind. This results in the visible jumble of campaign posters of 20 or more, and it is this that makes a chaotic and 'faceless' impression. But the ability of television to project a personality has had an impact on election campaigns, and its influence is still expanding. There has been a noticeable shift toward the packaging of an attractive candidate as a magnet for votes for the whole party slate. This is regularly denounced as an invasion of slick 'American' campaign practices, but as a matter of fact the impact of the modern media on election campaigns is a worldwide phenomenon. As we will see in a moment, it will take a great deal more than exploitation of mass media to change the character of the way Dutch elections are carried on.

What from the outside may look like a 'free-for-all' is usually quite orderly and even predictable. The whole spectrum of parties, down to the tiniest, has been able to count on a reasonably steady percentage of the vote from those who identify their own interests with its dependable program—or, to be more accurate if more cynical, its image. The traditional ideological purity of each party in standing for well-recognized principles was, for a long time, the basis on which the political system worked. The system lacks any one clearly dominant group, and political power is always dispersed. In the past decade or two there has been considerable erosion of party loyalty.

The voting public sees a set of lists of names, one list for each party participating in the election. The party has been assigned a number based on its percentage of the vote in the previous election, which naturally places the largest parties in the first spaces. Each party has drawn up its own list of candidates, putting the best-known names first, and the list is always headed by a *lijsttrekker*, the party's strongest candidate who can 'pull' the list along. When the voter goes to the polls on election day, he is given a ballot showing all the same lists, now with a block next to each name. The vote consists of filling in precisely one block on the whole ballot. Most voters simply mark the first name on their preferred party list, but any name on the list may be marked. When the votes are counted, it is the total number of votes, or better the percentage of the total vote, that decides how many names down the list are elected. The 'preferential' vote for names farther down the list is counted, and a candidate can move 'up' the list if he or she has gathered more than a certain mini-

Fig. 10.2
A portion of the official ballot

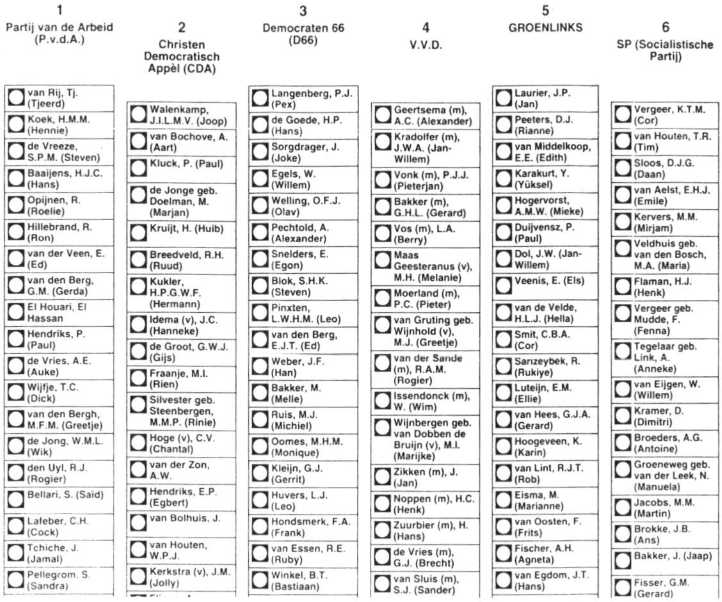

1 Partij van de Arbeid (P.v.d.A.)	2 Christen Democratisch Appèl (CDA)	3 Democraten 66 (D66)	4 V.V.D.	5 GROENLINKS	6 SP (Socialistische Partij)
van Rij, Tj. (Tjeerd)	Walenkamp, J.I.L.M.V. (Joop)	Langenberg, P.J. (Pex)	Geertsema (m), A.C. (Alexander)	Laurier, J.P. (Jan)	Vergeer, K.T.M. (Cor)
Koek, H.M.M. (Hennie)	van Bochove, A. (Aart)	de Goede, H.P. (Hans)	Kradolfer (m), J.W.A. (Jan-Willem)	Peeters, D.J. (Rianne)	van Houten, T.R. (Tim)
de Vreeze, S.P.M. (Steven)	Kluck, P. (Paul)	Sorgdrager, J. (Joke)	Vonk (m), P.J.J. (Pieter-Jan)	van Middelkoop, E.E. (Edith)	Sloos, D.J.G. (Daan)
Baaijens, H.J.C. (Hans)	de Jonge geb. Doelman, M. (Marjan)	Egels, W. (Willem)	Bakker (m), G.H.L. (Gerard)	Karakurt, Y. (Yüksel)	van Aelst, E.H.J. (Emile)
Opijnen, R. (Roelie)	Kruijt, H. (Huib)	Welling, O.F.J. (Olav)	Vos (m), L.A. (Berry)	Hogervorst, A.M.W. (Mieke)	Kervers, M.M. (Mirjam)
Hillebrand, R. (Ron)	Breedveld, R.H. (Ruud)	Pechtold, A. (Alexander)	Maas Geesteranus (v), M.H. (Melanie)	Duijvensz, P. (Paul)	Veldhuis geb. van den Bosch, M.A. (Maria)
van der Veen, E. (Ed)	Kukler, H.P.G.W.F. (Hermann)	Snelders, E. (Egon)	Moerland (m), P.C. (Pieter)	Dol, J.W. (Jan-Willem)	Flaman, H.J. (Henk)
van den Berg, G.M. (Gerda)	Idema (v), J.C. (Hanneke)	Blok, S.H.K. (Steven)	van Gruting geb. Wijnhold (v), M.J. (Greetje)	Veenis, E. (Els)	Vergeer geb. Mudde, F. (Fenna)
El Houari, El Hassan	de Groot, G.W.J. (Gijs)	Pinxten, L.W.H.M. (Leo)	van der Sande (m), R.A.M. (Rogier)	van de Velde, H.L.J. (Hella)	Tegelaar geb. Link, A. (Anneke)
Hendriks, P. (Paul)	Fraanje, M.I. (Rien)	van den Berg, E.J.T. (Ed)	Issendonck (m), W. (Wim)	Smit, C.B.A. (Cor)	van Eijgen, W. (Willem)
de Vries, A.E. (Auke)	Silvester geb. Steenbergen, M.M.P. (Rinie)	Weber, J.F. (Han)	Wijnbergen geb. van Dobben de Bruijn (v), M.I. (Marijke)	Sarizeybek, R. (Rukiye)	Kramer, D. (Dimitri)
Wijfje, T.C. (Dick)	Hoge (v), C.V. (Chantal)	Bakker, M. (Melle)	Zikken (m), J. (Jan)	Luteijn, E.M. (Ellie)	Broeders, A.G. (Antoine)
van den Bergh, M.F.M. (Greetje)	van der Zon, A.W.	Ruis, M.J. (Michiel)	Noppen (m), H.C. (Henk)	van Hees, G.J.A. (Gerard)	Groeneweg geb. van der Leek, N. (Manuela)
de Jong, W.M.L. (Wik)	Hendriks, E.P. (Egbert)	Oomes, M.H.M. (Monique)	Zuurbier (m), H. (Hans)	Hoogeveen, K. (Karin)	Jacobs, M.M. (Martin)
den Uyl, R.J. (Rogier)	van Bolhuis, J.	Kleijn, G.J. (Gerrit)	de Vries (m), G.J. (Brecht)	van Lint, R.J.T. (Rob)	Brokke, J.B. (Ans)
Bellari, S. (Said)	van Houten, W.P.J.	Huvers, L.J. (Leo)	Zikken (m), J. (Jan)	Eisma, M. (Marianne)	Bakker, J. (Jaap)
Lafeber, C.H. (Cock)	Kerkstra (v), J.M. (Jolly)	Hondsmerk, F.A. (Frank)	Zuurbier (m), H. (Hans)	van Oosten, F. (Frits)	Fisser, G.M. (Gerard)
Tchiche, J. (Jamal)		van Essen, R.E. (Ruby)	de Vries (m), G.J. (Brecht)	Fischer, A.H. (Agneta)	
Pellegrom, S. (Sandra)		Winkel, B.T. (Bastiaan)	van Sluis (m), S.J. (Sander)	van Egdom, J.T. (Hans)	

mum vote. The outcome for each party is predictable enough that each list consists of 'electable' and 'non-electable' places (though of course the printed lists themselves do not show this). Even small parties that know they will be doing well to elect one candidate still often submit full lists of twenty to forty names.

In parliamentary elections, the country is treated as a single constituency, while still divided for administrative convenience into electoral districts. This means it is in a party's best interest to put forward nationally acceptable candidates. Since votes are counted and election lists certified for the country as a whole, there is at best only a very weak identification with region, and national stability is thus enhanced. The representative elected to parliament accordingly carries an identification with a party and not with a local district. Of course everyone is interested in how well parties did in various places, so when election returns are published the next day, they are broken down by municipality. Any parties that have won enough votes to reach the minimum necessary to elect a single candidate are now part of the composition of parliament, (or of the Provincial or Municipal Council, depending on which elections are being held). The political coloration of the lower chamber has been decided by a system of nation-wide proportional representation that is almost unique in the world, and certainly unique in Europe.

The national figures for a typical parliamentary election always show that no one party has won a majority of the vote, which means that governing power has to be shared. In addition, only a small number of parties have won a significant percentage of the vote, meaning that realistically the choice of parties to share governing power is quite limited.

At this point in the process, with the political makeup of the lower chamber of parliament decided by the voters, the crucial step in the whole process begins. The executives have not been elected but must be chosen in some relation to this election outcome, eventually to be formally 'appointed' by the monarch. The whole trick here lies in those deceptively simple words 'some relation', and it is here that the real fun begins.

What happens next is based on tradition, there being no formal written rules or laws for how the cabinet ministers are to be selected. During this interim period of negotiations (the outgoing administration has already resigned but continues in office as *demissionair* until it is formally replaced) the queen has considerable discretionary power to keep the process moving. For private consultations, she summons the chairman of each party delegation in parliament, beginning with the largest and continuing through the one-member delegations, the chairmen of both chambers, and the vice-chairman of the Council of State (she could hardly summon its chairman, which as you will recall is herself). The queen first appoints an *informateur* to make the rounds of party leaders to assess feasibility of various combinations. The most significant step is the appointment of a *formateur* with the authority to confer with several parties and form some coalition of parties (all of which are 'minority parties') that can have its actions supported by parliamentary votes. Normally this person, if successful, becomes the prime minister in the administration formed.

Fig. 10.3
Summary of the election returns for the country as a whole. Total votes cast, percentage for each party, and the number of seats won.

Uitslag verkiezingen Tweede Kamer

	stemmen	%	1994 zetels
Opkomst	**8.966.151**	**78,3**	**150**
CDA	1.994.115	22,2	34
PvdA	2.150.035	24,0	37
VVD	1.787.358	19,9	31
D66	1.387.883	15,5	24
GroenLinks	310.292	3,5	5
SGP	155.177	1,7	2
GPV	118.990	1,3	2
RPF	158.702	1,8	3
CD	220.333	2,5	3
DNP	6.987	0,1	0
PSP'92	7.622	0,1	0
SP	118.535	1,3	2
SAPRebel	4.465	0,0	0
NWP	27.581	0,3	0
PMR	8.814	0,1	0
Unie 55+	77.953	0,9	1
SBP	9.347	0,1	0
AOV	325.997	3,6	6
CP'86	32.348	0,4	0
LP	2.841	0,0	0
Groenen	13.807	0,1	0
VIP	17.224	0,2	0
NCPN	11.701	0,1	0
ADP	5.334	0,1	0
S'93	7.865	0,1	0
PDA	4.845	0,1	0
Overige '89	-	-	-

Although negotiations are secret, the general lines they follow are usually guessed at rather accurately. They may also be protracted, since there is no alternative to everyone continuing until an administration is formed. Typically the whole process takes several weeks, although negotiations stretching on for months are not uncommon. When two or three (rarely more) parties find that they are able to reconcile their differences, they compose a joint statement setting down the program according to which they agree to govern together. If this is accepted by the lower chamber, the parties are given the authority to govern.

So the popular vote eventually, by a somewhat circuitous route, leads to consent to bestow executive power. But it is worth asking how this whole selection process has been relating to the mandate expressed in the election returns. It is evident that winning a larger share of the total vote than any other party is no guarantee of power to govern. All it does is assure voting power in parliament with all the potential for applying cooperative or oppositional pressure that this implies. Second, the two or three parties that have formed a coalition government cannot possibly match all the colors of the political spectrum of parliament, and in addition they must inevitably bend their own parties—principles somewhat in the interest of political realities. But after the election has already taken place, the compromise program that is drawn up is entirely out of the hands of the voters. And even the percentage of governing power—expressed most simply in the number of ministers' posts—given to each coalition party may not necessarily follow the vote percentage, although they normally stand in close relation to each other. And third, the delicate secret negotiations that eventually lead to the distribution of ministerial portfolios among the coalition parties are under no obligation to take detailed account of the electoral will: voters may perceive one party to have made a strong showing in the election on the basis of its stand on a certain issue, only to see the ministry with the authority to carry out that program pass into the hands of another party.

Once all the negotiations are completed and the result has been approved by parliament, the new cabinet is sworn in at the royal palace. By constitution, ministers are still formally 'appointed' by the monarch; the words 'at his pleasure' are merely a quaint survival of the past that has long since been overtaken by governing responsibility having been shifted to the ministers. The process of attempting to secure and hold the consent of parliament now begins. This consent will not be lightly withdrawn, as the political game seems to be played in some countries. Not only is there a strong consensus that an administration should have a fair crack at doing its job, but it is plainly not in anyone's interest to have to go back through the whole painstaking process. When a cabinet 'falls' before the end of its term, it is usually because an irreconcilable disunity has arisen within the cabinet itself, and only occasionally due to a clash between a party and the rest of its delegation in parliament.

Seen at a more subtle level, the administration is founded on a complex network of acts of accommodation and trust, and no party that looks ahead to the inevitable necessity of future consensus governments can afford to be seen as failing to 'play the game' without a good cause. Parties do not attack each other as enemies, and in fact well before the election they are already beginning to work ahead toward the coming consensus. It is precisely this constant sidelong glance at the inescapability of future cooperation that gives Dutch politics its characteristic staid respectability and even a certain blandness, something that today's world of media hype is unlikely to change much.

So notwithstanding all this attention to the cabinet, it is not here but in parliament that the individual 'personality' of each party comes out most strongly. Before looking at the political parties individually, it might be good to define what 'Religious' versus 'Non-religious' parties are. The idea of an important, major Christian political party is not known either in the US or in Britain, but such parties are a prominent part of the political picture in most European countries. In the past, political parties in the Netherlands were sharply polarized into those that based their concepts of social justice and progress on biblical principles and those that saw religious principles as having no direct relevance to political programs. Today the political air is far less overheated with the clash between 'confessional' and 'non-confessional' as they call it. This makes the polarization between them less wide but still very much a fact of political life.

CDA *Christen Democratisch Appèl* (Christian Democratic Alliance)

This Christian-Democratic party, one of today's large parties, is itself a merger of religious parties at or near the center. It has existed since 1975, and began participating in national elections in 1977. There were two reasons for the merger. One had to do with the growing political cooperation in Europe, especially the coming into being of the European Parliament which brought the necessity of a united front to cooperate with Christian-Democratic parties in other countries. The other was much more urgent. Decline in church membership in the '50s and '60s brought with it a disastrous erosion in voter strength for most of the religious parties, and a common effort was an obvious step.

The CDA is made up of three main groups which in not too distant memory were independent parties. The KVP, *Katholieke Volkspartij* (Catholic People's Party), was the strong Catholic party formed in 1918. Although vigilance against what was perceived as undue Catholic influence on social life—especially among orthodox protestants—has a long history reaching back to the Revolt in the 16th and 17th centuries, it soon became the strongest party in the political center, and by virtue of its discipline and electoral dependability it was the key to coalition politics. The Catholic party participated in every government since the war. But it included an unwieldy social diversity of voters, and it saw its strength drop from 31.9% of the vote in 1963 to 17.7% in 1972.

The *ARP, Anti-Revolutionaire Partij* (Anti-Revolutionary Party) was formed in 1878, and was the first political party along modern lines in the Netherlands. It was formed as a political home for the orthodox, conservative wing of the Calvinist Reformed Church, and throughout its history it has remained faithful to its strict adherence to religious principles based on divine authority. It owes its name to its stance in opposition to the egalitarian principles of the French Revolution, its model of society being a divinely-appointed hierarchy of authority. Representing a relatively small social group with a strong sense of loyalty and cohesion, it has always had a clearly-defined program.

The *CHU*, *Christelijk Historische Unie* (Christian Historical Union) was a center party that drew most of its support from the mainstream Reformed church. It has always been the smallest of the three, and the one with the weakest sense of party identity and loyalty. After the merger was completed, all three of these parties disbanded as independent units. Today, two decades later, the three constituent religious currents have by no means dissolved into a general 'Christian' identity; everyone is well aware of how political behavior inescapably points to which former party (now often known colloquially as 'blood types') each political figure belongs to.

The figures for the voting strength of the *CDA* parties (Fig. 10.4; combining them in parenthesis before 1977 for comparison) show that the decline was indeed reversed, but that in the '80s the slow slide of voter support continued until it swung upward once again. But recently its share of the vote has plummeted far more disastrously (the drop between the last two elections amounts to over 13 percentage points), as voters have abandoned the traditional center parties.

The CDA tends to see itself less as a regulator of society than as the protector of the weak, though the specifically Christian tone of its political rhetoric has been steadily watered down. Many in the party now openly express doubts whether a religious basis has any significant power to attract voters in today's society. In the present time the *CDA*, still dominated by its Catholic component, has continued to be regarded as the most secure power bloc. It has been the center of every government formed since the reconstitution of political parties in 1945, and in fact this has been the case with only two minor interruptions since 1918. It was only following the 1994 parliamentary elections that for the first time in history a coalition government was formed that did not include it.

	CDA	KVP	ARP	CHU
1946	(53)	32	13	8
1948	(54)	32	13	9
1952	(51)	30	12	9
1956	(51)	33	10	8
1959	(50)	43	10	8
1963	(51)	44	9	9
1967	(46)	28	10	8
1971	(39)	23	9	7
1972	(32)	18	9	5
1977	32			
1981	30.8			
1982	29.4			
1986	34.6			
1989	35.3			
1994	22.2			

Fig. 10.4
Parliamentary elections,
CDA % of vote

PvdA *Partij van de Arbeid* (Labor Party)

The modern party is a renaming of the Socialist party that first entered Dutch politics in the 19th century. Its predecessor was formally founded in

1894. From its beginnings, one of its chief aims has been to break through the traditional, narrowly-based ideological blocs based on class and religion, and form a political home for all. Its originally revolutionary line has been steadily modified in attempts to be a truly national, rather than a class party. Social Democrats (the generic category in which this party belongs) tend to see the government's role in the regulation of society and distribution of income as a strong one. In the '60s the *PvdA* attracted many new, younger voters and felt increasing influence from the Left.

Of late the party, like the one just mentioned, has also seen a disastrous drop in electoral strength, falling nearly 8 points in the 1994 elections. Whether the largest opposition party or part of a coalition government, it has been struggling to find its new identity in a changing society where some of the previous social issues seem less and less relevant to voters. With the disappearance of a true 'working class' its support has traditionally been based on, it appears to be evolving into a mildly-progressive party, championing lower-income voters while dropping its customary paternalistic tone and aiming much more determinedly at the middle class. The continued good health of the party is seen as crucial to the increasingly close network of European Social-Democratic parties.

VVD *Volkspartij voor Vrijheid en Democratie* (People's Party for Freedom and Democracy, usually called the 'Liberal Party')

This center party is the modern form of the 19th-century Liberal Party, the reform party that traces its origin back to those who first managed to wrest power from the monarchy and transfer it to the hands of a parliament and therefore of the people. Today it retains some of its distaste for large, powerful government, and it has an appeal to the privileged and upwardly mobile. Generally it favors programs that do not unduly restrict business interests, and that bring about economic and social reforms in orderly ways. It remains a modest-sized party, but nevertheless it has shared in coalitions for most of the past thirty years. Traditionally it has been a quiet, enlightened-progressive party with a comfortable old-guard group that worked by gentlemen's agreement along elitist lines, counting on a steady 10% of the vote. But now its strength in national elections has risen to more than double this. In the most recent provincial elections, the party even emerged as the country's largest.

These are the three main political streams—Christian-Democrat, Social-Democrat and Liberal—that have given form to Dutch political life since the 19th century. It might not have escaped notice that the familiar political term 'conservative' is not part of this. For many years this term was studiously avoided by the parties, all of which liked to present themselves as 'progressive', and it is only now that it is beginning to gain a new respectability.

D66 *Democraten 66* (Democrats 66)

This is normally a modest-sized but energetic moderate-left party whose name perpetuates the reminder of its birth in the turbulent atmosphere of the '60s. It burst onto the scene with a variety of new ideas about reforming the whole political system. The party appeals to young voters, and has been able to project an image of a fresh beginning thanks to its ability to propose credible anternatives to colorlessness and facelessness. Its main point was, and continues to be, increasing the influence of the voter on government, for instance by the direct popular election of the Prime Minister as a means of strengthening the executive's independence from parliament. The party's pragmatic proposals include the introduction of a system of regional constituencies and the evolution of a two-bloc system like the British model. The party has participated in two coalition cabinets in the '70s and '80s.

Recently it has showed unexpected electoral strength, partly profiting from left-of-center discontent with the *PvdA*, and partly no doubt from general voter weariness with the 'established' parties. The party, in its characteristic pragmatism, has been credited with being the first to see the citizen of today as an independent-minded electoral consumer. At one point it reached a surprising peak of nearly 25% in opinion polls, and as this is being written it continues to enjoy its unaccustomed status as one of the country's major parties.

All the rest of the parties are what is called 'non-governing'. That is, they are part of the composition of the political spectrum of parliament but, with only rare exceptions, they do not participate in national coalition governments. It should be added, however, that the 'splinter' parties are excluded only because they are not able to attract enough support on a nationwide basis and therefore the small number of parliamentary votes they could offer would not be worth the negotiating time it would take. It is also important to note that, since small parties regard themselves as standing for an ideologically undiluted principle, most would not be interested in any case in participating in a coalition, where compromise is unavoidable. In regions of greater strength, the splinter parties are often strongly represented on provincial and municipal councils. They readily fall into groups on the left and right.

The **PPR**, *Politieke Partij Radicalen* (Radical Political Party) is a 1968 split from the KVP. In 1970 it gained 7.8% of the vote, and in 1972 had two ministers in a coalition government, the first splinter party ever to do this. The **PSP**, *Pacifistisch Socialistische Partij* (Pacifistic Socialist Party) is a small radical group that broke away from the PvdA. The **EVP**, *Evangelische Volkspartij* (Evangelical People's Party), is a left-wing religious party formed by Christian-Democrats not satisfied with the CDA's dilution of religious content. The **CPN**, *Communistische Partij Nederland* (Communist Party of the Netherlands) was formed in the Netherlands in 1918, and until at least the Second World War it was primarily an urban working-class party. It enjoyed a wave of public support for its uncompromising stance during the five years of wartime occupation and resistance, but this eroded rapidly in the harsh realities of the cold-war years. Even though it evolved in middle-class and feminist directions, in 1986 for the first time it failed to win any seats in parliament. The **SP**, *Socialistische Partij* (Socialist Party), a newly-formed party standing for return to classic Socialist principles, has won two seats in parliament.

These first four small parties on the left (PPR, PSP, EVP and CPN) have recently merged to form the new party called *Groen Links* (Green Left), making common cause to avoid too great a splintering of efforts—which has not stopped groups of dissidents in the second and third of these from reorganizing national parties in an effort to keep the far-left voice alive. Opinion polls have given the party as high as 10% of the vote, but actual elections keep it closer to 4%. Here too, the former party identities have not yet begun fading away, and they are also coming to be called 'blood types'. The party is still searching for an identity in a shifting political world where yesterday's 'far-left' ideas for the radical reform of society no longer attract votes. But the party is still 'left' in standing for social justice, reduction of consumerism, and care for the environment (although it is hard to resist pointing out that that popular word 'green' in its name was originally intended merely to suggest freshness and growth, and in fact the party's logo prints the word in red).

An equivalent group on the right—though on some issues they find themselves 'left' of center—is three parties that collectively until recently were referred to as *Klein Rechts* (Little Right), all of them religious parties. The **GPV**, *Gereformeerd Politiek Verbond* (Reformed Political Union) split off from the orthodox Calvinist ARP (see above under *CDA*) and won its first seats in parliament in 1963. The **SGP**, *Staatkundig Gereformeerde Partij* (sometimes translated simply as 'Calvinist Party') was formed in 1918. It adheres uncompromisingly to orthodox protestant doctrine, opposing secularization of society, and has maintained a steady 2% of the vote. The **RPF**, *Reformatorische Politieke Federatie* (Orthodox Reformed Political Federation) is a home for conservative protestants who deplore the *CDA*'s increasing secularization but do not feel at home in the somewhat exclusive *SGP* or *GPV*. Together with the *CDA* these parties form the 'denominational bloc', which in the 1994 elections fell below 1/3 of the popular vote for the first time ever.

The **CP**, *Centrum Partij* (Center Party) is one which, in spite of its name, represents a decidedly conservative line and at one time captured public attention far out of proportion to its size or parliamentary influence. Its notoriety rests on its resolute opposition to the integration of all non-Dutch people into the society. Though the party insists it does not make racial distinctions, this opposition to foreigners had been universally regarded as racist in applying mainly to ethnic minorities. Disputes in the party have led to the formation of the **CD**, *Centrumdemocraten* (Center Democrats), and as such it continues to hold representation in parliament, which has now risen from the one seat first gained in 1982 to 3 seats. The original party, which together with the recently-formed *Nederlands Blok* is more avowedly racist than the *CD*, has been rechristened **CP '86**.

In the urbane Netherlands, the voice of these parties is relatively restrained compared to the shrill far-right sounds heard from some countries, though some are becoming increasingly bolder and noisy demonstrations are becoming more common. With their highly-publicized wrangling with and blackballing of each other, they have shown self-destructive behavior, and they are socially so isolated that they normally meet in secret. Still, they have had conspicuous success in some municipal-council elections, gaining as high as 9% (which is usually interpreted as a sympathy vote out of general disaffection with society), and the Dutch public's worried attention keeps them in the limelight.

In the first postwar period, political parties maintained their positions by representing the interests of a clearly-defined group. This depended on the party's projecting a sharp consciousness of its distinctiveness and the articulation of its principles. Within a party, it depended on discipline, a high degree of loyalty, and a certain deference to authority. The rank-and-file membership, in other words, was not only socially isolated from that of other parties but kept aware of a highly competitive atmosphere. The compromise and accommodation between parties took place only at the top, in the hands of an elite at the head of each party. This picture is what Lijphart called 'the politics of accommodation', the title he gave his famous book presenting to the world the outlines of the unique Dutch political system—as it used to be.

This strong tendency to stand up for 'principle' is still noticeable in parliament today. But since the mid-'60s parties have no longer been able to count on the old deference and loyalty, voters do not feel so strongly that a party stands up for 'their' interests, people are no longer so suspicious of each other, and an estimated 30% or more of voters are 'independents', moving from party to party as they vote on issues. More and more, the political elites must expose themselves directly to the voters, and demonstrate the legitimacy of power rather than assuming it. The unquestioning ties between voter and party leadership have largely disappeared, and many perceive no one at all as representing their interests. This vacuum goes a long way toward explaining what many perceive as the current alarming popularity of the far-right parties.

The breakdown of unquestioning loyalty to the party as the bearer of Principle has not only stood the traditional Dutch political system on its head and made things far less predictable. It has also heralded the breakdown of the religious / non-religious polarization. Only the small GVP and SGP still regard the political arena strongly as a struggle for or against religious principles, while the CDA, today's large religious party, assigns first importance to social and economic issues. The steady weakening of the religious hold on political life means a resulting decrease in distance between parties along this dimension. This and the continuing, often more subtle influence of religion and morality on political discourse are both closely connected to the role of religion on the social life of the Netherlands.

FURTHER READING

Daalder, Hans, and Galen A. Irwin (eds.), *Politics in the Netherlands: How much change?* London: Cass, 1989.

Gladdish, Ken, *Governing from the Centre: Politics and Policy-making in the Netherlands.* London: Hurst, 1991.

Lucardie, A. (et al.), *Driestromenland. Liberalisme, socialisme en christendemocratie in Nederland.* Leiden: Stichting Burgerschapskunde, 1993.

Daalder, Hans, 'English language sources for the study of Dutch politics.' In: Daalder,H. and C. Schuyt (eds.), *Compendium voor politiek en samenleving in Nederland.* Alphen: Samsom, 1986- [Loose-leaf; the individual sections are updated regularly, the one quoted from January 1990].

Religion and pluriformity

The close ties between politics and religion in the Netherlands go back to the Reformation; religion has always been everybody's business. Today the on-going debate is seldom purely theological any more, but political dialogue often carries a religious tone. The table shows the principal religious groups and their relative membership strength in approximately 1995.

Religious	Christian	Catholic		Roman Catholic	22
		Protestant	Calvinist	Gereformeerd	7
				Hervormd	11
			Non-Calvinist	Remonstrant Doopsgezind Lutheran etc. }	1.5
	Non-Christian			Jewish	1.2
				Moslem	2.8
Non-religious	Organized			Humanist + other	} 54.5
	Non-organized			No affiliation	

Fig. 11.1
Religious belief
in the Netherlands

The difficulty with this type of statistics comes in assessing what a claim of membership in a religious organization should be taken to imply. Many claim that the non-affiliated category should show over 50%; a study in 1987 showed that non-affiliation in 11 of the 17 largest cities was over 60%, with Amsterdam at the top showing 79% non-religious.

The following survey does not attempt to profile all the denominations but selects the main currents.

The **Hervormde Kerk** (Reformed Church) is the mainstream Calvinist protestant church that emerged from the Reformation and the 16th and 17th-century revolt against the Spanish. In being the only church allowed full public worship in that time, it came close to being a state church, but it has never been the 'established' church in any more formal sense than being the church adhered to by the establishment. The Orange family today is nominally and by tradition *Hervormd*, though in a society where Protestant and Catholic have coexisted in an uneasy balance for centuries, not in conspicuous ways. This church has the honor of being the one at the cultural center of Dutch history and national identity. But this is a rather dubious honor because through these centuries it has been so taken for granted that it has not had to struggle for its place in society and thereby develop a strong sense of group identity and cohesiveness.

It has always been dominated by a confident middle class, a social class whose outlook was strengthened by the modernism of the 19th century, and who played a leading role in adapting Dutch religious movements to the modern world view. But the tolerance and liberalism this brought with it has proved to be the church's undoing. Of all the churches in the Netherlands, the *Hervormd* has been the most vulnerable to the secularization process that easily dissolved theological unity and made exit from the church in the liberal direction simple. Today it is in the weakest position with respect to watering-down and loss of membership. Surveys of church members' attitudes toward a variety of religious and social matters show the *Hervormd* to have the most liberal stance toward abortion, disarmament, and living together unmarried. They rank lowest in the measures of church attendance, contact with the minister, reading the Bible, and interpreting the world in religious terms. Along with the liberal and middle-of-the-road members, the Reformed Church has a very conservative right wing called the *Gereformeerde Bond* 'Reformed Alliance'.

As long as we are talking about 'mixed blessings', another one not often noticed as such is the very large number of church buildings that were 'inherited' from the Catholic church after the Reformation and that are still the homes of relentlessly shrinking congregations. Immediately on transfer of ownership they were altered to suit the sober Calvinist taste (the 17th-century painter Pieter Saenredam, more than any other, has shown the world how to feel the serene atmosphere of their interiors), and today none of them can be maintained and used without government subsidy. Increasing numbers of them are being sold by congregations—not by any means only *Hervormd*—and converted to other uses.

The **Gereformeerde Kerk** (Orthodox Reformed) is actually composed of a number of churches originating in past doctrinal splits. It owes its ultimate origin to conflicts between a liberal and conservative wing of the Calvinist church in the Reformation time. Its membership came mostly from an originally underprivileged and economically disadvantaged class, and in the 19th century they set about the task of emancipation under strong leadership and with a powerful sense of cohesion. Characteristic of the *Gereformeerd* way of thinking was discipline, self-sacrifice and obedience to divinely-instituted authority, and unswerving commitment to religious doctrine. Part of their continued success in resisting the trends of the 20th century toward secularization is due to their image of themselves as a people set apart and threatened by the secular society around them. They formed the Anti-Revolutionary Party, fought for public funding of church schools in an effort that made common cause with Catholics and gave new forms to Dutch society, and collected pennies from their members to found and support their own university, the Free University in Amsterdam. Numerically they have never amounted to much more than about 10% of the population, but their impact on society has been far out of proportion to this. *Gereformeerden* have, for instance, held a conspicuously large number of high government posts.

Today they show the highest percentages when asked for attitudes about church attendance, contact with the minister, reading the Bible, and seeing the world in religious terms.

The 'chosen people' mentality has served the Orthodox Reformed well, even in its current modified form, in maintaining a sense of community. And yet, it is an attitude that is by no means restricted to them nor is it a particularly new one. The welcoming of large numbers of displaced Jews in the late 16th century was undoubtedly made easier thanks to a partly unconscious identification with another 'chosen people'. And it was this way of viewing the world that Dutch settlers took with them in the 17th century to South Africa, and in the 19th century to America. In many ways Gereformeerd communities in both South Africa and the U.S. have preserved a purity and cohesiveness that is now more and more diluted in the home country.

Recently these two churches, the Hervormd and the Gereformeerd, have been making moves toward reuniting. Complete organizational merger under the new name *Verenigde Protestantse Kerk in Nederland* 'United Protestant Church in the Netherlands' is expected to be a fact early in the next century.

In any Dutch protestant church, whether the above or another denomination, the service is apt to have the same readily recognizable Dutch flavor. A member of the Church Council escorts the minister up to the front and takes leave of him with a handshake (a constant reminder that he is merely a servant of the congregation), ministers have the same style in addressing the congregation, the same psalms and hymns are sung—the more orthodox churches favoring the former and the more liberal the latter—, the singing is done in unison, at a stately pace but at full volume. The service is sober, reserved with little show of emotion, and the privacy of the visitor is not intruded upon. The only truly exuberant side of a church service, especially in old churches, is likely to be the organ, one of the Netherlands' richest cultural heritages.

The **Rooms-Katholieke Kerk** (Roman Catholic) has been disadvantaged—political liberty in the 17th century was identified with Protestantism—though never physically persecuted. Catholics were excluded from many public offices but were permitted worship under the condition that the place not be visible to the public. This restriction, placed on Catholics and many smaller protestant churches, resulted in the construction of a large number of *schuilkerken* 'hidden churches', the best-preserved example of which today is *Ons Lieve Heer op Zolder* 'Our Lord in the Attic' in Amsterdam. They are nice illustrations of the Dutch talent for practical accommodation.

Catholics in the Netherlands developed a close-knit community, even a ghetto mentality in which life revolved closely around a narrowly-conceived Catholic life. Thanks in part to this isolation from the rest of the world, the church hierarchy kept a strong hold, and the church in the Netherlands became a model of solidarity, loyalty, orderliness and obedience that was held up to the world. The Pastoral Letter the Dutch bishops issued in 1954 sternly warned Catholics of the dangers of association with Socialists and threatened religious sanctions against them. Around Catholic life there grew up a whole range of organizations, activities and eventually schools and newspa-

Fig. 11.2
An editorial cartoon that
appeared in May 1985

pers that insulated Catholics still further from outside social contacts. This all looks reasonable enough under the appropriate lens: Catholics were engaged, alongside the Orthodox Reformed, in a struggle for social emancipation in which unity and organization were the first prerequisites. The isolation of Catholic social institutions was an aspect of the pluriform society evolving in the 19th and 20th centuries.

Liberalizing currents, largely resisted by the Church, have been sweeping Dutch Catholicism. At one point in the recent past, the church hierarchy in the Netherlands was probably unique in the quickness of its grasp of people's need to think for themselves. Since then a more conservative hierarchy has been substituted. But the widespread resentment in the liberal-thinking Dutch atmosphere of what looked like heavy-handed attempts to assert authority from outside was the atmosphere in which the Pope's visit took place in May 1985. The Dutch Catholic church had become decentralized and, like the rest of society, what it did was based on discussion and consensus and not on anyone's mere say-so. The cartoon (Fig. 11.2) comments eloquently on the Pope's inability to grasp the strength of this. After a long period of decline, the Catholic church today is experiencing a revival of interest, and the membership loss is beginning to turn around.

Jews have had an important impact on urban society since the 16th century. Many prominent Jewish families in the Netherlands today with names like Coelho, Jessurun d'Oliveira or Coutinho are reminders of the welcome extended in the late 1500's to that other 'chosen people', refugees from Spain and Portugal, a wave of immigration that included the ancestors of Spinoza. The Portuguese synagogue in Amsterdam is a reminder of the prominent role played by the Jewish community in the 17th- and 18th-century Republic. In succeeding centuries, the originally Sephardic Jews were overtaken by Ashkenazic immigration from eastern Europe. Jews continued to have a strong impact on Dutch society, particularly urban society, right up to the Second World War.

The deportations and mass executions of the wartime German occupation left the Netherlands with only a fraction of its Jewish population. In Amsterdam, a tight cluster of four synagogues of the 17th and 18th centuries, one of them the oldest public synagogue in western Europe, has now been converted into the permanent Jewish Historical Museum displaying a long Jewish history and the flourishing culture that used to be. It is a somber reminder full of the ghosts of a vanished way of life. In another part of the city a large synagogue built before the war, whose congregation has also vanished, now houses the Resistance Museum.

Jewish religious life today has to contend with the same secularizing tendencies other churches do, the drift away from any strong commitment to a religious organization. In the years immediately following the Second World War there was an overwhelming tendency to assimilate, but now many younger Jews are reaffirming their religious heritage. Jewish identity today is supported by a combination of identification with those in other countries beyond the border, the state of Israel, and keeping alive the memory of the wartime experience.

Islam has become the second largest religious group after Christianity. At a time when churches are closing, mosques are opening. Mosques are still usually buildings converted from other purposes, including synagogues. The Moslem community in the Netherlands is now about 450,000 strong. Roughly two-thirds of these are Moroccans and Turks originally brought into the country as laborers, and the rest is made up mainly of Dutch citizens from the former colonies, Indonesia and Surinam. Moslems are rapidly acquiring a permanent stake in the complex of social systems including the church ones, and they are developing into one of the country's established religions.

Taken as a whole, the Moslem community in the Netherlands has a relatively strong religious identity. What are rightly or wrongly perceived as its conservative aspects are probably magnified by being transplanted into an alien environment. Some of the many complications attaching to the Dutch perception of their Moslem community will be explored a bit in a later chapter. Part of the unease about Islam in the Netherlands comes from their being perceived as a great deal more monolithic than they really are. The Moslem identity does not necessarily build a cohesive religious community, and there tends to be relatively little communication between Islamic groups of different national origin. In the case of the immigrant minorities, the religious links with 'back home' are much stronger.

Aside from the small protestant denominations, **Humanists** and anti-clerical movements make up the rest of the picture. In the social culture of the Netherlands thirty or forty years ago, equal rights to a share of recognition and benefits tended to come by way of identification with a group based on belief, most of them religious but not necessarily so. The *Humanistisch Verbond* 'Humanistic Society' was formed in 1946 in an effort to create an organizational home for those who needed a secular belief that would stand up to that of the churches. It fell into the religious pattern of meetings on Sunday morning, songs, leisure activities, social work, youth organizations, official visits and the like, but gained wide recognition for its stance founded on human values rather than divinity. Though its actual membership is small, as much as 20% of the population applies the term 'humanist' to itself. It has had an influence on social attitudes that is far out of proportion to its numbers.

Secularism and anti-clericalism have always been one of the important currents of thought in the Netherlands, going back at least to the 18th century. Religion has exercised a strong influence on Dutch literature, but at the same time many of the most highly respected writers have stood on the principle that religion is to be blamed for much that is wrong with Dutch society. The most famous is probably the essayist Menno ter Braak, in *Afscheid van domineesland* (Farewell to the Land of Preachers, 1931) and *Van oude en nieuwe Christenen* (Of Old and New Christians, 1937).

The Netherlands is a fascinating laboratory for the sociology of religion. The trend away from commitment to religion and church membership has affected every western society, but nowhere as dramatically as in the Netherlands —the first European country in which religious affiliation has slipped into a minority percentage. The Dutch themselves claim that they have developed greater momentum here because they had farther to go. The result has been that the Netherlands, once the most devotedly religious country in Europe, has quickly become its most secular. Independence from all religion is a positive stance proudly claimed by more and more voices. The Dutch have not tired yet of exploring and debating this phenomenon. One writer speculating on the future of the Catholic church made the wry remark that the church is indeed built on a rock, but that viewed through a sociological lens that rock is 'slowly sinking in the marshy soil of the Low Countries'.*

But what is disappearing? How much of our national cultural identity, the Dutch ask, was based on religion?

Notwithstanding all this, discourse about religion is still an accepted part of Dutch social life—whether for or against—and it is still a 'presence' in an increasingly secularizing country. Belief has become more general, as the previous sharp lines between us/them, clergy/laity, men/women have become steadily more indistinct. Non-church religion is growing strongly, as many seek to experience a liberal form of religion on their own. And as elsewhere, Evangelical movements are taking root vigorously. Religious principle still affects behavior in various social areas, and there are still correlations between religion and class, status and occupation. Religious attitudes, for instance those that have to do with the sabbath, still permeate society: On Sunday most stores and gas stations are closed, and daily newspapers do not publish Sunday editions (although Sunday newspapers are available on the Internet). A recent attempt to publish a Sunday-only newspaper to fill just

* W. Goddijn et al., *Hebben de kerken nog toekomst*. Baarn: Ambo, 1981, p. 137.

this gap ended after a year and a half in failure. Dutch society now finds itself in the stage of debating the mutual roles of church and state in modern times. Government has tended more and more to regard churches not as a conscience for all of society— a role they still claim for themselves—but as service organizations aimed at a specific group.

This religious heritage is intimately interwoven with an idea that has been appearing in these pages a number of times now, the pluriform structure of society in the Netherlands. Social organizations formed along odd and unexpected lines become intriguing when they show signs of falling into a pattern. Recall: there are two labor federations, one 'general' and one 'Christian'; social benefits are distributed via a network of private organizations partly coinciding with religious and political groupings; the school system is duplicated several times over by sub-systems; the political-party system is divided into religious and non-religious. Even some historical events participate in this: When the new IJsselmeer polders were settled in the 1930's, the government's population selection preserved 'in triplicate' ('protestant', 'Catholic' and 'general', the latter term to be explained in a moment) the demographic and ideological composition of the Netherlands at the time. Religious groups were settled into their own villages and regions, and the new polder became something like a scale model of Dutch society as it was perceived in the 1930's.

In spite of sweeping changes in society, there is still a noticeable place for matters that come down to ideology. Since the strength of religion itself does not seem to be sufficient to account for this attitude, it must be based on something more fundamental to the social fabric. In the Netherlands as it was from about the 1930's on to about the mid-'60s, we find a society that

Fig. 11.3
'Playing democracy'

was fragmented into blocs based on ideology—religious or otherwise—and strongly isolated from each other. This bloc organization, along with the resulting isolation, was highly institutionalized. That is, the pattern ran through all types of social organization and there were ways in which its perpetuation was assured. The blocs were relatively independent of each other, had little or no contact at the level of ordinary people, and tended to regard each other with suspicion—rarely with hostility but usually mixed with a kind of guarded respect.

The key term used in the Netherlands for describing these blocs was and is the word *zuil* 'column'. Society is referred to through this metaphor as a 'building' supported by 'columns' or 'pillars', all of them necessary to hold it together and form the 'roof' of cooperative democracy. The language goes on to derive other words for this system of sub-societies: *verzuiling*, usually translated 'pillarization', *verzuild* 'organized according to ideological blocs', *ontzuiling* 'breakdown of the ideological-bloc system', *herzuiling* 'reintroduction of ...' and so on. For many years *verzuiling* was the subject of jokes and innuendoes. The Greek column became the favorite symbol for referring to the whole system, indeed for evoking Dutch society itself.

Talking about belief has a very long history in the Netherlands. The system of *verzuiling* brought with it the necessity of being sharply aware of where one stood and what the philosophical position of one's group consisted of. People developed a variety of ways for recognizing each other's religion or position, and most were—and still are—highly skilled at reading the signs that are invisible to an outsider.

A 'column' was really a collection of often interlocking social organizations. An individual's life was oriented around a whole set of these, which usually meant almost exclusive association with one's own kind. They consisted of

church or *equivalent*
school, and often *university*
political party
trade union, including *farmers' and employers' unions*
professional society
leisure organization (sports, amateur music, hobby clubs, ...)
newspaper, radio, in a later period also *television*
public library, hospital

and many others besides. To be sure there is nothing unusual about a wide variety of volunteer organizations, but what makes these unique is that all of these organizations were partially or fully subsidized by the central or the municipal government. The government's financial stake in the system of course guaranteed its perpetuation.

For most people, relationships were formed and long family traditions shaped within a particular 'column'. Leaving one meant entering another, and since this often meant severing old associations, it was an emotional uprooting similar to emigration. The blocs are striking in being based on no familiar sociological concepts such as class, hierarchy, region, ethnic origin or caste. Although the system was not compulsory for anyone, it had a strong tendency to be exhaustive. Power and influence derived directly or indirectly from the competition among the blocs, and playing this social game meant fitting in—even by those who opposed all ideology and indeed the bloc system itself.

The main unanswered question at this point is: How many blocs were there? It may be a bit anticlimactic to have to say that after oceans of ink have been spilled on the subject, no single answer is possible. There is universal agreement on at least three (Protestant - Catholic - General), but often enough four are insisted on because 'Protestant' so clearly consists of two distinct blocs, *Hervormd* and *Gereformeerd*. And if 'General' is divided into two (Socialist and Non-organized), we end up with five. The commonly-accepted usage is

1 *Roman Catholic*
2 *Orthodox Reformed (Gereformeerd)*
3 *Reformed (Hervormd) and other Protestant*
4 *Socialist*
5 *General and Non-church*

The roots of this complex social system go far back in the cultural history of the Netherlands, and ultimately it is based on cleavages as much as four centuries old. The system developed along the lines of pragmatic acceptance and accommodation that are habits reaching far back in Dutch history. The style of interaction that evolved gave a form to religious and political debate that it still retains. Political power came to be so dispersed and fragmented that decision-making was channeled into a consensus process. The system had the effect of minimizing radicalism and withdrawal from the political process, and it prevented a strong left-right polarization. In no other country in Europe were there states within the state like this, nor can we find so exact a balance of blocs, the practically equal weight of Catholic and Protestant being the best example. In no other country have religiously-based political parties so thoroughly dominated the political system.

With all its restrictiveness, *verzuiling* can be seen to have had a number of positive effects. At the end of the Second World War, many hoped the old pattern of isolated, competing blocs was gone for good and that society could be reorganized on a new, cooperative basis. But as recovery got under way, *verzuiling* reemerged more strongly than ever. It was not until the '70s that it became possible to look back and see the deeper social role it had been playing: innovative ideologies and ideas about social progress came not from one or two but from numerous rival centers, and because of the long-established principle of equal treatment, all benefited from whatever one was able to achieve. The competition itself seems to have made rapid social change manageable. The system did not itself become one of the objects of social change until the '60s, when for the first time people confronted each other on an individual basis. There were new political parties, radicalization, less deference to leadership, weakening of the hold of religious establishments, changing attitudes toward religion itself—old certainties were being lost and the familiar outlines of society were suddenly and disorientingly blurred.

Not a word of all the above would have been worth saying if the picture of *verzuiling* did not have some connection to today's society. Much of it has been modified almost out of recognition, and yet much of it is still there. The word *verzuiling* is heard less and less frequently in referring to current conditions, and the image of the column has had its day in parody and satire. Whether one is for or against, all agree that *verzuiling* in the old familiar sense is just not alive any more. In fact, some members of an older generation are already heard complaining that the young are so ignorant of their own recent past that they hardly know what the term means. A little observation readily confirms this. There is a steadily decreasing identification with organizations exclusively on the basis of one's ideological position, and in general association with others across the old invisible lines is much freer. It is now no longer common for children to be warned against buying something in a particular store because it is run by people of the 'wrong' religion, something that used to be an accepted part of upbringing.

But we are interested in today's *verzuiling,* and here the catch lies in those words 'in the old familiar sense'. The old sense is something like 'historically evolved ideological blocs consisting of long lists of associated organizations', but what if we change the sense to imply something like 'a general mentality that sees competing blocs as natural but with variable content'?
In terms of general attitude, the past decades show a clear erosion of support for institutions on a religious or ideological basis. Labor union federations have gone from a whole field down to two, and there are moves to do away with even this division. The two main protestant churches are far advanced in the merger process, and ecumenical services with Catholics are no longer unthinkable. Once it was possible, as we saw, for the Catholic bishops to issue their notorious Pastoral Letter warning Catholics they would be refused the sacraments if they joined Socialist organizations or even so much as listened to Socialist radio programs, an attitude that sounds almost medieval today forty years later. Where in 1964 a TV program that satirized the 'worship' of television by applying religious symbolism to it caused a national uproar that filled newspaper columns for weeks with the rage of the offended, religion is now satirized much more openly and without serious consequences. The formation of the Christian Democratic Alliance erased the three-way church rivalry on the political front.

But that old habits die hard is nicely illustrated by the 'P.C.Hooft Prize' affair of a few years ago. The writer Hugo Brandt Corstius, widely known for his sharply satirical columns attacking any and all self-important moral leaders, was nominated for the P.C.Hooft Prize in literature, the highest national literary honor. But the government refused to award the prize, saying that it could not be seen as giving approval to someone who deliberately set out to insult people. The government, it was implied though not stated in so many words, felt a responsibility for safeguarding the respect due each segment of the population and could not be in the position of rewarding offense to some. In the storm of protest in the press over this assumption of moral paternalism for an entire society, many did not hesitate to point out that the minister had shown himself to be precisely the kind of self-righteous moralist that Brandt Corstius skewered with such gusto. The awarding of the prize was quickly taken out of government hands and awarded to Brandt Corstius anyway, but the point is that even today it is possible for the attitude of observing the sanctity of the blocs to spring to life.

Does the Netherlands remain a divided, pluriform society? In other words, is it a system in which a fragmented form is not so much modified into homogeneity as it is given new content? In spite of all the changes that have taken place, there is good reason to see something like a national commitment to pluriformity, in the sense that an ongoing process of accommodation and consensus among relatively independent and competing equals is widely accepted as the best model for society. Dutch society remains committed to a cultural pluralism that does not promote one ideology or set of values as the only right one.

An example of this cultural pluralism is the integration of ethnic minorities into Dutch society. The Netherlands has always been culturally pluriform, and what we are witnessing now is a continuation of an old pattern as these groups are integrated in the time-honored Dutch 'culturally semi-autonomous' style. Many have proposed, for example, that Moslems be fully incorporated into Dutch culture while at the same time being given ample room to preserve their own culture and form their own set of organizations. This means a reactivating of the old *verzuiling* model on a new basis. But Moslems are more heterogeneous than most people realize, and so far a bloc based on belief has not proved practical. Nevertheless, cultural pluriformity seems to be increasing in strength, and a social experiment is still under way. There can be no doubt that understanding the recent evolution of pluriformity into its many faces today is crucial to understanding how contemporary Dutch culture is put together.

In view of these unambiguous trends, to say nothing of the precipitous decline of religion with which this chapter opened, it may seem a bit surprising that so much of the formal structure of the *verzuiling* system is in fact still in place. In politics, most parties—particularly on the denominational right *(klein rechts)*—continue to attract the same segments of the population as always. Besides the innumerable leisure organizations that identify themselves publicly as 'Catholic', 'Christian' and the like (an exclusiveness that in practice usually does not extend much beyond the name), there are two major social institutions whose form today is only understandable through grasping the way in which they perpetuate the bloc structure: the education system and the broadcast media.

As we saw above, the school system consists of public education and, parallel to this, sets of government-subsidized 'particular' schools *(Bijzonder Onderwijs)* administered mostly by religious groups. In practice many communities are not large enough for more than one type of school, and parents must often be content with whatever school is available. In the Catholic south, for instance, this is almost certain to be a Catholic school. Since today approximately 70% of all schools nationwide are 'particular', the chance is not great that a school that is available will be a public one. The highly productive principle of the past, actually a progressive one, held that any gain made by one group must be extended to all. This has turned the school system organized along *verzuiling* lines into vested interests that are extremely resistant to change. And the system is becoming increasingly deeply entrenched: annually 80% of the applications for secondary schools is in the 'particular' category.

The majority fails to support *verzuiling* in education, and there are increasing signs of organized resistance to it. It has been shown that only 20% to 45% of the Dutch population (the percentage depending on the ways the questions are asked) believes that education along *verzuiling* lines is worth the expense. 60% of parents have no interest in religious content—even their own—and prefer that importance be attached to quality of education.

At a very early stage in the evolution of *verzuiling,* it was grasped that the mass media were crucial to group identity and cohesiveness. The vastly expanded modern media show clearly the marks of this pattern, but in varying degrees. It is in the debate over the immediate future of some of the mass media that some of the lines of a pluriform style of thinking emerge most clearly.

FURTHER READING

Daalder, Hans, *Ancient and Modern Pluralism in the Netherlands.* Cambridge, Mass.: Harvard University, 1989.

Felling, A., J. Peters and O. Schreuder, *Dutch Religion: The Religious Consciousness of the Netherlands after the Revolution.* Nijmegen: Instituut voor Toegepaste Sociale Wetenschappen, 1991.

Goddijn, Walter (et al.), *Hebben de kerken nog toekomst. Commentaar op het onderzoek 'Opnieuw God in Nederland'.* Baarn: Ambo, 1981.

Hoekstra, E. G. and M. H. Ipenburg, *Wegwijs in religieus en levens-beschouwelijk Nederland. Handboek religies, kerken, stromingen en organisaties.* Kampen: Kok, 1995.

Post, Harry, *Pillarization: An Analysis of Dutch and Belgian Society.* Aldershot: Avebury, 1989.

Reesink, P. (ed.), *Islam. Een nieuw geloof in Nederland.* Baarn: Ambo, 1991.

12 Mass media

Not many years ago, watching TV was an exercise in being persuaded, if not indoctrinated, and the ideological messages were clear and unmistakable. Each ideological bloc of the population had a 'right' kind of programming intended for it, the content of which constantly reinforced group cohesion and identity. In the earlier days of television, most people carried over habits formed in radio days and avoided most 'other' programs. The organization of the most powerful of the mass media still follows in the nineties the lines laid down more than half a century ago when access to radio time was first allocated and society was far different.

When radio came to be widely used after the First World War, no national broadcasting corporation was ever set up, but instead a group of interested 'amateurs' was allotted broadcast time, and soon other competing groups—organized according to 'columns'—followed. In the rigid system of *verzuiling*, each 'column' was allotted its fair share of time on the air, and TV later followed this same system. Each bloc formed its own independent broadcast association (*omroepvereniging*), the term still in use today. The organization that evolved was thus a faithful reflection of the society of the Netherlands at the time, and knowing this fact about its background will help account for what will at first seem like a quite a curious structure. Though today society, as we have seen, has evolved away from these isolated blocs, the Broadcast Associations are still in place.

These radio and television associations are, briefly:

AVRO Since the forerunner of this association was the one that made the first claim to radio time, it is one of the oldest, but in fact the first four associations listed here all date formally from the year 1925. From its beginnings, the AVRO has been 'neutral' and has always steered clear of any specific ideological position. In the heyday of *verzuiling*, it proved attractive to many from both the secular and liberal Reformed blocs. At present it is the largest of the associations. It has been gradually shifting its emphasis in the direction of entertainment programming.

VARA The association representing the Socialist bloc has always adopted the tone of the rebel challenging the taboos of the others. It was the VARA that in 1964, as we saw in the previous chapter, tested the limits of freedom of expression with its program using religious symbolism for satirical purposes. It managed to maintain in its programming a focused, identifiable ideological content longer than most of the other associations did. With the crumbling away of most of the former Socialist bloc's marks of identity, the VARA has lost some of its justification for being different, and terms like 'identity crisis' are often heard. Its current byword is *groot en rood*, popular and 'red' at the same time.

VPRO This is another of the old associations that trace their origins back to the beginnings of radio. The VPRO represented the *Hervormd* or liberal Reformed bloc, though by now most of this identity has disappeared and the association has a generally 'humanist' outlook. It has remained one of the smallest of the main group of associations.

KRO This association began as an institution serving the Catholic bloc of the population, and it retained this identity into the early days of television. In the '60s it began drifting away from its strong ideological position, but in the '70s was able to reverse this trend, and now the programming includes low-key but clear emphasis on Catholicism. It has always insisted on maintaining a high degree of informative content. It strives, as it puts it, to remain 'A and K' that is, both an 'A' association (the category of the largest ones) and Catholic.

NCRV The 'C' stands for *Christelijk*, as it does in the names of a great many other organizations. This association, another of the original ones, represented the orthodox Reformed bloc, the *Gereformeerden*. During the TV years of its existence, its emphasis on religious content has become very watered down, to the point where many former supporters have moved into more recently formed and more orthodox associations such as the following. Still, today it continues a discreetly religious tone.

EO The 'E' stands for *Evangelisch*, an association that began relatively recently in an attempt to recapture the biblically-oriented outlook that used to characterize some of the other associations. Its programming is not preachy, but via adherence to strict moral standards still carries reminders of the religious aspects of modern life. It has quickly become one of the largest associations, and is now the main voice of evangelical religion in the country.

TROS This association began its existence as a pirate transmitter offering entertainment in a straightforward market approach, and hoping to break through the *verzuiling* mold. Its initials also stand for a formal name, but at the same time the acronym spells the word *tros*, which means 'bunch of grapes' or 'ship's cable'. After it went legitimate it continued to put heaviest

Fig. 12.1
TV program listings
on a typical day

NEDERLAND 1	NEDERLAND 2	NEDERLAND 3	RTL 4	RTL 5	SBS 6
KN 07.00 Alles kits extra. NCRV 07.00 Iet wakkere woud. AVRO 07.25 Pippi angkous. 07.49 Lava lava. KRO 07.55 atjetoe. AVRO 08.18 Droomshow. JCRV 08.46 (TT) Willem Wever. KRO 9.11 Professor Poopsnagle. NCRV 9.38 'n Goeiedag met Jos Brink. OHM 0.28 Meera. NCRV 10.53 Rondom ien. ZVK 11.30 Alom klinkt het woord. JOS 11.54 NOS-Tekst tv. KRO 5.45 De wonderbaarlijke sneeuwpop Amerikaanse jeugdfilm. 7.06 100 Jaar Nederlandse cinema. AVRO 7.16 Alies kits. Kinderprogramma. KRO 8.13 Star Trek: The next generation. Amerikaanse sf-serie. NCRV 9.01 The nanny. Amerikaanse comedy-serie. AVRO 9.30 Alle dieren tellen mee. NOS :0.00 (TT) NOS-Journaal. AVRO :0.25 (TT) NOS-Weeroverzicht. AVRO :0.34 Avalon. Amerikaanse speelfilm uit 1990. Sam Krichinsky en zijn broers zijn emigranten en wonen in Baltimore. Ze laten familie overkomen en dan ontstaat een strijd tussen de ouderen en de jongeren die openstaan voor nieuwe idee-en. :2.37 Karel. Talkshow. :3.24 The two Jakes. Amerikaanse speelfilm uit 1990 van Jack Nicholson. Met: Jack Nicholson, Harvey Keitel, Meg Tilly e.a. l1.33 Einde.	TELEAC/NOT 08.30 Koekeloere. 08.45 Beestenboerderij. 08.55 Kerstmis, een feest van licht. 09.10 (TT) Nieuws uit de natuur. 09.30 (TT) Schooltv-Weekjournaal.10.00 Einde. 11.30 Een tuin voor het huis. 12.00 Knoop in je zakdoek. 12.15 Milieu: doen en laten. 12.30 Starting business English. 12.45 Hos Geldiniz (Turks voor beginners). EO 13.00 Het elfde uur. 13.52 Gospeldip. NOS 14.00 (TT) NOS-Studio sport. TELEAC/NOT 16.55 (TT) Fotograferen. NOS/TROS/EO 17.29 (TT) 2 Vandaag. Met om: 17.30 (TT) NOS-Journaal. TROS/EO 17.35 (TT) Actualiteiten. Presentatie: Victor Deconinck. NOS 18.00 (TT) NOS-Journaal. NOS 18.15 (TT) Actualiteiten. NOS 18.39 (TT) NOS-Hoofdpunten uit het nieuws gevolgd door het weer. EO 18.48 Sea rescue. Documentaireserie over het dagelijkse werk van de Amerikaanse kustwacht. NOS 19.20 (TT) België - Nederland. Rechtstreeks verslag van deze WK-kwalificatiewedstrijd. 22.06 (TT) Man/Vrouw. Praatprogramma over mannen en vrouwen. 22.46 Trits. Kennisquiz. 23.13 (TT) Omega. 6-delige informatieve serie over bovennatuurlijke zaken. 00.03 Songs of the seasons. Lied. NOS 00.05 NOS-Journaal. EO 00.10 Middennacht klassiek. TROS 00.40 Kunst... omdat het moet. Serie kunstprogramma's. 01.32 Einde.	NOS 07.00 NOS-Tekst tv. 13.00 NOS-Journaal. 13.09 Noorderlicht. Herh. 13.36 (TT) Twee voor twaalf. Herh. 14.12 Panorama vrijdag. Herh. 14.54 (TT) Ju Ju. . Met:. Herh. 15.47 Een dag om nooit te vergeten. NOS 16.00 (TT) NOS-Journaal. 16.05 Frasier. Herh. 16.30 Alle kinderen zingen. NPS 17.00 Urbania, een stadstriptiek. Reportageserie. RVU 17.30 The factory. 8-delige documentaireserie. VPRO 18.00 Villa Achterwerk. NPS 18.15 Sesamstraat. Kleuterprogramma. NPS 18.30 (TT) NOS-Jeugdjournaal. VARA 18.45 (TT) ZaterdagavondLINGO. 19.10 (TT) Oppassen!!! Nederlandse comedyserie. 19.40 (TT) Twaalf steden, dertien ongelukken. Serie. 20.10 (TT) Unit 13. Nederlandse politieserie. 21.05 (TT) De show van je leven. Serie portretten. NOS 22.00 (TT) NOS-Journaal. VARA/NPS 22.16 (TT) Nova. Actualiteitenrubriek. NOS 22.45 (TT) NOS-Studio sport. VARA 23.40 Spijkers: actualiteit en satire rond de nachtspiegel. Amusementsprogramma. NOS 00.20 (TT) Unit 13. Nederlandse politieserie. Herh. NOS 01.10 NOS-Tekst tv.	07.00 Telekids. Kinderprogramma. 12.00 Great expectations. Klassieke cartoon. 13.15 Fairy tales: The brave little tailor. Tsjechisch sprookje. 14.50 De jukebox van RTL 4. 15.05 Agenda 21. Serie waarin mens en milieu centraal staan. 15.40 Jenny Jones. Amerikaanse talkshow. 16.25 Snowmagazine. Wintersportprogramma. 16.55 Het staatslot op lokatie. 17.25 Gezond & wel. Gezondheidsmagazine. 18.00 Zes uur nieuws. 18.10 Eigen huis & tuin. Informatief programma. 19.00 5 tegen 5. Spelprogramma. 19.30 Half acht nieuws. 19.50 Weer. 20.00 Het beste van Nederland Muziekland. Compilatie. 21.00 Commissaris Rex. Duitse politieserie. 21.55 Parodie parade. Showprogramma. 22.55 Heb ik dat? Themaprogramma. 23.55 Late nieuws en sportnieuws. 00.20 Ärztin in angst. Duitse thriller uit 1994 van Bruce Seth Green. 02.05 Nachtprogramma. **EURO 7** 07.00 Euro 7 club. 10.00 Dossier aarde IV. 10.30 Passie, liefde en relatie. 11.00 Schilderen met Bob Ross. 11.30 Vermommingen.12.00 TV Shop. 13.00 Een wereld verdwijnt. 14.00 Dossier aarde V. 14.30 Passie, liefde en relatie. 15.00 Over de grens van de geneeskunde. 15.30 Exotische huisdieren. 16-delige reportageserie. 16.00 Schilderen met Bob Ross. Cursus. 16.30 Gone fishing. Reportageserie. 17.00 Einde.	17.35 Streets of San Francisco. 18.30 Alles over veilingen. Engelse documentaireserie. Herh. 19.05 Hunter. Amerikaanse detectiveserie. 20.00 Het movie weekend - How the future began: The right stuff (1). Amerikaanse dramafilm uit 1983 van Philip Kaufman. Met: Sam Shepard, Scott Glenn. 21.40 Zaterdagavondcafé. Nederlandse comedyserie. 22.10 Maniac cop II. Amerikaanse thriller uit 1990 van William Lustig. 23.55 Teachers jazz nights. Serie jazzconcerten. 00.50 Nachtprogramma. **VERONICA** 07.00 Veronica Call tv. Met om: 07.00 Op en top. 09.00 Winkel van Sinkel. 11.00 Way of life. 12.00 Game time. 14.00 The lounge. 15.30 Als je van paarden houdt .... de hoefslag. Herh. 16.00 Miami vice. Amerikaanse politieserie. 16.55 Big N.O.W. TV. 17.50 Ajax! Voetbalprogramma. Herh. 18.20 Dinosaurs. Familieserie. 18.45 The Baldy Man. Amerikaanse serie. 19.20 TV Woonmagazine. Informatief programma. 19.55 Home improvement. Amerikaanse comedyserie. 20.25 Bird on a wire. Amerikaanse speelfilm uit 1990 van John Badham. Met: Mel Gibson, Goldie Hawn, David Carradine. 22.30 Mariska. Talkshow. 23.25 Genuine risk. Amerikaanse erotische thriller uit 1991 van Kurt Vos. 00.52 Einde.	14.45 Happy days. 15.15 Chopper squad. 16.05 New Mission Impossible. 17.00 Koken met Cas. 17.45 In en om het huis. 18.20 Rabo top 40. Herh. 19.30 Jag. Amerikaanse detectiveserie. 20.30 A cry in the dark. Film. 23.15 Revenge of the ninja. Film. 00.50 Silk stalkings. 01.40 Horoscoopjournaal. **KINDERNET** 07.00 Wekservice. 07.15 Ovide. 07.30 Dino babies. 07.50 Toeters & bellen. 07.55 Bassie en Adriaan. 08.30 Kinno Kiepert. 08.40 Little Rosey. 09.00 Toeters & bellen. 09.05 Superworm Jim. 09.30 Albert de vijfde musketier. 09.55 Toeters & bellen. 10.00 Tom Sawyer. 10.25 Ghostbusters. 10.50 Popeye. 11.00 Dino babies. 11.20 Knock outs. **MUSIC FACTORY** 07.00 The morning after. 09.00 The bass-ment. 12.00 The pitch. 13.00 Clip-parade. 16.00 Best of. 17.00 Dance Top 40. 19.00 The young ones. 19.30 ïxter 8. 21.00 Weekend special. 23.00 Sylvana's soul. 02.00 Clip Gallery. **TV 10** 12.45 TV shop. 13.45 Pearl II. 15.20 Vijf op een rij. 15.55 To the manor born. 16.25 The saint. 17.15 Bewitched. 17.45 The man from U.N.C.L.E. 18.40 Fame. 19.30 Vijf op een rij. 20.00 Scoop!20.30 Ruth Rendell. 22.15 The Agatha Christie hour. 23.10 Sanford & son. 23.40 De versierders. 00.30 Saturday night live.

emphasis on entertainment at the expense of any more than the required minimum of informative programs, and fears were expressed on all sides about *vertrossing*, a general lowering of standards. These somewhat sneering complaints are still heard, but TROS did help turn TV from a medium with a selective appeal into one with mass appeal.

The *Nederlandse Omroep Stichting* or *NOS* (Netherlands Broadcasting Foundation) is a separate foundation that coordinates the work of all the associations, and provides business and legal advice. It provides program facilities for all associations and for small religious or cultural groups that do not maintain their own. It is the sole producer of all the daily news broadcasts, so that news is ideally kept free of the ideological bias of any association. The *Nederlandse Programma Stichting* or *NPS* (Netherlands Programming Foundation) has the function of producing programs that all Associations draw on. The *Nederlands Omroep Bedrijf* or *NOB* (Netherlands Broadcasting Company) was recently formed to take care of all the technical equipment the individual associations are not able to provide for themselves.

This last function needs a word of expansion, because it is more important than it may sound, being a fundamental feature of the Dutch way of organizing their broadcast media. Along with the licensed associations with their significant numbers of members (we will return in a moment to that key word 'member'), legislation provides for access to broadcast time by *kleinere zendgemachtigden* (minor licensees), which are recognized groups without membership, and whose principal function is other than broadcasting. Any group that can form an organization and demonstrate that its point of view is not reasonably represented within the existing structure—and that what they have to say will make a positive contribution to its diversity—can apply for broadcast time and facilities. This is how the *Nederlandse Moslim Omroep* (Dutch Moslem Broadcasting Foundation) was granted guaranteed annual broadcasting time on TV and radio.

The daily program listings (Fig. 12.1) will regularly show the names of many of these 'minor licensees' without memberships.

As the name suggests, broadcast associations are required to be legally incorporated and to be able to show formal memberships. 'Member' in this context does not mean the same as 'viewer'. Though all who pay the basic annual user fee are free to watch whatever programs they wish to, all associations compete with each other for members, since their allocation of broadcast time is dependent on this membership total. There is a total of just over 5,000,000 memberships of one Association or another. But since practically all these are household memberships, this means that in fact between 80 and 85% of all Dutch households have membership in a public association.

Becoming a member implies general support for the association's programming objectives, which in the time of *verzuiling* meant the propagation of one's own belief. Today it means little more than a preference for the general outlook or program emphasis of one association over others. Membership involves a fee paid to the association, and this includes a subscription to a program guide. Since only the day's programs without commentary are published in the newspapers, the magazine is one of the primary lures to members, and the associations are free to make these as attractive and as commercially profitable as they choose.

The first source of financial support for television is the user fees, and the second is membership and subscription fees. The third source is revenues from broadcast advertising. All advertising broadcast by these public associations is in the hands of a separate organization, the *Stichting Ether Reclame* (*STER*; the acronym means 'star') 'Airwave Advertising Foundation'. Advertising is allotted its own blocks of time, and its content is regulated by this commission, which collects revenues and distributes them to all the associations according to a proportional formula.

The system according to which television is organized in the Netherlands shows several remarkable features. Formally it is still in the steadily weakening grip of competing ideological interest groups that control the programming content, but at the same time it has been made so open that no single outlook is able to dominate it. The unwieldiness of competing views has been transformed into the means for guaranteeing freedom of expression. The influence of government is largely restricted to its regulatory role.

One of the most difficult points in the debate accompanying the coming of commercial cable TV—which more than once has almost brought about the collapse of cabinets—is the extent to which the expansion of the commercial side can be handled by way of the present system. There are several non-cable channels that are nevertheless commercial. The present distribution of broadcast time among groups is based on restricted access to the medium imposed by limitations on technology. But cable-TV technology has meant a vast expansion of the possibilites, and over 90% of Dutch homes are now connected. Drawn up opposite each other, as it were, are the established associations on the one hand, and on the other the commercial interests ready to exploit the new media possibilities on a free-market basis. On the commercial side, the year 1995 saw the formation of the 'Holland Media Group', a conglomerate of commercial channels and large newspaper and publishing groups. This HMG in turn competes with several other large media conglomerates, all of them resulting from a constantly shifting succession of mergers.

The associations are based on a bygone structure of society, and their attempts to hold on to any group exclusiveness on TV is in direct conflict with the medium's powerful universal attractiveness. They are going through an agonizing process of fighting a rearguard action, determinedly reorganizing in an effort to meet the rising tide of commercial TV (with a market share at present of around 50%). It seems rather safe to predict that they are destined to lose the last remainder of their 'bloc' identity and that they will rather attempt to represent broad social currents to meet the varying needs of the viewing public.

After seemingly endless debates about urgent reforms, it was recently decided to move away from the old representation of belief blocs and evolve toward three 'network identities', representing three different types of programming the public presumably wants. The groupings can be seen in Fig. 12.1. It remains to be seen whether these associations can learn to cooperate closely enough to offer more effective competition to the non-subsidized commercial channels surging in popularity. On cable TV the commercial competition is even greater.

This national picture has tended to ignore the growing strength of regional radio and TV broadcasts, both of which are probably well-positioned to take full advantage of the accelerating pace of regionalization and decentralization.

Broadcast media legislation provides for a special fund for the purpose of ensuring the continued vigor and diversity of the print media. This fund represents a surcharge on radio and TV advertising revenues, and is intended to help shield the print media from the competitive blow administered with the beginning of broadcast advertising.

As everywhere, newspapers have had to face the challenge of sharply rising costs and competition from television. From the '20s on to the '50s, the press was firmly locked into the *verzuiling* pattern, each paper with its own constituency and a steady, reasonably predictable readership. But it was economic necessity rather than social progressiveness that swept the press out of this phase. In order to survive, newspapers had no alternative to broadening their appeal to readers of various persuasions, and this meant steadily modifying and eventually giving up a narrow ideological stance. So the press has evolved from an instrument for the perpetuation of *verzuiling* into the diverse, vigorously critical free press that it is today.

Though criticism of government can be sharp and unsparing, government and press are not in adversarial roles. The former could probably not mold the latter to its own liking even if it were inclined to. Being based on coalition politics, the government itself is always relatively diffuse and has no single clear ideology. This same diffuseness also makes the government a difficult target for the press, and criticism most often has a restrained tone.

Traditionally Dutch newspapers have favored a somewhat bland staidness in their makeup—at least compared to some papers in the US and Britain —though present-day competition has tended to increase overall brightness of look. The Dutch have a distaste for flashiness, and newspapers do not need to compete to attract attention on the newsstand. Papers are sold mostly by subscription and delivered at home, a family orientation that affects both appearance and content.

The six largest dailies, listed below, have all moved away from *verzuiling*. If we were to move farther down the list of the national dailies into those with a smaller readership, we would find more and more that still retain their specific religious or other ideological orientation inherited from older times.

De Telegraaf Conservative and middle-brow, it is a morning paper aiming as a mass appeal. It is the boldest in makeup, though still far from 'tabloid' in appearance.

Algemeen Dagblad Mildly progressive, middle-of-the-road morning paper attracting a large audience. As that code-word *algemeen* 'general' indicates, it has never had an identification with any of the ideological blocs of former generations.

De Volkskrant For the first decades of its existence, this morning paper served the Catholic segment of the population. The reference to its religious orientation was removed some years ago, as it attempted to become general

and progressive in content. It is generally regarded as one of the two best dailies in the country.

Het Parool This evening paper began as one of the main voices of the postwar Socialist movement, although it was never seen as a party paper in the strictest sense. This specific orientation it has since given up, although it remains mildly progressive. Its present goal, as a daily centered on Amsterdam, is to continue its existence as a 'popular quality paper'.

NRC Handelsblad The product of a merger of two 19th-century dailies, *Algemeen Handelsblad* and *Nieuwe Rotterdamsche Courant*. As an evening paper it continues the tone of mildly progressive solidity for an educated, business-oriented readership. Along with the *Volkskrant*, it is a 'quality' national daily. Both have been able to increase their readership markedly in recent years.

Trouw Previously one of the voices of the Orthodox Reformed bloc, this morning paper has, like the rest of the large dailies, to a great extent muted its previous specific identification. However it retains some discreet Christian character, and its occasional loyalty to traditional values has been known to lead to its being labeled the 'most Dutch paper'.

Most subscribers to daily newspapers also read an opinion weekly, a category that gives the makeup of the Dutch press picture its distinctive flavor. The largest ones are

Elsevier
Vrij Nederland
HP-De Tijd
De Groene Amsterdammer
HN **(Hervormd Nederland) Magazine**

The latter two have the most clearly identifiable editorial positions. The last has abandoned its former tie with the church, and maintains a stance that is both Christian and politically radical.

Today the opinion weeklies are just emerging from a struggle for survival as it looked as though the dailies were taking over more and more of their traditional cultural-commentary function. They have all been forced to adapt to modern times by softening their bold ideological stance into a less controversial tone that is more attractive to the advertisers they depend on. *Vrij Nederland*, for instance, continues its tradition of investigative journalism emphasizing the forgotten and underprivileged, and it has been steadily adopting a more colorful format as its leftish image gets progressively diluted. The weeklies are returning to a healthy market share.

During the five years of German occupation, most of the prewar papers were forbidden publication if they refused to comply with the press restrictions imposed. *De Telegraaf* was the only one permitted publication all through the occupation years, a fact that many of an older generation have still never been able to forget. The restrictions resulted in resistance papers, some of which have survived to become today's dailies and weeklies. Many of the names still proclaim their origins. *Trouw* is 'faithfulness', *Het Parool* is 'the Watchword', and *Vrij Nederland* 'the free Netherlands'. The latter, not the largest but widely regarded as the best opinion weekly in the country, became the foremost symbol of the resistance and today, as it has passed its fiftieth year of publication, it is still identified with it.

Finally, significant competition to all these is offered by the large number of regional dailies. The sharpness of the competition comes in the one way in which they differ most strongly from regional or local papers in other European countries or the US: they offer very full coverage of international news. They are able to do this by sharing the services of correspondents and background stories. As is the case with the national dailies, most of these papers tend to be owned and run by large publishing groups able to take advantage of regional markets.

At present the press serves the Dutch-speaking domestic population, but at the time of the very beginnings of something we can call 'the press' its reach extended much further than this. In the 17th century the Netherlands, most notably Amsterdam, served as a press center for all of western Europe. Though there will no doubt always be some dispute over where the first real newspaper was published, the Amsterdam ones earned an international reputation at a very early date. Informal newsletters began appearing on a regular schedule to help merchants plan their activities, and these were called *corantos*. The first one of these appeared in 1618. The Dutch newspapers that evolved from this beginning had two sizable advantages over their competitors. There were Dutch nationals living in all major European seaports who could supply information, and the Netherlands was the only country at the time where private persons could publish news. In London they read and quoted from The *Amsterdam Courant*, and the number of competing native and foreign enterprises grew. Amsterdam was a center where newspapers and books could be published with a freedom possible nowhere else. Let us take a look at how this all came about.

FURTHER READING

Bardoel, Jo, and J. Bierhoff (eds.), *Media in Nederland* [vol. 1]. 6th ed. 1990; *Informatie in Nederland* [vol. 2]. 2nd ed. 1989. Groningen: Wolters-Noordhoff.

Fact Sheet (described in chapter 1). See the issues 'Broadcasting' and 'The Press'.

Hilversummary. Broadcasting News from the Netherlands. Hilversum: NOS [A magazine].

Verschuren, P., and R. Memelink, *Media-atlas van Nederland*. Den Haag: SDU, 1989

13   The historical dimension

The Seventeenth century in the Netherlands is not nearly as remote a time as one might suspect it to be. In important ways the Dutch still follow today the distinctive patterns of social life their ancestors laid down nearly four hundred years ago. The phrase 'the Netherlands in the 17th century' evokes in the minds of most of us vivid images of a comfortable, quiet, sober middle-class social life in a setting of clean, colorful cities and a peaceful, idyllic countryside. These images come from the vision left to us by the Dutch painters. In a way their world is part of the experience of all of us.

In the portrait, both of individual and of group, they evolved a new vocabulary for putting a personality in a setting that reflected personal achievement rather than birth—a rather novel idea in paintings of the time. But it was in the genre paintings, scenes of everyday life, that they gave their world a form in which, rightly or wrongly—and it is some of both—we still see it. They painted with such a photographic eye that we are tempted to see the pictures as realistic renditions of what we could have seen then. But the self-contained, other-worldly stillness of their atmosphere never really was. No painting was without some moral content. The genre paintings and the still-lifes (a term which the Dutch invented) are carefully arranged messages full of symbolism.

But though they are idealized and stylized, the paintings can still serve as our entry point to a period that is remote and present at the same time. The society they depicted was after all not just invention. Hundreds of paintings show a self-confident, modestly affluent, soberly industrious society the general nature of which historical records tend to confirm. The houses they built for themselves in their expanding cities, the second principal source of the image that involuntarily enters our mind today, are concrete confirmation of this impression. The houses along the canals in Amsterdam—but also in comparable sections of many other cities—were built by people of middle-class tastes. They are all nestled close to each other, each with its own 'personality' and yet none out of harmony with the rest or even much larger than the rest. To our modern eye, the difference between these homes of an affluent class and those built for those without wealth seems relatively slight.

The centers of most Dutch cities today continue to testify to the form and style of 17th-century society. Indeed, the large number of Dutch paintings from the 17th century allow us some revealing glimpses into family life. They show us beyond any room for doubt that the Dutch attachment to domesticity, family life, and the affectionate nurturing of children awakened at an early date, before it did anywhere else in Europe. The interiors of most Dutch homes today still reflect the same priority given to comfortable, orderly family life.

No time in the Netherlands is more richly documented or easily available in books than the 'Golden Age'. This was the cultural expression of a society that engaged in a lengthy war against the Catholic king of Spain and at the

Fig. 13.1
Pieter de Hooch (1629-1684),
A Woman Peeling Apples

same time allowed Catholics in the Netherlands freedom of worship, where freedom of expression was secure enough that the Netherlands became a center of publishing of all kinds, and where dissidents from other countries could find a haven. In a time when princes elsewhere were turning wealth into conspicuous palaces, the charitable and social-welfare institutions provided a model for the world.

It was a society that built a whole educational system on the concept of the practical and useful. A good example of an outlook on life that ran throughout the 17th-century society was the *Nederduytsche Academie*, which we might translate as the 'Netherlands Academy', founded in 1617. The Academy was based on the idea that instruction and education in a variety of subjects at university level should be available to everyone, and in the vernacular at that—a highly progressive idea. The Academy offered classes in such useful subjects as science, arithmetic, history, astronomy, public speaking, art, politics and ethics. Much of the instruction, especially in subjects such as the last two, was done by means of plays written especially for the curriculum. These put a strong emphasis on the profitability of the 'proper leading of life' in the practical world, a moralistic strain in the Netherlands that can be found in the earliest literature and one that has never left it. But the Academy was established in the midst of a social atmosphere that was not as broadly tolerant of such free thinking as we might like to think, and in 1622 church officials forced it to close.

The closing of the Academy proved to be only a minor setback (15 years later the climate had relaxed enough that a new theater enterprise could take its place) in the much larger picture of the emancipation of the mind that was being carried on. This same society was the home of the mathematician Simon Stevin we have already met, of Leeuwenhoek, Huygens and the many other determined observers of the world. Mapmaking reached a peak of development and served a worldwide market, thanks to years of careful recording of places combined with a highly developed engraving technique that came from the printmakers. Astronomy developed out of practice in the art of finding one's way around at sea, and the design and production of better telescopes stimulated the making of better lenses. This, in turn, is inseparable from the optical glass technique that made microbiology possible and provided the fundamental means for early science. The surrounding world is knowable in new and entirely different ways, they were convinced, and the route to it is by way of seeing and representation. The Dutch devotion to seeing helped make their universities centers in which the new scientific outlook was practiced. A commitment to precision and accuracy of observation took the place of superstition and reliance on inherited authority.

The figures that look out at us from the portraits made in the Netherlands tend to give us an 'everyday' impression. Most often they are a middle-class couple having a wedding portrait painted, a prosperous merchant, an officer of the military or militia, a stern-looking burgomaster dressed in black with a white collar, or a group of severe-looking governors of a charitable institution. What we are looking at is the faces and the self-assured demeanor of the urban patriciate, the representatives of the merchant class of the cities. They are called 'Regents', and it is their practical, unostentatious tastes that gave shape to a whole culture and gave cities throughout the Netherlands their characteristic look. Their 'benevolent paternalism' put such a pervasive stamp on the society that the Dutch today still refer to any official who exhibits too much authoritarianism as a 'Regent'.

Fig. 13.2
Bartholomeus van der Helst (1613-1670),
Portrait of Andries Bicker,
mayor of Amsterdam

All the early maps of Amsterdam (for instance Fig. 4.7) show plainly a pride in the fact that the city was 'born out of the water' and owed its prosperity to it. The concept of 'freedom of the seas', a phrase that formed the title of one of the best known works of Hugo Grotius, was a Dutch idea that was a novel one at the time. Amsterdam depended on its strategic location on the trade routes between Flanders and the Baltic, and the southern route to Spain. From the 13th century on, Amsterdam became an important port, and by the 17th century it was the warehouse and trading center for all of Europe. Amsterdam replaced Venice at the front of the world stsge, and ultimately it was eclipsed in turn by London. The city is often referred to by historians as the last flourishing of the city-state. This term inplies a trading empire carried on by a city—and immediately surrounding countryside—and not by a state in the modern sense with all the forces and resources that implies.

It is admittedly somewhat lacking in romance to point out that Amsterdam's prosperity was based on the Baltic trade plus its ability to serve as warehouse and credit supplier for all of Europe. In the popular imagination its main activity was not this but its trade routes to the Indies. The *Verenigde Oost-Indische Compagnie* (United East Indies Company), founded in 1602, is the best-known symbol of the Dutch trading empire. The corporate voc model was imitated almost immediately by other countries. In 1621 the Dutch set up another company along the same lines, the West Indies Company, but the West proved for various reasons to be a less fortunate venture. In any case, the Netherlands became one of the first true bastions of capitalism, an economic commitment from which they have never since departed.

The Dutch Republic in the seventeenth century was a confederation of provinces that had formed a union for the purposes of securing political liberty, but that still thought of themselves as to a great extent autonomous. These ministates acted independently, each running its own affairs by means of a legislative assembly (not truly democratic in the modern sense but more like an oligarchy) called the *Staten* 'States'. For the unavoidable coordination of efforts and the achievement of at least minimal coherence in economic and military policy, the provincial States sent representatives to the States General in The Hague—still the official name of the parliament in today's centralized state. The absence of centralization went considerably farther than this. Each town considered itself autonomous as well, a claim that was based on economic power and the resulting authority exercised by the urban patricians, the Regents. It was a type of organization inherited from earlier centuries, with endless rival laws, customs barriers and tolls, coinage systems and dialects, in which both authority and law enforcement were spotty. This local semi-autonomy was a direct outgrowth of liberties secured by cities in the Middle Ages. It was one of the primary factors in the 16th-century revolt against the Spanish.

These loosely confederated provinces had only a feeble hold on something that might be called a state, which accounts for the difficulties that arise in what to call the political unit. It was sometimes referred to as the 'States-General' after its unique administrative institution, sometimes the 'Seven Provinces', but most often as the 'United Provinces'—though in 1672 the visitor William Temple remarked that 'Disunited Provinces' might be more ap-

THE DUTCH REPUBLIC
in the 17th century

Fig. 13.3
The Dutch Republic
in the Seventeenth century

propriate. Nevertheless, it was within this seemingly chaotic fragmentation and geographic particularism that the Dutch were able to form a system in which some measure of freedom for all was assured. The freedom was none the worse for being based on self-interest: toleration was good business. This shaky, but effective, state was made up of several competing forces.

The first of these was the Regents, the class whose power and influence was based on the far-reaching independence of the manufacturing and trading cities. They not only controlled city administrations throughout the country, but created their own coordinating bodies at the provincial level. The details of organization and the titles varied from province to province. In Holland the leadership of the Regent structure was in the hands of the *raadpensionaris*, often translated 'Pensionary', a name that suggests little to an English-speaking reader. The word simply meant 'salaried adviser'. He had a function something like that of Minister of Foreign Affairs or Secretary of State and even some powers of a governor, all this based on the consent of his peers and not on any popular election. Since Holland far outweighed all the other provinces economically, it inevitably did politically as well. The Pensionary of Holland became, in effect, the Regent head of the Republic.

The second of the forces was that of the *stadhouder* and the administrative structure that went with it. Originally the stadhouder was an official appointed by the king of Spain to govern in his place in a distant province—a 'lieutenant' in the literal sense, the Dutch word being a translation of the French. At the time the revolt against the Spanish began, the stadhouders in the provinces of the Netherlands were members of prominent families such as the house of Nassau. The stadhouder in Holland was William of Nassau, who also held the heritary title 'Prince of Orange' and was therefore usually called William of Orange, better known by his nickname 'William the Silent'. Though the office of stadhouder was not originally hereditary, in the 17th century it remained in the hands of William's descendants, first by custom and later by law. The stadhouder was the closest to a titular head that the Republic possessed. When the authority of the Spanish king was renounced, the stadhouders of the various provinces—mostly military people with slight interest in the commercial world—assumed for themselves the right to govern the country and assure its continued independence from the Spanish.

Prince Maurice, the first of William's sons, not only replaced his father but turned into one of the foremost military leaders in Europe. He developed his armies along modern professional lines, forming a 'school of war' that trained military people from far outside the borders. And they tended to be somewhat less sober than their patrician counterparts: In the first part of the 17th century Frederick Henry, the second of William's sons, developed a court life of such luster and glamour as to give the new Republic considerable sovereign status in the eyes of the world.

From the first attempts in the last part of the 16th century to break the hold of foreign rule and attempt independent government, all the way down to the final end of the Republic in the last years of the 18th century, the social forces supporting the Regents and those supporting the stadhouder were in an uneasy alliance with each other that several times degenerated into hostility and outbursts of violence. The two chief rivals, the Pensionary and the stadhouder, often cooperated smoothly but, depending on the period, the function of head of state was fulfilled sometimes by one, sometimes the other.

The third force was that of the Calvinist church organization. The Reformed Church in the Netherlands, one of the products of the Reformation, began its existence with a strong and independent organization based on firmly established local communities. These 'consistories' were an early form of dem-

ocratic organization forming their own rules and assuring their own perpetuation. This form of organization was strong enough to retain its democratic
structure even when their ministers accumulated more and more authority
and began to assume leadership. In the last years of the 16th century and the
beginning of the 17th, the Reformed Church took more and more seriously
the enterprise of establishing a theocratic state. Its leaders guarded ortho-
doxy and attempted to root out secularism and blasphemy. They were powerful enough to force the closing of the Academy mentioned above. These,
then, are the three forces the interacting of which gave shape to the moment-
ous events that brought an identifiable Dutch society into being and gave it
the form it still retains.

In ways too involved to go into here, the Church provided the ground on
which the above-mentioned rivalry between the Regents and the stadhouder
was contested. To put things as simply as possible, the former tended to be
allied with the theological liberal wing, and the latter with the orthodox
wing. These two sides were called the *rekkelijken* and the *preciezen* (latitu-
dinarian and orthodox, literally 'pliable' and 'precise'), terms that were part
of the polemics of the time, and, as a pair, still part of the Dutch vocabulary.
In the early 17th century a clash between the two rivals for secular authority,
clothed as a theological dispute, resulted in the execution of Johan van Ol-
denbarnevelt, Pensionary of the Province of Holland. But the hold of the
Regents, who had no intention of allowing Church authorities to take civil
power away from them, was not seriously shaken.

The serenity of the paintings is apt to mask political realities. Each of the
three forces mentioned had its own stake (in turn trade, political liberty and
religion) in resistance to their feudal overlords the Spanish. With the stage
now set, let us take a look now at the further political events unfolding, this
time on a somewhat larger stage.

Europe in the 17th century showed the world the first models of the modern
nation-state with its strongly centralized authority. In England, France and
Spain the competing claims of a variety of mini-states and local authorities
had been subdued by a central administration under a strong absolute monarch. People were no longer citizens of a town or principality with its own
laws and identifying insignia, but of a nation that by way of royal display was
able to create a sense of identity. Part of the nation-state's claim to the loyalty of its citizens was, and is, its mission of assuring them enough space to live
in comfortably and of defending them from the threats posed by other states.

In the 17th century we are witnessing a world just forming along modern
lines. It was on this fiercely competitive stage that the United Provinces of
the Netherlands found themselves. The competing claims of local and regional authorities were the same as those in all the surrounding countries,
but here there was a curious difference. There was no centralization of administration, no absolute head of state, and only a weak sense of nationhood
ever developed. Its neighbors looked with a mixture of wonder and disbelief
at the unprecedented spectacle of a people trying to govern itself and evolving the political means by trial and error as they went along. Its governmental system was a throwback to the traditions of the past, modified to meet radical new demands. It was a fiercely-defended preservation of the custom by

which local regions and towns exercised some of the governing of themselves, a custom that was being abolished elsewhere. But at the same time it was also a large-scale experiment in the development of democratic forms such as had never been seen before.

The provinces of the Low Countries (a rather general term intended to cover the region included, roughly speaking, in the present-day Netherlands and Belgium) were a rationally organized but highly fragmented and decentralized system. The provinces were inherited intact from what had evolved in the preceding centuries under the Dukes of Burgundy. This was a succession of dukes who were rivals to the king of France and who, by means of dynastic marriages, during the 15th century added most of the already prosperous and culturally advanced Low Countries to their possessions. They did not attempt to impose anything like a centralized authority in the modern sense, but confirmed the host of local charters and privileges that had been won from various local feudal princes centuries before. These 'privileges' mostly concerned rights to a limited self-rule and authority to collect taxes and tolls, and they formed a legal basis for self-government that was an important aspect of the later conflict with the king of Spain. The original duchy of Burgundy was in central France, but during the course of the century the dukes found that the wealth and prestige of the cities in the northern part of their realm were more attractive, and the court activities—which always had a way of being rather peripatetic anyway—shifted from Dijon northward to Brussels.

The 15th-century Burgundian Netherlands left a cultural heritage that, to the modern imagination, rivals that of the Republic in the same area only two centuries later. The 'Netherlandish' or 'Flemish' school of painting influenced all of European art. Van Eyck's paintings immortalize many wealthy and prominent Burgundians. The period from the mid-15th to the mid-16th

Fig. 13.4
The court of Duke Philip
of Burgundy

centuries in music is sometimes called the 'Age of the Netherlanders', and the terms 'Netherlands School' and 'Burgundian School' are used interchangeably. In a sense, the Burgundians are still with us in the Dutch consciousness: the word became synonymous with splendor to such an extent that today the word *bourgondisch* refers to a taste for lavish living and carefree consumption.

By the end of the century, the Low Countries provinces had passed, through a series of marriages, into the hands of the German-Austrian Habsburgs. The Habsburg Charles V, elected emperor in 1519, had been born in Gent, in the Burgundian Netherlands. The ruling of this empire, which also included territories in the Americas, was now centered in Spain, and the king was obliged to leave the administration of the Netherlands in the hands of stadhouders, under the supervision of a relative appointed as regent (which is not the same as 'Regent' as used above, referring to the urban patricians in the Netherlands).

Liberal ideas about religious experience were not new in the Netherlands, but until the first decades of the 16th century they remained the property of an urban, educated class. The first Reformation movements that had their origins in the Netherlands appeared about 1520, but most of the impulses came from outside. Even in this time, the Netherlands formed a crossroads where ideas collided and were traded and adapted. In spite of all the Spanish efforts to eliminate the heresy of protestantism in the Netherlands, threats, prohibitions and executions were not able to stop movements that continued to multiply.

By 1560 church organization was becoming well established. The Reformed, 'Calvinist' congregations began in the South. During most of the 16th century they remained far stronger in the South than in the North, the region that, ironically enough, in only a few decades was to become the independent protestant Republic. As the new religion grew steadily more assertive in the Netherlands, Spanish attempts to suppress it became more determined. The regents in the Netherlands provinces had the task of mediating and trying to defend the rights of the people the best they could. The stadhouders and other noblemen in the North tried to assure as much respect as possible for the local legal privileges that were being continually invoked as a basis for a restricted autonomy.

Now, in the second half of the 16th century, differences became so great that peaceful reconciliation was no longer possible. The result was full-scale revolt, known as the Eighty-years War. The incorporation of prosperous provinces, duchies, counties and seigniories into the Duchy of Burgundy in the 15th century had led to their becoming the duchy's center of gravity and had molded them into a rudimentary political unit with a beginning sense of cultural identity. Economic power produced an increasing sense of a right to political independence which, in turn, came to be identified with the new religion. In this way religion and politics came to be thoroughly intertwined, a circumstance that has been one of the facts of life in the Netherlands ever since.

Charles V's son and successor Philip (who became king of Spain as Philip II) had been born and raised in Spain, with no particular familiarity with the

cultural traditions of the Burgundian provinces. Spain in the 16th century was an old-style feudal empire that was developing into a centralized, absolute monarchy without any significant urban middle class like the one that was so prominent in the Low Countries. Protests against repressive rule became more insistent and more urgent. Messages and delegations were sent to the regent and to the king, but the gap only widened. When in 1566 a delegation of noblemen personally brought a petitition to the regent for the relaxation of sanctions against heretics, one of her courtiers sneeringly called them *gueux* 'beggars', and the term *geuzen* became a symbol of revolt against Spanish oppression.

The term joined the Dutch language permanently, not only as a word for 'protestants' long in use in the Catholic South, but today for any ordinary people who engage in an uphill struggle for a worthy cause against constituted authority perceived as repressive. The first group of unorganized resistance to the German occupation in 1940 called itself by the same name. Calvinist groups became more and more bold and met in public. When a wave of destruction of Catholic church images broke out in the same year—what is called the *Beeldenstorm*—many Catholic churches in the North were turned over to protestant congregations.

King Philip's reaction to all these protests was military force headed by the Duke of Alva, whose brutally repressive regime had the predictable consequence of strengthening the resistance. One of the focal points of resistance to Spanish rule was William of Orange, who as stadhouder of three of the provinces was by far the most powerful. Philip saw in him his principal antagonist, even though he and the other stadhouders continually reaffirmed their loyalty to the king. The actual armed revolt is counted as beginning in 1568, when William for the first time directly engaged Spanish troops.

Fig. 13.5
Prince William of Orange (1533-1584) (left), Philip II, King of Spain 1556-1598

The commonly-used phrase 'the revolt', as if an entire people rose at once with singleness of purpose, is in actuality a much later invention covering an uncoordinated and directionless series of local uprisings. Armed revolt also began from another side, which at first was unrelated to this. In 1572 a band of *geuzen* landed at Den Briel, the present Brielle west of Rotterdam, and occupied the town. They raised their flag and succeeded in repulsing the Spanish counterattack, and the first town in the Netherlands found itself on the side of the revolt. It was only a short time before these bands and the stadhouder's forces made common cause, and nearly all the towns of Holland joined in. The 'revolt' was the first in history, by the way, to make full use in its propaganda of the relatively new invention of printing and of printmaking. Thousands of one-page broadsides satirizing the enemy have survived.

Efforts to break away from Spanish rule proved to be considerably more successful in the northern provinces than in the southern. This was partly because of the presence of better natural defenses such as the great rivers, and partly because of the still growing economic independence of the province of Holland. The 'Union of Utrecht', formed in 1579 as a set of agreements to cooperate and coordinate efforts, was an agreement between mainly northern provinces, while a competing treaty of the rest was formed in the South. The political division of North and South had become a fact.

In 1580 the king declared William an outlaw and set a price on his head, and in 1581 the seven provinces of the Union of Utrecht responded with an Act of Abjuration, formally terminating recognition of Philip as king. In 1584 William of Orange was assassinated in Delft, and even though he felt despair at his failure to secure the political liberty of all the Netherlands, self-rule was already so far advanced that his death did no real harm to the cause. In 1585 Antwerp was captured and held by the Spanish, and the large numbers of Calvinists there were allowed to migrate to the cities of the northern provinces. This last date is a milestone for two reasons. It marked a final cultural separation of the northern and southern provinces—the further course of the war for over a half century did little to change the basic division—which is still present today in the cultural gap between the Netherlands and Flemish Belgium (Chapter 17). Further, since the city was promptly blockaded, Amsterdam's main rival was eliminated at one stroke. This assured the rapid economic rise of the northern provinces.

After the death of William of Orange, the state (if it can be called that yet) was left without a sovereign head, and at the time nobody knew how to fill this kind of gap. When attempts to find some member of aristocracy or royalty in France or England to head the country failed, in 1598 the States of the seven provinces took a bold step into the unknown and decided they would go ahead and exercise sovereignty themselves. With this decision, the 'Republic of the Seven United Netherlands' came into existence. The relative stability achieved in the first uncertain steps in self-government made possible the famous 'Golden Age', and at this point we have finally come full circle, back to the quietly confident 17th-century Dutch culture that is part of the world's image.

The revolt is very much alive today in popular Dutch consciousness in the form of colloquial expressions, folksongs, and names of famous figures and battles learned in school. The revolt was seen by contemporaries in terms of a religious struggle against the forces of evil. There is a tendency in the Netherlands to see the experience of the Second World War in some ways as a replaying of the revolt and the Eighty Years' War, as was illustrated by the early resistance *geuzen* mentioned a few paragraphs back. These same *geuzen* did not hesitate to call the German occupation governor 'the new Alva'. The revolt began as a protest movement, the first time a people had claimed political independence for themselves and formed a new state. The right of collective or individual protest, and acceptance of it as a normal part of the political process, has from the beginning been part of the Dutch way of thinking.

With the signing of the Treaty of Westphalia in 1648, the existence of the United Provinces as an independent state was formally recognized. The Republic remained economically strong until well into the 18th century, and formally it continued to exist until it was abolished by the French invaders in 1795. In its best years it served not only as the economic and commercial but also as the diplomatic capital of Europe. The strands of international agreements joined in The Hague, and four major treaties by which the European powers settled their differences were signed on Dutch soil. Through these treaties the Dutch were able to remove progressively more obstacles from the pursuing of their trade.

From here we can move toward modern times with a few large strides. Economic prosperity brought growing rivalry with England, which between 1652 and 1780 broke into hostility on four occasions. The Republic tended to think of itself as safe behind its water defenses, with the Spanish Netherlands to the south forming a convenient buffer against the aggressiveness of the French. The Regents in Holland had become powerful enough to govern without the stadhouder, and in 1667 had declared that the office was abolished. But when England and France joined against the Republic and invaded in 1672, the government was caught militarily unprepared and the stadhouder had to be reinstated as a rallying point.

The two long 'stadhouderless periods' in Dutch history are concrete outgrowths of the continuing debate over just what—if any—role the House of Orange should play in the Dutch democratic system. In the 18th century there was a stadhouderless period of 45 years, and this time, when one of the Orange princes was called on to restore a symbol of national unity, the office was for the first time made hereditary in the male line for all the provinces together. But notice that these people are still far from being 'king'. There have always, from the 16th century on, been strong voices of opposition to monarchical pretensions, and the usefulness of the monarchy is still questioned today. Here we see the absorbing spectacle of a people debating for some four centuries the pros and cons of monarchy within a democratic system until they finally put them together.

It is a curious fact that even though the Dutch Republic had long since assumed legendary proportions in the world, something we can call a Dutch national identity was only beginning to show signs of forming. But by the end of the seventeenth century it was about to be put to a severe test. In the 18th century a variety of weaknesses of the Republic combined to bring about its end. Shipping to the Baltic declined, and the cities of the Netherlands were bypassed. Amsterdam no longer functioned as a commercial transshipping and trading center, and more and more confined its activities to operations of financing. Competition with the English and French was not pursued aggressively, and control of the commercial empire overseas was neglected. The Republic was no longer the technological 'research lab' of the western world. The decentralized habits inherited from the 16th century were part of the problem. No one was able to create or impose an efficient organization. The Republic had to a great extent ceased to function as a sovereign state and lost most of its independent identity.

Developments that took place at this point, poised at the edge of modern times, revolved around how citizens' interests were to be recognized and represented. Oligarchical rule had not been able to evolve an effective representational system. The Regents were widely distrusted, and the stadhouder proved to be no solution to the visible crumbling away of the state. The first revolutionary outburst came in 1747. The most fervent anti-Orangists of the time were the 'Patriots', who by 1786 had formed a strong enough force that a full-scale revolution was attempted, three years before the French Revolution. It failed in its ideal of turning the confederation of seven provinces into a truly unified national state with a meaningful central administration, but this did not discourage popular sentiment. There was increasing identification with revolutionary movements in France. When the French, reinforced by Dutch Patriot units, invaded the Netherlands in 1795 they found little real resistance.

FURTHER READING

Because historical surveys of the Seventeenth Century in the Netherlands are so numerous and readily come by, no attempt will be made to list any here.

Duke, Alastair, *Reformation and Revolt in the Low Countries.* London: Hambledon, 1990.

Haak, B., *The Golden Age: Dutch Painters of the Seventeenth Century.* New York: Abrams, 1984.

Kossmann-Putto, J.A. et al., *The Low Countries: History and Language.* Rekkem: Stichting Ons Erfdeel, 1993.

Parker, Noel G., *The Dutch Revolt.* London/New York: Penguin paperback, 2nd ed. 1990.

Prevenier, Walter, and Wim Blockmans, *The Burgundian Netherlands.* Cambridge: Cambridge University, 1986.

Schama, Simon, T*he Embarrassment of Riches: An Interpretation of Dutch Culture in the Golden Age.* Berkeley: University of California, 1988.

Struik, Dirk, *The Land of Stevin and Huygens: A Sketch of Science and Technology in the Dutch Republic during the Golden Century.* Dordrecht/Boston: Reidel, 1981.

14   The modern Netherlands

The course history took in the Netherlands was that, for the making of a modern nation, first all traces of the identity of the outmoded order had to vanish. In 1795 the stadhouder fled to England, and the former Republic of the United Provinces was transformed amid general rejoicing into the new, revolutionary Batavian Republic. The transition to the new order on the French model seemed simple. A new, centralized government system was formed, and work was begun immediately on a new constitution. Among other things, this provided for complete equality of religion, which meant taking exclusive rights to hold office out of the hands of the Reformed church for the first time. But this republican form of government could last only as long as it lasted in France, and when in 1804 Napoleon became Emperor, the Republic turned briefly into the 'Batavian Commonwealth' under a Grand Pensionary (a title recalling the old Regent rule), and then into the Kingdom of Holland under the emperor's brother. This, in turn, lasted only until 1810, when the kingdom was dissolved completely as an independent state and incorporated into the French empire.

The separate identity of the Netherlands had vanished, and yet this complete absorption into the French system had the effect of introducing modernizations on a scale that might not have been possible by less drastic means. The country now saw the abolition of the old guilds which had been outside most government control, the introduction of a postal system and uniform coinage, standardization of weights and measures, reformation of the tax system and codification of civil and criminal law, and the founding of libraries and museums. Coming closer to home perhaps, it was also in this period that the Dutch, like most other peoples in Europe, inherited the requirement of family surnames that made modern civil record-keeping possible.

For all the reforms and modernizations, the Netherlands found itself in the complete control of the same people, who, only fifteen years earlier, had been greeted as liberators. But though national identity seemed on the surface to disappear, foreign occupation and control had the same strengthening effect it always does. By around 1813 the fall of Napoleon was imminent, and the Netherlands proclaimed itself independent. It formed a government and invited stadhouder William VI over from exile in England to assume sovereignty of the new state. In 1815 he became King of the Netherlands as William I. But he became king of a much larger country than his predecessor had left as stadhouder. The Congress of Vienna was convened to redraw the map of Europe in line with the power balance following Napoleon. It resurrected an ancient concept of a powerful state between France and Germany, and decided to unite the former Republic with the former southern Netherlands provinces that had been under Habsburg rule since the 16th century, to create the Kingdom of the United Netherlands. This was the way the Netherlands first acquired a monarchy.

But the differences between the two halves were not to be papered over so easily. The North had had centuries of independence and prosperity while the South had been a remote province of the Spanish and later Austrian empires. The constitutional provision for equality of religion had not changed the fact that protestantism was dominant in the North and Catholicism in the South. The union lasted only fifteen years, and in 1830 the two went their separate ways again. Chapter 17 will look at how all this affects present-day cultural relationships between the Netherlands and Flemish Belgium.

The loss of the southern half of the kingdom was greeted by many in the North with a feeling of 'good riddance'. But it did nothing to solve the problem of an autocratic king who failed to recognize the winds of change and preferred to rule by royal decree rather than by constitutional procedures. The strand of distrust of Orange rule was still strong, and the constitutional reformers were determined to bring about true representative government. By 1848, in a new constitution, the Lower Chamber of parliament emerged as the real center of power. It was now elected by direct vote and had secured a series of rights to handle and approve legislation. It was at this point that the king's power to appoint and dismiss ministers at his pleasure was reduced, as we have seen, to a merely symbolic act. This revolution in the Netherlands was a quiet one. The Dutch people did not have to undertake an armed uprising to win democratic government, but had it presented to them.

The events of this first half of the 19th century set the stage for the making of the modern Netherlands. Other than centralization, reforming the national administration so that it could operate as a single whole, and industrialization, the really significant 19th-century step into the modern world was the series of emancipation movements that created the social and political systems of the Netherlands today. It was not until orthodox Calvinists and Catholics organized their own political parties to form an opposition to the supposedly benevolent Liberal oligarchy that the beginnings of the modern political-party system were launched. When the political field was formally entered by the Socialist movement in 1878, all the main lines of the modern system were in place. And taking one more 50-year leap, the emancipation movements contained the seeds of the pluriform system of social blocs that was to develop increasingly more structured forms through the first half of the 20th century.

On May 10, 1940, the German army invaded the neutral Netherlands and, after brief resistance, surrender followed on May 14. But this was not before a German deadline had passed and a threat to fire-bomb Rotterdam had been carried out. The center of the city was destroyed and 78,500 inhabitants were homeless. The day before this, Queen Wilhelmina and the Cabinet left the country, and from London became all through the war a symbol of defiance to the occupiers. The Netherlands was under civilian administration, and at first efforts were made to win the cooperation of the Dutch population. Political parties were not abolished but only the National Socialist party had full freedom of activity.

In this first period of the occupation, Jews were not persecuted physically, but the occupiers tried to isolate them from the rest of society by surrounding them with petty restrictions and prohibitions. Pressure was put on businesses to declare Jews unwanted, and Jewish figures in public life were forced to re-

Fig. 14.1
'The Devastated City',
by Ossip Zadkine in
Rotterdam, a reminder of
the bombing of the city in
1940 (left)
'The Dockworker' by
sculptor Mari Andriessen
in Amsterdam, commemo-
rating the strike in 1941

sign. It was the increasingly heavy-handed German treatment of Dutch Jews that in February 1941 led Communist dock workers in Amsterdam to organize a general strike in protest, for which the Germans were unprepared. The statue of the 'Dockworker' in Amsterdam commemorates the origin of the strike. In 1947 Queen Wilhelmina officially added the words *Heldhaftig, Vastberaden, Barmhartig* 'Heroic, Resolute, Merciful' to Amsterdam's coat of arms.

Resistance movements began almost immediately, on a small scale and organized rather haphazardly. Bulletins and clandestine news sheets were printed and distributed, and the first of the underground newspapers began. In 1942 an organization was formed for coordinating resistance movements and supporting those who had gone into hiding. Teams undertook sabotage, assassinations and other similar activities. Still later came an even tighter organization of resistance activities of all kinds and planning of increasingly massive interference with the German occupation machinery.

In 1942 the yellow Jewish star was required for the first time, and more and more Jews chose to go into hiding. Anne Frank in her diary kept during two years of hiding has given the world a feeling for what it was like. In July 1942 came the first deportations of Jews, a stream that was to continue until 1945. In 1941 there were 141,000 Jews in the Netherlands. Approximately 111,000 were deported to the camps in the east, and only 5,450 returned. This means that over 104,000 Dutch Jews were killed during the war, the highest percentage of any country—including Germany.

After 1941, the harshness of the repressive measures of the occupation increased rapidly. Rationing became stricter, men were rounded up for labor in Germany, punishments for a variety of infractions became severer. Political parties were banned entirely, and most newspapers had stopped publishing as the only alternative to refusal to comply with German restrictions. With the entry of the United States and the Soviet Union into the war, the Resistance became bolder and more extensive. In November 1943 the first hostages were executed by the Germans, and this form of punishment turned into a regular practice. By the end of the war, about 600 had died in concentration camps in the Netherlands and about 20,000 in Germany, and between 2000 and 3000 had been executed.

The number who participated actively in the resistance always remained relatively small. Since by its nature it was an organization without detailed records, after the war it was possible for many to claim resistance activity on the basis of small acts of non-cooperation. The numbers tended to become inflated when it was realized what an irresistibly high prestige was attached to the word 'resistance'. Resistance groups in the Netherlands were forced to operate in a geographical setting that did not permit guerrilla or countryside operations, and there was no free border to escape across, so their style of operation had to be that of remaining submerged in the midst of society.

It is especially the final months of the war that have impressed themselves vividly on the minds of those who lived through that time. Following the Allied invasion of Normandy in 1944, Belgium and some of the southern provinces of the Netherlands were liberated, but for the rest of the country the worst was yet to come. The Germans had up till now made some attempts to perpetuate the pretense of being stern but fair governors, but now they treated the Netherlands as enemy territory. Making matters much worse was the unusually severe winter of 1944-45, the *Hongerwinter,* when most food supplies were cut off and starvation resulted. Harry Mulisch has preserved a glimpse of this world in his internationally acclaimed novel *The Assault.* Resistance had now become overt, almost a form of open war. When the Allied advance resumed in March 1945, it continued until the final liberation of the Netherlands came on May 5.

Fig. 14.2
A typical May 4th
commemoration

It was not just a historical accident that the first resistance efforts, the first underground newspaper, and one of the important cores of the organized resistance came from the uncompromising orthodox Calvinist side, the *Gereformeerden*. From the first days of the occupation, the war was seen by them in terms of a struggle between good and evil, with no shades in between. The common word *fout* narrowed its meaning 'wrong' down to the specific area of whatever had to do with the side of the ememy, and now over fifty years later it still preserves this specific meaning. But it is also interesting to speculate on another background to the Dutch perception of the war and occupation in terms that allowed no middle ground. Would it have found itself separating 'good' and 'evil' quite so cleanly if the royal family, the primary symbol of national identity, had not gone into exile immediately in 1940, before there was any chance of cooperation with the Germans?

There is a reason for going into this much detail, and the reason is that to an unanticipated extent the war and occupation have become central to the Dutch national cultural identity. The national experience of war and occupation was sensed, from the beginnings of reflection on it after the war, as one of the most important periods in Dutch history. The process of mythologizing it began almost immediately, and the Resistance assumed legendary proportions. In the popular view, the people of the Netherlands had undergone a period of testing and had emerged with its honor intact. The extent of small acts of collaboration, and the lack of wide national resistance to the decimation of the country's Jewish population, were quietly forgotten.

L. de Jong's massive history of the Netherlands in the Second World War is now complete at 29 volumes and a total of nearly 18,000 pages. *Het Koninkrijk der Nederlanden in de Tweede Wereldoorlog* (The Kingdom of the Netherlands in the Second World War) has achieved a widespread popularity—the entire set has now been published in paperback—not usually enjoyed by the work of professional historians. This is precisely because it confirmed this view and projected a picture of a crucial break in history from which moral lessons could be drawn. As the volumes appeared they were reviewed in detail in the popular press. It is likely that no five-year period in history anywhere has had so much written about it. De Jong, with his sharp eye for human events, has become the nationally celebrated historian of the collective conscience.

The Dutch public's need to talk about all aspects of the experience has so far refused to disappear. By now over four thousand books have been written about the war, most of them factual and about ten percent fictionalized. The experiences of resistance, hiding, and coping with the *hongerwinter* were told and retold, and not allowed to pass into history. Indeed, with the passage of time it seems as though the war becomes more immediate rather than less so. It is as if it fulfills a national need for part of a collective identity and, as it taps into deep cultural roots, needs to be guarded and endlessly debated. Each year since the war the country has observed *Dodenherdenking* 'Commemoration of the Dead' on May 4, still including a two-minute observation of silence throughout the country, and celebrated *Bevrijding* 'Liberation' on May 5.

A second generation, and now a third, has had all this passed on to it, often with a vague sense of guilt for not having experienced it itself or being sufficiently comprehending and sympathizing. Whole generations born after 1945 have inherited their parents' attitudes toward Germany, including the sound of the German language. In the half century that has elapsed since the war, perceptions of it have changed in a variety of ways. The national tendency to interpret the war and occupation in religious or moral dimensions has become more diffuse over the years, partly through the inevitable passage of time and partly due to the weakening of religious thought in the Netherlands. For many in a younger generation, the war is not really over and the struggle won, but it serves as just one more episode in a continuing contest between good and evil. Fascism, racism and other conspicuous evils are always present, and 'resistance' is an appropriate stance to take against them.

The national wartime attention to opposition to the occupier was replaced immediately after liberation by the claims of national reconstruction. After five years in which all the familiar social structures had been dismantled, calls for a new unity of purpose in the spirit of the resistance were ignored as the old social structure of *verzuiling*, with all its competitiveness and isolation, promptly dominated politics again. The thing that did allow reconstruction to succeed so well seems to have been convincing the pragmatic and realistic Dutch that their backs were really to the wall. The lines of the present welfare state began to be laid down, continuing a process that had already begun in the '30s. It is ironic that it was precisely the socially divisive *verzuiling* system that, through its success in creating a national welfare state, assured a strong national integration and hence its own dissolution.

Immediately after the war came more traumas. First was the loss of the East Indies colonies and a few years later of New Guinea. Then in 1953 came the disastrous winter flood that inundated 5% of the total area of the country and resulted in a loss of 1800 lives. Once again a national effort was required, and the immediate outcome was the organization and approval of the Delta Plan described in chapter 2.

The primary task of postwar reconstruction required a stable, relatively unchanging society along old familiar lines, and by the beginning of the '60s national recovery had been assured. But by the mid-'60s the national consensus supporting this structure began to evaporate on several sides at once. The result was the rebellion and disorder of the '60s. Upsets like these occurred practically worldwide at that time, but they proved especially disorienting to a society accustomed to a calm, orderly life organized along well-recognized authoritarian lines.

The Dutch live in a small, densely populated country where people of all kinds and persuasions have to live in constant close proximity with each other. Where social problems take on a special intensity thanks to crowding, we have a right to look for the evolution of forms for handling dissidence. The Netherlands' unique pluriform system was long the main response to this disorderly side of society. The worldwide image of the Dutch as orderly and tolerant (and their favorite image of themselves) is certainly deserved. Over the centuries they developed an elaborate system of mutual respect and middle-class morality that made them into a people valuing obedience and constituted authority. But the Dutch have another side not often enough recognized. Their nationality owes its first origins to an act of dissidence and protest, an attitude that has always occupied a secure place in the Dutch way of approaching the world.

At the beginnings of the '60s society had gotten rather contented, and it was this that was rudely prodded once again by disorderly protests. There were unfocused and unconnected stirrings of discontentment about a variety of issues all at once: the nuclear threat, the continually more visible excesses of the consumer society, deterioration of the urban environment because of increased traffic, the TV culture, and—particularly to the young—the heavy hand of Authority in general. Many officials in this time were unhesitatingly called by the disparaging term 'Regents'. The main goal of the most publicized movement that coalesced was the provocation of authority. It adopted the name *Provo* and, from its center in Amsterdam, regularly dominated the news media and overshadowed other, similar protest groups.

When the controversial engagement of Princess Beatrix to the German Claus von Amsberg was announced in June 1965, Provo had another cause, and it was the organization that staged the disturbances—banners and smoke bombs—the world saw at the time of the royal wedding in Amsterdam in 1966. But Provo's 'program' (and the quotes signal that many Dutch observers decline to dignify it with such a term) was not merely the negative provocation of authority. It developed a series of 'white' plans designed to answer urgent social needs such as the elimination of car traffic from the center city, provision of more housing, and improvement of relations with the police. More than one 'crazy' environmental idea of the '60s was eventually enacted into public policy.

Whether or not Provo made any permanent impact on Dutch society or was merely a creation of the publicity media is a matter long debated. It survived mainly because of its ability to administer shocks to society, but when it turned out that society itself was moving at its own pace in the same anti-authoritarian directions, Provo was deprived of much of its force and petered out. At the very least it helped set Amsterdam on a course from which it has never since deviated. In the eyes of the world Amsterdam remains the focus of the 'permissive' Netherlands and a widely recognized and accepted part of rebellious youth culture.

Provo showed something that is important for understanding protest movements in the Netherlands in general, and one that is unwittingly illustrated in an amusing way by the photograph (Fig. 14.3) taken in one of the clashes of the eighties. As soon as the police began reacting to Provo, a complex game of response and counterresponse was set up that took on some aspects of the stage, and formed a ritual the rules of which were exploited by both sides. Just as the riot policeman and the protester on the bridge have been captured in a perfect geometrical reciprocity with each other, protesters and police continually found themselves choreographed actors in a public theater.

These anti-establishment provocations have an unfortunate tendency to eclipse the serious protest movements of the same period, and to mask the

Fig. 14.3
A news photo from 1980. Note the remarkable symmetry and reciprocal pose of the two figures.

real social change going on under the surface. One of the most significant of these is the women's movement in the Netherlands. The graph (Fig. 14.4) shows some of the statistical result of what has taken place since 1960. Women in the Netherlands were traditionally assigned homemaking roles, and as of 1994, the proportion of married women with full-time employment was only 7%, compared to an EU average of nearly 19%. In spite of the increase in the percentage of working married women, the goals are far from fulfilled. In the UN's 1995 Report on the status of women, the Netherlands even finds itself in the company of developing countries.

Even today, 44% of all students (13% in technological fields) and 6% of professors, 20% of the Lower Chamber of parliament and 9% of mayors are women. Even though women have had the vote since 1919, it was 1955 before the country saw its first woman Cabinet minister, and it took another 30 years before there were two women in the Cabinet. The administration formed in 1994 included four women ministers for the first time in history—though still less than a third of the Cabinet.

The Dutch now have a highly literate women's movement that supports a large number of periodicals of all persuasions. There is now a prestigious prize awarded annually to women writers.

The anti-military movement also had its real beginnings in the '60s, though pacifism is anything but new to the Netherlands—Erasmus, in the beginnings of the 16th century, was a determined and outspoken pacifist. In the Netherlands, the armed forces have never been seen as playing any part in power politics. There was a long series of massive anti-war demonstrations throughout the '80s. By the mid-eighties the Dutch peace movement (mainly the *Interkerkelijk Vredesberaad* 'Ecumenical Peace Conference') had grown to become the largest social movement the Netherlands had ever known, and was famous around the world. When in 1986 the government was debating the placing of NATO medium-range missiles in the Netherlands, the peace movement was able to present a petition to parliament containing nearly four million signatures. The placing of the missiles was approved by a narrow margin (though as it turned out they were never placed). The movement is now somewhat reduced but still a force to be reckoned with.

Lack of enthusiasm for militarism in the Netherlands still manages to capture attention now and then outside the borders. In the '60s a union of military personnel was recognized, and in the '70s it won many rights such as freedom of expression, a standard work-week with overtime, the abolition of saluting and—by far the most famous abroad—the wearing of long hair. It was perceived as moving so far from expected army discipline that the question was often asked in military circles whether the Dutch army really took combat preparedness seriously enough. Today the army's union is still unique in the world.

A third critical social issue of the past few decades is housing. The country as a whole has been suffering from a housing shortage ever since the Second World War, and this has been most acute in the large cities such as Amsterdam. With years of crowding, doubling up and the frustrations of seeing apparently available housing unoccupied, the situation has been a constant source of unrest and social tension.

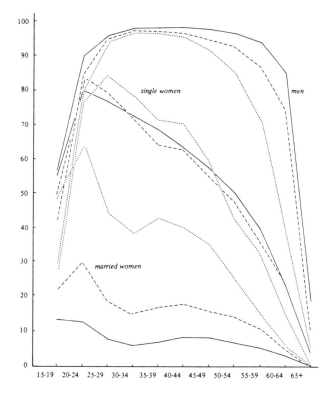

Fig. 14.4
The status of women in Dutch society in the period 1960 - 1983

```
——————— 1960
- - - - - - - - - 1971
............... 1983
```

It was this situation that provided the medium for the main protest movement of the '70s and '80s, the *krakers* (squatters) in their characteristically high-profile and often confrontational style. Entering and squatting in unoccupied housing had been practised on an unorganized basis for years in Amsterdam, so all they had to do was coordinate activities that were already familiar. The city's decision to demolish old housing in the *Nieuwmarkt* neighborhood, one of the oldest in Amsterdam's center city, for construction of a new sub-way line gave the *krakers* a highly publicized issue and an opportunity to side with the residents in protest demonstrations. It also launched them on a crusade they have never abandoned: saving the old city center for its traditional residents by holding back what they saw as a tide of *cityvorming*. The *krakers* continued to develop the entering and occupation of empty housing —much of which was held by speculators—with characteristic Dutch efficiency into an organized activity with local units, a communication system that included a radio station, and a guidebook to squatting.

Although they originally showed the same grasp of public street-theater that Provo had, the *krakers* soon became more stubbornly uncooperative. In addition to their housing activity, they have turned into a rough-and-ready public-interest group against large-scale commercial invasion of the center city, and some have developed an effective form of independent neighborhood administration that defends the interests of minorities. While they once enjoyed a measure of sympathy and even admiration for their public-spirited role in exposing speculation and governmental indifference to residents' needs, they are now steadily shrinking in size, and their growing social surliness has cost them most of their public support.

But this 'urban social movement', like Provo before it, has assured itself a permanent place in Dutch history. It has changed the makeup and diversity of Amsterdam by its championing of the young, the poor and the isolated. It is not hard to predict that it will inevitably be succeeded by some other movement responding, in the Dutch way, to social issues with a fresh approach. The urban guerrilla of some European countries is not part of the Dutch 'style', which is one with a marked distaste for violent confrontation. The activity of the *krakers*—with all its unruliness—is well understood as a logical extension of, and operating within the boundaries of, the socially familiar concept of *actie*.

The word *actie* is difficult to translate because it covers a wide variety of forms of public expression. An *actie* is any means by which an individual or a group attempts to make a public point on an issue or on behalf of any cause, and it may range from the national to the strictly personal. A brief sample of some acts that were called by this term will illustrate the range of meaning:

- protesters stop a tour boat in a canal and throw paint on it, to protest the construction of large tourist hotels in the city
- a group walks through the city with flags and pamphlets protesting the presence of immigrants in the country
- a campaign is started to raise money for the restoration of the Concertgebouw
- someone paints a slogan on a wall to make a point
- a small group (or an individual) makes the rounds of bars and discos to test the level of discrimination of ethnic minorities

- an individual offers a tray of fruit to a cabinet minister, and when the fruit 'accidentally' rolls off, a pointed message is seen on the tray
- workers demonstrate their invisible contribution to a public organization by working for a day only as fast as they are required to
- a newspaper campaigns for new subscribers
- a large group forms an incorporated organization on behalf of environmental issues
- workers in a plant go on strike

As these scattered examples show, *actie* may be individual, or on a momentary impulse, or it may be something undertaken with significant nationwide support. Most often, the undertaking of *actie* presupposes the existence of a supporting organizational structure, the *actiegroep* or *actiecomité*. The most successful of them have well-considered, concrete aims including that of raising money; many, though, are simply unfocused expressions of discontent.

The Netherlands has no formal lobbying system, and public expression in the form of *actie* is the accepted means by which protest is communicated to government. Even confrontational, often illegal *harde actie* falls well within the accepted range of this form of public expression, and indeed, studies show that it tends to achieve more of its aims. Protest in all but its most hostile forms is treated as natural and expected (see Fig. 14.5), an accepted part of the democratic process that is everyone's right. It is well to note, though, that this easy tolerance of dissent ends abruptly as soon as one reaches one's own circle. Here, as we have seen, consensus is worked toward, the alternative being not the 'thrashing out' of dissent but the forming of a new independent dissident group. Through its own social means evolved over the centuries, the Netherlands is able to form protest and *actie* into a growing edge of change by not allowing it to become a socially isolated opposition.

The need to keep things in proportion by diluting total seriousness, what the Dutch call *relativeren,* is a central one that we will return to in a later chapter. At this point we would do well to notice its manifestation in what

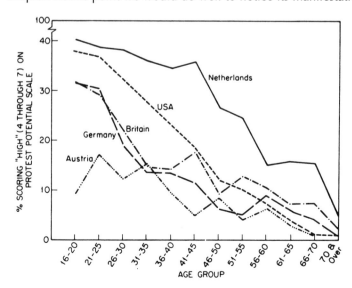

Fig. 14.5
Protest potential by age by country

the Dutch call *ludiek*. The Provos of the '60s seized the term *ludiek* borrowed from the historian Huizinga's book *Homo Ludens* and gave it a new popularity as their key word for their attitude toward society. Much of the style of the *krakers* in the mid and late '70s followed the same habit of introducing a light-hearted tone into the hardest and most confrontational of *acties*. Outbursts of protest usually seem to manage some light touches. Those that accompanied the investiture ceremonies in 1980 included both rock-throwing and a festival atmosphere that were often hard to distinguish from each other.

So we see a society that seems to be none the worse for putting democracy into practice according to its own style. At its best it could even provide a model for those of us on the outside. The Dutch are often seen as over-permissive, but they take some satisfaction in the fact that a great deal is tolerated as long as there is no clear national consensus against it. As we have seen, even those addicted to the illegal hard drugs are part of the social welfare system and have their own union. Prostitution, euthanasia and abortion are all regulated in a matter-of-fact way, and many other controversial issues of society are resolutely kept part of the ongoing public discussion. Just where all the areas of public consensus are is constantly being discussed and readjusted. Whether or not those in other societies always agree with the result, it seems only fair to say that the Dutch are doing more or less what a true practicing democratic society ought to do. They are doing it in their own inimitable way.

FURTHER READING

Ter Borg, M. B., 'Publieke religie in Nederland' in O. Schreuder, *Religie in de Nederlandse samenleving.* Baarn: Ambo, 1990 [the Occupation experience has developed into a 'public religion'].

Deben, L., *Urban Landsquatting: Another Way of Living in Amsterdam.* Amsterdam: University of Amsterdam, 1990.

Hirschfeld, G., *Nazi Rule and Dutch Collaboration: The Netherlands under German Occupation, 1940-1945.* Oxford/New York: Berg, 1988.

De Jong, L., *Het Koninkrijk der Nederlanden in de Tweede Wereldoorlog.* Rijksinstituut voor Oorlogsdocumentatie. The Hague: SDU, 1969-1990.

Kroon, Liesbeth, and Tineke de Rijk, *Positieve actie: Een strategie voor verandering.* Leiden: Stichting Burgerschapskunde, 1991.

Mamadouh, Virginie, *De stad in eigen hand. Provo's, kabouters en krakers als stedelijke sociale beweging.* Amsterdam: SUA, 1992.

Presser, J., *Ashes in the Wind: The Destruction of Dutch Jewry.* Detroit: Wayne State, 1988.

Steggerda, Monica, *Vrouwen in Nederland. Verscheidenheid in sociale contexten en opvattingen.* Nijmegen: Instituut voor Toegepaste Sociale Wetenschappen, 1993.

Women and the State. Dutch Government Policy for the Advancement of Women. The Hague: Ministry of Social Affairs and Employment, 1989.

15 The ethnic heritage

On the west side of the royal palace on the Dam in Amsterdam, in the pediment high above the traffic, is an allegorical sculpture originally made when the building was the city hall of the capital of a vast commercial empire. At the center stands a woman's figure, and she is graciously receiving gifts and riches from other figures representing the different races from other continents. For centuries goods and riches flowed into Amsterdam, but so did people. From even before the 16th century they came to the provinces of the Netherlands from all corners of the world. Traders from other European countries, protestant refugees from the Spanish-held South and later from France, Jews from Spain and Portugal and later eastern Europe, peoples of other races from all over the trading empire. Practically from their first beginnings, cities of the Dutch provinces were open to influences from outside. Cities like Amsterdam have never in their history been of a purely 'Dutch' culture but rather homes to a cultural and racial mixture that played the main role in forming the Dutch reputation for hospitality and tolerance. At the same time, the assimilation of this varied cultural heritage has never been smooth.

Today there are some in the Netherlands who look up at the allegorical sculpture with different eyes, those who see themselves not as the figure at the center but as one of those grouped down lower and around the edges, the outsiders helping to supply the riches but not part of the 'center'. The Netherlands as a whole, and the large cities in particular with Amsterdam occupying first place, is an ethnic mixture of great complexity. Much of it is well assimilated into the dominant culture but a significant part remains only partially or hardly so. What is loosely termed 'ethnic minorities' amounts today to something like 6% of the total population. Since ethnic minorities tend to be concentrated in the large cities such as Amsterdam and Rotterdam, the percentage there is far higher (average over 20%) and the social adjustments more intense. If we were to look at only the minority population below age 20 in the large cities, the percentage would be far higher yet. Today the Netherlands is said to have the most varied multicultural society in Europe.

The East Indies The Dutch began their extensive trading empire in the East Indies in the 16th century, and from the first the East Indies occupied an important place in the economy and, inescapably, acquired a strong hold on the Dutch imagination. Practically from the first descriptions by traders and explorers, the cultural magnetism of the East has been part of the Dutch view of the world. The East has long been in a sense the opposite pole to the Netherlands, a place where natural man is a tiny element in a lush, wild and unforgiving nature.

Whole generations of civil servants grew up in an 'Indies' tradition and returned to flavor the home culture with it. This influence went far beyond artistic and culinary broadening. In the period when colonialism was at its

Fig. 15.1
'The Landscape and
its Children' (1939)
by Walter Spies

peak, from the mid-19th century down to about 1920, The Hague was the Indies capital of the Netherlands, a role still reflected in many of the city's street names. Migration went in both directions, resulting in a large 'Indies' colony in The Hague that created a whole sub-culture from which many writers have drawn inspiration. These original settlers from the Indies have become as good as completely assimilated into Dutch society and lost most ties to the old homeland. Colonial society in its peak period was a stratified one completely in European colonialist hands, where ideally everyone knew his proper place. This situation is called *tempo doeloe* 'the [good] old days', a name that at least to an older generation still evokes romance and no little nostalgia.

A darker aspect of this picture is the reality of colonial exploitation. The Dutch colonial administration never assumed an exclusive right to govern the Indies, but depended heavily on the native hierarchy on all but the uppermost levels. Dutch rule was of the 'Regent' form, an elite expecting the unquestioning deference of those below them who did not know the job as well. Native nationalism was never absent, but it did not become significant until the 20th century when such movements became increasingly stronger.

The Second World War, a time when the Indies were under Japanese occupation, released many other anti-colonialist forces and allowed independence movements to gain a firm hold. Immediately following the Japanese surrender in 1945 the independent Indonesian Republic was proclaimed. The Dutch government underestimated the strength of Indonesian nationalism, and since the leaders under Soekarno had relied on Japanese support to evict the Dutch, they were regarded as collaborators. When no peaceful compromise seemed possible and the Dutch saw all of Indonesia coming under the control of political radicals, they began a 'police action' in 1948 as a last attempt to salvage some authority. By this time world opinion was heavily against them and in 1949 sovereignty was turned over to the United

Indonesian Republic. New Guinea was withheld and became the subject of sharp controversy in the Netherlands. It was finally added to Indonesia in 1963.

On the breakup of the colonial empire in the East, a new wave of immigration was added to the already present numbers of settlers from the Indies. On independence everyone was given the choice of accepting Indonesian citizenship or leaving for the Netherlands. In the '50s and '60s many more thousands of Eurasians, persons of mixed blood called *Indo's* in Dutch, joined the flood of immigrants that had begun during the war. Their numbers are difficult to estimate because these too have become largely assimilated. Probably about 300,000 have been absorbed into the society.

Another group from the East Indies presents a very different picture. The South Moluccas, one of the groups of islands in the Indies with a strong cultural identity of its own, which was reinforced by large-scale conversion to Christianity in the 19th century, had developed a separate independence movement. They resisted incorporation into Indonesia, and in 1950 proclaimed an independent Republic of the South Moluccas. The alienation from Indonesia was made more complete by the fact that the Netherlands Army of the Indies (called the KNIL) had recruited a high percentage of its native troops in the Moluccas. In 1951, 21,300 South Moluccans were brought 'temporarily' to the Netherlands until the question of their sovereignty could be resolved. They brought with them the name, administrative structure and popular ideal of their Republic. From their first arrival, they resisted assimilation into Dutch society and kept alive the ideal of their independence. They relied on the Dutch government to continue the pressure on Indonesia, but the latter showed no interest in the matter and the Dutch government's need to preserve good relations with Indonesia was of much higher priority. The South Moluccans in the Netherlands thus found themselves without a home. They had little taste for integration into Dutch society, fading hopes for an independent homeland, and saw less and less interest back in the Moluccas themselves in independent status.

Fig. 15.2
The Dutch East Indies

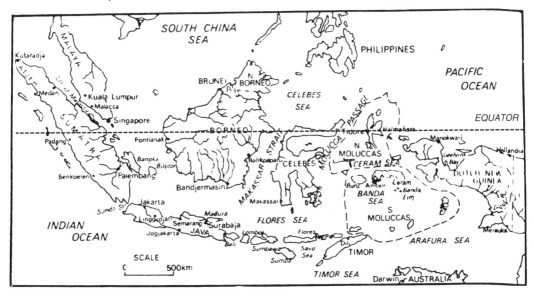

As frustration grew, some of the more radical younger generation turned to acts of terrorism as a means of putting pressure on the Dutch government. In 1975 and 1977 trains were hijacked, and a consulate and provincial government offices were occupied. All were eventually resolved by force. This was all repudiated by the Moluccan community leaders, but for a time it had the effect on the Dutch mind of equating the whole South Moluccan community with violence.

The following year, in spite of the government's general sympathy for the plight of this group of citizens, it announced that it would not recognize or support an autonomous republic, and this was the blow that deprived the South Moluccans of their only ally. At the same time, the Dutch government announced a social and cultural package designed to help the South Moluccans in the integration process. Increased financial help was supplemented by commitments to build new homes scattered around the country. This last was a reversal of the original policy of helping to preserve identity in exclusive communities, which prevented assimilation.

In the years since their arrival, the South Moluccans have maintained the strongest ethnic identity of all the minority groups in the Netherlands. They have done this by way of the ideal of the republic, and also by strict adherence to the web of village bonds and traditional laws brought intact from the islands. But this identity is progressively weakening in the current more relaxed atmosphere. The steadily increasing percentage of the group born and raised in the Netherlands and the rise in the mixed-marriage rate to over 40%, coupled with a vast increase in visits to and from the 'home' islands, have resulted in a fading of the ideal of an independent republic.

The West Indies The West presents a very different picture from the East. In the East the Dutch found a variety of languages and cultures that nevertheless had underlying similarities. Both geographically and culturally, the West is far more heterogeneous. Possibly because of the scattered nature of the West Indies, probably because of the absence of a highly developed culture of its own, and certainly because of its relatively minor economic importance, the West has never had the emotional hold on the Netherlands that the East has. Nevertheless, in terms of the present-day ethnic picture the West Indies plays a far larger role than the East Indies.

Suriname (see map, Fig. 15.3) is a large, geographically varied territory that was first settled by the English in 1650 and in 1667 turned over to the Dutch in exchange for the New Netherlands territories in North America. In the centuries since then, it has been both exploited and neglected. Plantations were established, and peoples of a wide variety of ethnic origins brought in for working them. This has resulted in the ethnic variety of Surinam today. Eventually the colony was incorporated into the Kingdom of the Netherlands. Having the same Dutch citizenship as those in the Netherlands included, among other things, the right of residence in any part of the kingdom. In the postwar period, moves for the independence of Surinam gained momentum, and these met with little resistance in the Netherlands, where the dubious prestige of a colonial empire no longer seemed worth the financial drain it caused. Independence was simply presented to Surinam. In addition to this, the Dutch government was even more accommodating in a

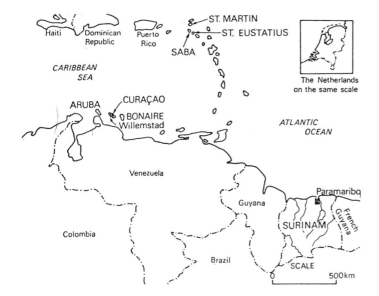

Fig. 15.3
The Dutch West Indies

period when it was determined to avoid a repeat of the Indonesian mistakes and especially the miscalculation with New Guinea.

Lengthy negotiations were carried on to assure an orderly transition to a democratic government, and unusually large amounts of development aid were made available. Nevertheless, when it became clear that independence would come in 1975, large numbers of Surinamese—including most of the professional top—moved to the Netherlands to avoid the economic and political chaos they feared at home. Fully one third of the former population of Surinam now lives in the Netherlands. Surinamese are now the Netherlands' largest minority. The history of all this is complicated; somewhere in the process the Dutch lost control of the steps toward the democratic administration they envisioned, and Surinam got a leftist military government. This drove many more Surinamese to the Netherlands and polarized the sides at home. The period of military dictatorship has now been left behind, but in a country with extremes of ethnic diversity nation-forming has proved unusually difficult. Recently there has been talk of reestablishing closer bonds, as the two countries enter into a type of 'commonwealth' agreement, a move strongly supported by the Surinamese population. The close ties with Surinam will not be severed in the foreseeable future. The identification is still so close that newspaper reports on Surinam are still apt to appear under 'domestic news'.

In the Netherlands, Surinamese have been steadily becoming absorbed into the rest of the population. Some 35% of all Surinamese households are ethnically mixed. Although their unemployment figure is still far higher than the overall average for the country, it is still well below that of other minorities.

In the end of the 16th century, the Dutch were making regular expeditions to the Caribbean for salt to use in the vital herring trade, for smuggling and privateering, and later for the slave trade. In 1621, following the model of the

East Indies Company, the West Indies Company was formed to coordinate expeditions for salt. The island of *Curaçao* was seized from the Spanish in 1634 and turned into a base for commercial activities. *Aruba* and *Bonaire* were taken in 1636 and used mainly as havens for privateers. Of the northern group of islands, *Sint Maarten* was claimed by the Dutch in 1630 and used as yet another privateering base. It has been shared with France since 1648. *Sint Eustatius* and *Saba* were first colonized in 1636. All six of the Antillean islands (Fig. 15.3) began their modern European period in somewhat doubtful enterprises as part of the darker side of the Dutch colonial past, and they have fared little better since then, repeatedly acting as pawns in international politics.

The northern group is separated from the southern by some 800 km (500 miles). The southern or Windward Islands are called the 'ABC Islands' by the Dutch, and of these the largest and most important is Curaçao. Dutch influence on the island was strong, the language of government and education being Dutch, and the rows of houses along the harbor in the capital Willemstad have an unmistakable Dutch urban look. Even in the mid-eighties, KLM was advertising Curaçao as 'A piece of home in the tropics'. By now the influence of the Dutch language and culture has largely vanished. The Papiamento language, a Spanish-Portuguese creole language with a mixture of Dutch words that is the native language of the ABC islands, is now being taught in the schools as the standard language. Aruba received a strong economic boost in this century when refineries were built there to process the oil from Venezuela. Both Aruba and Bonaire are under strong and by no means friction-free cultural domination by Curaçao.

The Dutch Antillean islands were all joined into a single administrative unit in 1845, with Willemstad on Curaçao as capital. In the present system in which the Antilles are all members of the kingdom, the government is of the same structure as in the Netherlands. The Antilles still remain parts of the kingdom, but the ties are maintained largely out of a sense of responsibility. The hope is that eventually a United Antilles can go its independent way, but for the present the islands will remain in the kingdom as long as they are able to keep reasonable order at home and avoid contributing to Caribbean political or economic instability. The difficulty has been that the Antillean islands are in no hurry to sever the advantageous ties with the Netherlands. All the islands are now following the lead of Aruba in bypassing the present Antillean administration and seeking individual direct ties with the Netherlands.

The urging of independence on former colonial territories before a strong local demand for it has developed (in fact Antilleans continue to resist any attempts of the Dutch government to cut them loose) may be novel in the history of colonial empires, and there is still considerable controversy over the long-range dangers of any overhasty piecemeal cutting of the ties. The combination of economic and political uncertainties has led large numbers of Antillean Dutch citizens, the majority from Curaçao, to move to the Netherlands.

The Mediterranean All that has been described up to this point is what has been inherited from the colonial days. The other major source of the present ethnic mixture of the Netherlands belongs to more recent history, and it can be stated more briefly because here the Netherlands is very little different from the other industrialized countries of western Europe. In the 1950's and 1960's, during the period of greatest economic growth, agreements were signed with several of the poorer countries to supply laborers—mostly un-skilled—on a temporary basis. These workers were originally called *gastar-beiders*, a term which has been replaced since then by a succession of bu-reaucratic euphemisms. In the long period of full employment they were es-sential to the running of the industrial machine, but when recession came in the early '70s, the Netherlands, like its neighbors, was left with several hund-red thousand immigrant workers for whom even an uncertain life in the Netherlands was preferable to the certainty of unemployment back home. Despite the only limited degree of acceptance by Dutch society, over the years a significant proportion of the immigrant workers has become well set-tled in the Netherlands, and acquired a stake in the social-welfare system. Where in the beginning only the laborers themselves were permitted res-idence, in recent decades families have been allowed to immigrate to reuni-te with the workers. This has also encouraged more permanent settling, as has the increasing numbers of children born in the Netherlands and comfor-table with Dutch language and culture. All ethnic minorities are now offi-cially called *allochtonen*.

Each of these immigrant groups has carried over from the days of 'temper-ary' residence the self-protective habits of clustering in a distinct communi-ty, and most of them still have relatively little contact with each other or feel much in common other than the disadvantaged status in Dutch society. Each group has had its own difficulties in assimilating, but the greatest are faced by those from Moslem countries, which in the Netherlands means principal-ly Turkey and Morocco. Close adherence to the religious traditions of the home country has enabled immigrant minorities to maintain a strong sense of identity, but inevitably it has also created tensions.

The 1993 estimates of the approximate numbers within each minority group are

Mediterranean	435,000
Turkish	207,000
Moroccan	168,000
Surinamese	264,000
Antillean	84,000
Moluccan	50,000

'Mediterranean' is larger than the two sub-groups under it because the figure includes people from other countries in this region.

These figures also do not include several other important ethnic groups: Chinese (about 25,000), Pakistanis (about 8,000), Gypsies (about 2,000), and various other foreign-worker groups such as Spanish, Portuguese, Ital-ian, Yugoslav and Greek, for a total of another 95,000. In addition, the Netherlands has admitted since the '70s a total of about 33,000 refugees, a number that continues to increase. The Netherlands' lagging behind most other neighboring countries in its admittance of those seeking asylum (over the last five years, an average 84.5% of applications were rejected, the highest percentage in Europe) is still a painful point in a nation that takes great pride in its tradition of hospitality to all seeking escape from repression. It is usually excused, not without some unease of conscience, with the thought that the Netherlands is already too full to serve as a haven for refugees. Finally, it is estimated that there are somewhere between 30,000 and 150,000 illegal immigrants in the Netherlands.

Ethnic minorities entered a society that was not prepared to become multicultural and multi-racial at quite the pace that events have required of it. Discrimination experienced by members of ethnic minority groups has taken all the predictable forms expect the most violent. It ranges from the polite indifference and vague discomfort of middle-class citizens—with whom ethnic minorities have relatively little contact—to more bluntly expressed prejudice in the working-class neighborhoods where most of them have settled. An article surveying racial name-calling in the Netherlands recently listed 143 terms of abuse for Turks, 182 for Surinamese and Antilleans, and an almost equal variety for all the other ethnic minorities. Members of minority groups have been subjected, at one time or another, to name calling, graffiti, mostly vague but occasionally pointed threats, and scattered acts of physical violence. Abusive yells and banners and complaints about unfairness on the part of referees became common at sports events. These incidents may have contributed to the fact that some minority groups such as the Turks still have their own clubs and play matches within their own leagues.

The huge *Bijlmermeer* apartment complex south of Amsterdam (originally designed as an ultramodern housing development) has such a high percentage of minorities that it has been called a 'Third-World city'. It was largely ignored and avoided until the highly publicized plane crash in 1992, that resulted in extensive loss of life and destroyed one of the large buildings, helped bring this sub-society up into Dutch consciousness. The perceptible rise in Dutch consciousness of ethnic minorities and their place in society—whether for or against—dates from about this time, although of course it has a complex of causes.

It is the forms that the Dutch reaction to its minorities takes that will tell us the most about the society. Many Dutch have a vague fear that the flood of Moslem immigrants, with their attitudes toward church and state, women, democracy and the like, will turn back the clock on ideas that have been hard-won by many emancipation movements ever since Reformation and Revolt. It does not deny the reality of these fears to point out that in fact it is normally immigrants who do most of the assimilating.

Dutch society has long cherished its traditional reputation for tolerance, and when in the 1970's newspaper articles, books and documentaries first exposed the level of discrimination already in existence and getting worse, the reaction was mainly one of shock at what it saw in this mirror. The most determined response on the official level was the enactment of strict and unambigious anti-discrimination legislation making any act of discrimination a punishable offense. Municipal administrations directed police to follow up all complaints vigorously, and the police, sensitive to the importance of being perceived as enforcing the public will, was so quick to issue warnings that it occasionally seemed to be overreacting.

In March of 1986, anyone who had lived in the Netherlands for at least five years on a valid residence permit was allowed to vote in the municipal elections, which for the first time gave immigrant minorities an opportunity to participate in the process. Instructional booklets and posters explaining the system and urging participation were made up in the languages of all the main immigrant groups, and they are still available at all times. In the TV and newspaper coverage of the election returns, considerable attention was paid to the ethnic-minority participation.

Particularly in the neighborhoods where there is daily contact with members of ethnic minorities, frustrations build up. They are blamed for unemployment—even though they are usually the first ones to suffer from it—and the quickness of some to cry 'discrimination' at any disagreement or rejection breeds resentment. Both national and municipal governments are often perceived as bending over so far backwards to avoid any suspicion of discrimination that they have in effect renounced their own responsibility to keep order and treat those with full citizenship fairly.

This is the state of affairs that the *Centrum Partij*, the *Nederlandse Volksunie* and now the *Centrumdemocraten* (chapter 10) stepped into in their attempts to exploit unrest via their rhetoric of 'us versus them', even though appeals to nationalism traditionally find little resonance in the Netherlands. The vote in national parliamentary elections of close to 3% (and up to 9% in local municipal elections) may be largely a generalized protest vote, but the figures are interpreted by many as a covertly racist statement of a strength that sounds a national alarm. The Dutch public attitude has raised these parties, ineffectual as they are in some ways, to the status of a new fascist enemy against whom a new Resistance must be mounted. The ritualism of the strong taboo against racism has resulted in a certain brittleness in the Dutch stance with respect to its ethnic minorities. Acts of violence against minorities are still on the rise.

Little by little the Netherlands is learning to adjust to the previously unanticipated reality of a multi-cultural society in a world rapidly becoming international in which countries are no longer the airtight units they once were. But increasing unease can be anticipated as the Dutch perceive the open borders of today's Europe bringing an even greater watering down of their traditional culture. It is estimated that by the year 2010, about 15% of the Dutch population will be of ethnic-minority origin. Steps toward integration have proceeded very much in a characteristically Dutch style. Discrimination is overwhelmingly perceived as incompatible with the national tradition of tolerance, but the practice is proving far more elusive than the ideal.

In spite of vigilance, racism and prejudice enter in largely unconscious ways into people's communication with each other. Even among those who are quick to protest that they are free of any discriminatory intent, some words contain hidden, racist meanings that do not appear on the surface but are well understood by everyone. One example out of many is the current range of meanings of the common phrase *Nederland is vol*. The current 'pregnant' implication of the innocent word 'full' used in this way is that the Netherlands is crowded and therefore cannot accept any more outsiders, which everyone knows—though most do not say—really means those of other races.

'Integration' is the high-minded ideal, but it is never precisely spelled out. So far the Dutch pluriform approach to society has adapted to multiculturalism rather readily, and policy has tended to assure equality of treatment from a base within the minorities' own culture, rather than an assimilation to a general 'Dutchness'. Ethnic minority children receive in school several weekly hours of instruction in their own language, and most ethnic education is funded by the state as part of the Dutch system of 'particular schools' (see chapter 7; the allocation of broadcast time to the Moslem community was mentioned in chapter 12).

In 1995 a new national organization addressing minorities and society was launched: FORUM, *Instituut voor multiculturele ontwikkeling* ('Institute for multiculturel development') to replace a number of separate minority organizations. From then on governmental financial support—formerly given to the minority organizations—was transferred to this new institution. FORUM assists various institutions and minority groups in dealing with the development of a multicultural society.

Soms of those former minority organizations still exist. One of them is the *Nederlands Centrum Buitenlanders* (NCB) 'Netherlands Center for Foreigners', a national organization with the broad purpose of improving the social position of minorities in a variety of ways. The NCB develops and carries out various projects and activities regarding minority groups; it operates independently of FORUM and without government financial support. The projects and activities concern employment opportunities, educational matters, health care and welfare.

In the Dutch system each group has wide latitude to maintain its own identity, but in the case of ethnic minorities the danger is that isolation and thus minority position become institutionalized and perpetuated. The education system reflects some of this: the percentage of Dutch children pursuing the prescribed route toward higher education is just twice that of minority children, while the percentage of the latter in vocational education is well over twice the Dutch average. Younger generations are rapidly assimilating to Dutch ways, though often not throwing off the handicaps of minority status.

It is of considerable significance that minorities are steadily occupying new places in Dutch society, in ways that were previously unanticipated. At a time when various economic developments are forcing increasing numbers of people from the traditional class of small independent shopkeepers and café owners out of business, ethnic minorities are rapidly stepping into this gap. Larger and larger numbers of Turks, Surinamese, Moroccans, Indians and Pakistanis are able to retail selections not available elsewhere. This represents a major shift by minorities from a still-narrowing labor market to a more permanent stake in communities. Like all the rest of Dutch society, all of this is a social experiment the future development of which nobody can foresee.

FURTHER READING

Ankersmit, T. et al. (eds.), *Minderheden in Nederland. Statistisch vademecum*. Rotterdam: ISEO [annual].

Goslinga, C., *A Short History of the Netherlands Antilles and Surinam*. The Hague: Martinus Nijhoff, 1979.

Landman, N., *Van mat tot minaret. De institutionalisering van de Islam in Nederland*. Amstelveen: VU, 1992.

Muus, P.J., *Migration, Minorities and Policy in the Netherlands: Recent Trends and Developments*. Amsterdam: University of Amsterdam, 1986.

Penninx, R. (et al.), *The Impact of International Migration on Receiving Countries: The Case of the Netherlands*. Amsterdam: Swets en Zeitlinger, 1993.

16   Dutch literature

In the opening paragraph of her 1948 novella *Oeroeg* about a boyhood friendship in the setting of the Dutch East Indies, Hella Haasse distills in symbolic, almost poetic form the attitude of a whole culture toward its relationship with another one.

> Oeroeg was my friend. Whenever I think back to my childhood and my boyhood years, the image of Oeroeg never fails to appear to me, as if my memory were one of those magic pictures we used to buy, three for a dime: pieces of shiny yellow gum-coated paper that you had to rub with a pencil to get the hidden images to appear. Oeroeg too comes back to me in just that way when I immerse myself in the past. Even though the setting may vary depending on how long ago the period is that I summon up, I always see Oeroeg ... Oeroeg and I, playing and on expedition in the wilderness—Oeroeg and I, bent over our homework, over stamp collections and forbidden books—Oeroeg and I, invariably together in all stages of development from child to young man. It's not too much to say that Oeroeg is branded into my life, like a seal, a trade-mark. Now more than ever, when any contact, any chances to be together belong unalterably to the past. I don't know why I want to come to terms with my relationship to Oeroeg, and with all that Oeroeg meant and still means to me. Maybe it's his irrevocable, incomprehensible otherness that stimulates me, that secret of flesh and blood that for a boy created no problems but that now seems all the more tormenting.

Through the means of exploring the relationship between two boys, all the emotional attraction, incomprehension, and sense of loss in the Dutch attitude toward the East Indies are summarized. A work of literature takes on a certain authority to speak for, and to, the society. Independent of the subject chosen, an author sometimes—often unconsciously—distills his or her own culture's collective experiencing not so much of historical events as of basic human responses. In this way, works of literature provide a far more direct reflection of this experiencing than is possible with any other art form. In this chapter we will adopt this somewhat narrow view of literature, and look for a few salient reflections of a society's ongoing thought.

The place occupied by the experience of the Indies in the Dutch imagination is a good—if entirely arbitrary—place to begin. For centuries writing about the East Indies has been distilled into the permanent record of the national literature. Descriptions of voyages began in the 17th century, and in the middle of the 18th, dramas first began using the Indies as a setting for the action. The first really strong impact on the literature was Eduard Douwes Dekker's novel *Max Havelaar*, published in 1860. Written under the pseudonym 'Multatuli', the novel describes both the splendor of the Indies and the brutal realities of the Dutch colonial administration. It held a mercilessly satiric mirror up to the self-satisfied society in the home country that supported the exploitation. Louis Couperus was a member of the class of upper-level Indies civil servants in The Hague around the turn of the century. In *De stille kracht* (1900; The Hidden Force), the mysterious East is seen through the uncomprehending eyes of a colonial administrator who is rigidly practical and blind to the unexplainable forces around him that eventually drive him away. After Multatuli's *Max Havelaar*, the Dutch generally regard Edgar du Perron's *Het land van herkomst* (1935; Country of Origin) as the most important writing inspired by the Indies and reflecting something fundamental about the Dutch attitude.

Successive generations of Dutch citizens who went to the Indies, or were born and raised there, experienced life in the colonies at first hand and wrote about it, and the list of them by now is very long. Since the end of the colonial era and the independence of Indonesia, writing in the Netherlands by those who grew up with an intimate first-hand knowledge of the Indies has continued just as vigorously. On a more popular level, the 'Indo' experience was put into words best by Tjalie Robinson.

The loss of the colonies might be said to have released a flood of attempts to record and reflect on an era now concluded. The Dutch public is still fascinated by its Indies past. In her psychologically acute historical novel that was on the bestseller lists for many months, *Heren van de thee* (1992; The Tea Merchants), Hella Haasse showed that after more than forty years she is still able to resonate just as powerfully with this need. The older generations have been succeeded by younger ones who knew the Indies only as small children or at second hand. The East-Indies experience becomes increasingly diffuse as it becomes background and setting, or as newer writers try to see from the Indonesian perspective rather than that of 'tropical Holland'.

This Indies aspect of Dutch literature probably has greater power to speak to the world than do those—for instance most of what is talked about below—that arise from the experience of life in the Netherlands itself. A greater share of it, and a much more representative selection, has been published in translation. But the rest of the literature of the Netherlands, while it is possibly less appealing and certainly less readily accessible, is just as

Fig. 16.1
Aelbert Cuyp (1620-1691),
A Dutch merchant in
Batavia (Dutch East Endies)

much a reflection of collective experience over the centuries. In spite of all that is said above, literature about the Indies does not occupy as prominent a place in the Dutch perception of their literature as it does in the world's perception. It is not at all surprising to find the 'brokering and mediating' aspect of the national collective experience reflected in the literature as well.

From the first medieval knightly romances translated into the vernacular, the Low Countries eagerly laid hold on each new literary form and fashion, adapted it and passed it on. In these few pages, we will ask a rather down-to-earth question. It is: In what ways do literary works reflect Dutch collective experiences, habits of thought, and ways of looking at that society? We have been observing a society that tends to approach the world in a matter-of-fact, businesslike way that leaves little room for the heroic or the flamboyant. It is also a society that tends to like fine detail, whether in planning and organization or in attitudes toward life. A literature in which little that is grand or bold can be anticipated might well hold little attraction for us. If painting in the Netherlands were as unfamiliar to the world as its literature we might hesitate to look at it for the same reasons—but when we did we would be in for a surprise.

The comparison of literary writing to painting in the Netherlands is not as far-fetched as it might seem. Just as a taste for the accurate representation of everyday reality found expression in Dutch painting in the 17th century and before that in the Flemish painters, detailed realistic description has been one of the specialties of the written word from the beginnings. Louis Couperus was a meticulous observer of society; a half century before him, Nicolaas Beets, writing under the pseudonym 'Hildebrand', called his sketches of the social life around him 'little paintings'. The *Camera Obscura* (1839) is still considered one of the enduring classics of the literature. The play *De Spaansche Brabander* (1618; The Spanish Brabanter), a series of pictures of life in late 16th-century Amsterdam and another of the literature's classics, was written by the professional painter Gerbrand Bredero. Only four years before Bredero's play, Roemer Visscher published a book of emblems with explanatory texts, and in the foreword urged the reader to 'pay more attention to the amusement of the images than to the sobriety of the explanations.'

In the creation of sharply observed and focused pictures of daily life, Bredero and Beets have had a great many successors, the most popular of whom in our own time was Simon Carmiggelt, whose widely admired miniatures of personalities began as newspaper columns and soon became classics in their own right. A few years ago Peter van Straaten, one of the Netherlands' best known pen-and-ink artists, began illustrating Carmiggelt's predominantly melancholy world in a way that seemed to be saying in a few sharp lines what the writer had been trying to say all along in words.

Capturing the mood and atmosphere of a setting is still one of the strongest sides of Dutch writing, just as it has never been absent from Dutch painting. Lyric poetry, often claimed to be the highest achievement of Dutch literature, shows in all its periods a remarkably strong attachment to the environment, whether natural or artificial. It continues to draw heavily for its inspiration and imagery on the physical setting of the Netherlands.

Social life in the Netherlands shows a strong sense for the ordered living of life. Along with this there often comes moral responsibility to others, which we saw in the 17th-century organization of charity. If we look back well before the 17th century to what was being written and circulated when vernacular writing first appeared, we can hardly help noticing a strongly didactic tone. Stories told, whether religious or secular, contained a moral lesson and were intended to be useful for the 'right' living of life. The noticeable practicality and down-to-earthness make it easy to conclude who these works were intended for. They were intended to be read not by an aristocratic class, as was the case in neighboring countries, but by a citizenry that was something like what today we would call middle-class. In the early 16th century Erasmus of Rotterdam was writing in Latin and for an educated audience, but his writing never fails to betray his Dutch origins. The *Praise of Folly*, the *Colloquia* and the *Adages* are all full of practical advice for the sensible and balanced living of life, the first in the form of a mock public address, the second collections of lively dialogues and the third mini-essays.

From around Erasmus' time on into the 17th century, the creation and dissemination of moral instruction in the vernacular for ordinary people was mostly in the hands of literary guilds called Chambers of Rhetoric. It was Chambers of Rhetoric that produced plays in the cities. The Dutch devotion to moral instruction found its most enthusiastic preacher—and, as many now claim, Dutch literature reached a low point—in Jacob Cats, whose books of pious and uplifting verse remained popular down into modern times. Cats is an intriguing example of something that used to be possible when society was less stratified. His being a member of the ruling Regent class did not prevent him from sharing all the main social values with the public down to the lowest educational levels, and communicating effortlessly with them.

The Dutch instinct for the pictorial representation of everyday reality and for moral instruction are nowhere more elegantly harmonized than in the emblem. Books of emblems, typically a carefully-executed drawing accompanied by an instruction and a few lines of explanatory text, were popular in the 16th century and reached a peak of popularity in the 17th. Roemer Visscher's *Sinnepoppen* ('Emblems') of 1614 and later years, mentioned a moment ago, is the best known of the many collections in circulation. Dutch emblems have a strong preference for realistic references to everyday life such as ordinary useful objects, activities, or features of the polder landscape. In other cultures such humble objects are not the usual bearers of symbolic moral sense. Neither an overall philosophy not church nor state make any claims on conduct, which is simply a matter of practical, purposeful and useful living.

Emblems were a popular genre everywhere in western Europe at the time, but the heart of the emblem-production industry seems to have been in the Netherlands. In modern times we realize that many of the 17th-century paintings are really carefully composed emblems with a moral message, and that probably no painting of the time is without some emblematic content.

Dutch society tends to be a rather practical arrangement keeping some accommodation going, so idealization of society, nationhood or some grand ideal is not easy to find. Dutch people are more apt to be skeptical or cynical

VAN DE SINNEPOPPEN

XIX

Exonerat et arcet*

Exonerat et arcet.

DE kracht van de Sluysen zijn by wey-nigh natien bekent: maer de Hollan-ders houden by naest al haer landt van dit ghebou* te leen*, 'twelck sonder behulp van dien, luttel of niet waert en soude we-sen: want het tapt de overtollige wateren af, en verhindert dat de schadelijcke niet wederom mogen komen: daer om ist won-der dat de botte Hollanders van den eersten vinder gheen Sant* ghemaeckt hebben, schryvende zynen naem met gul-den letteren in het hooft van den Brevier. Is de rechte Sinnepop van een vroom* Vorst, die't landt suyvert van ghebeoft, door justitie: soo dat de inwoonders die deughdelijck zijn, te beter moghen groeyen en bloeyen.

about whatever takes on too many pretenses. Criticizing society as it is and complaining about it are Dutch traditions, but so also is the surrounding of complaint with irony and the casting of analysis in the form of satire. Litera-ture that is not imported but original in the Low Countries first appears in the 12th century with a work that is magnificently satirical in nature, the animal epic *Van den vos Reinaerde* (Reynard the Fox). As in the classic tradition, all the animals represent thinly-veiled human shortcomings, stupidities and vices. But taken as a whole, the work seems to be a ridiculing of feudal aris-tocratic society by a prosperous urban class that was becoming self-confi-dent and independent.

From its first beginnings, a mixture of strong realism, moral-didactic pur-pose and a satiric attitude toward society is the tone that gives Dutch litera-ture a continuously recognizable voice of its own. In the *abele spelen* the Low Countries produced the first genuine secular dramas, but in some ways even this is overshadowed by the six comedies *(kluchten)* that are inter-spersed with them in the manuscript. These short farces are social satire at its best. Popular literature that came from the earliest printing presses was full of this kind of satire—sharply-drawn characters and a useful point. The writers of the 17th century used the old popular satires for their own more elegantly formulated reflections on society, and the tradition continued on into the plays and 'spectatorial' essays taking an ironic look at society in the 18th century. Elisabeth Wolff and Agatha Deken's epistolary novel *Sara Burger-hart* (1782) is a penetrating and witty observation of society and personali-ties. Hildebrandt's *Camera Obscura* is a gentle but coolly realistic reflection of society at the threshold of modern times.

This chapter began with writing inspired by the world of the East Indies, a distillation of a collective experiencing of history. The national experiencing of historical events has always found reflection in the literature. The protes-tant Reformation in the Netherlands inspired religious poetry of an often stridently partisan nature. The revolt produced polemics, poems and religious-political songs such as the *Nederlandsche Gedenck-clanck* of Adrianus Valerius, and in Marnix van St. Aldegonde's *Wilhelmus* the song that became the national anthem. Revolution in the 18th century, the Napoleonic period and religious renewal in the new kingdom all inspired reflections in the literature.

We might expect that liberal reform and the great emancipation movements in the century between the *Camera Obscura* and the beginning of the Second World War would have produced a new outburst of inspiration. But at least in fiction a real 'outburst' is hard to find. Modernization came more placidly to the Netherlands than to some of its neighbors. With the almost isolated exception of *Max Havelaar*, novel writing does not place society in the foreground or show much taste for crusading against its wrongs. Though this did take place in other forms, for instance in the essays of Conrad Busken Huet. The social critics are by far the best known and most highly regarded of the writers of the time. These polemicists brought new life into the first period of the independent kingdom, and with a vigor that went beyond what was going on at the same time in neighboring cultures. The strongest voice in social criticism was the literary journal *De Gids* 'The Guide', founded in 1837 and still in existence. It did not hesitate to proclaim its moralizing mission in its title, and championed liberal ideals of social progress and middle-class faith in practical common sense. Its moralizing stance put such a stamp on the Dutch perception of their culture that today it is common to hear them referring mockingly to their country as *Gidsland*.

Frederik van Eeden's *Van de koele meren des doods* (1900; The Deeps of Deliverance) and *De kleine Johannes* (1887; Little John), among the best-known works of this period, are both preoccupied with society's effects on the individual personality and emotions. Literature's confrontation with social reality came toward the end of the century in the Dutch response to 19th-century European Naturalism, especially in Marcellus Emant's novel *Een na-*

Fig. 16.3
A woodcut illustrating Reynard the Fox

gelaten bekentenis (1894; A Posthumous Confession), and in the dramas of Herman Heijermans such as *Op Hoop van Zegen* (1910; The Good Hope). The novels of Arthur van Schendel in the 1920's and '30s such as *De waterman* (1933; The Waterman) give a meticulous description of a society—in this case the fervently religious life of those who lived on the river and canal system—but do not focus on what was behind it.

The impact of all historical events on Dutch literature pales when compared to that of the five years of war and occupation from 1940 to 1945. The first writing, some of it set down during the war years, was an attempt to capture various aspects of the experience itself while they were fresh. Even here the satiric instinct surfaced early. Simon Vestdijk's *Pastorale 1943*, published in 1948, shows the hard reality of the resistance but also the less heroic side of the groups and their amateurism in the early years of the occupation. Marga Minco's *Het bittere kruid* (1957; Bitter Herbs) distilled into a series of brief vignettes the naive innocence of Jewish families who were blind to the scale of what was happening. Etty Hillesum's diary was published only years later as *Het verstoorde leven* (1981; An Interrupted Life), but it had a powerful effect in its wartime immediacy along with its reflections on the problems of hatred in the world. Willem Frederik Hermans' *De donkere kamer van Damocles* (1958; The Dark Room of Damocles), a suspense novel set in the time of the occupation, had the advantage of a decade and a half for reflection but records faithfully the wartime dissolution into violence of the best aspects of humanity.

Writing on the war receded somewhat into the background during the '60s and '70s, though it continued to appear as setting or an important part of the personal experience of the personages. It was not until the beginning of the '80s, with the 40-year commemoration of the Liberation coming into view, that reflection on the wartime experience took on a new intensity. Seen in this lengthening perspective, the war took on many different and more subtle aspects. Marga Minco's *De glazen brug* (1986; The Glass Bridge) is about a young Jewish woman who survived the war under a false name and identity, only to discover afterwards that she was no longer able to return to her previous 'real' identity. The principal character in Koos van Zomeren's *Otto's oorlog* (1983; Otto's war) is someone who is also unable to detach himself from the war as his real identity. The best known reflection on the wartime experience from a lengthening perspective is Harry Mulisch's *De aanslag* (1982; The Assault), which records the black-and-white attitudes during the occupation sliding gradually into new shades of gray in the whole question of guilt and questions about what is the 'right' side in the postwar decades.

In the years since then, as younger generations emerge, preoccupation with the war is still common but it continues to become more diffuse. Some writers deal with the theme of children of collaborators: Dirk Ayelt Kooiman's *Montijn* (1982; A Lamb to Slaughter). More than one writer even used the painful absence of wartime experience as a theme. The writer Armando continues to debate what 'good/evil' and 'enemy' mean, as in *Voorvallen in de wildernis* (1994; Events in the Wilderness). Tessa de Loo's *De tweeling* (1993; The Twins) tells the story of two twin sisters who grew up separately in the Netherlands and Germany, and who as adults attempt to reestablish communication. As is the case with Haasse's story about the boys in Indonesia, it is not difficult to see that these personages personify communication between two separated cultures.

Jewish writers have continued to draw on their own unique experiencing of the war's aftermath. Frans Pointl's melancholy bestseller *De kip die over de soep vloog* (1989; The Chicken that Flew over the Soup), Marcel Möring's *Mendels erfenis* (1990; Mendel's Inheritance), and Leon de Winter's *De ruimte van Sokolov* (1992; Sokolov's Space). And this shows no sign of disappearing. In rapid succession have come Carl Friedman's return to Jewish war experiences in her *Twee koffers vol* (1993; Two suitcases full), Gerhard Durlacher's postmodern *Quarantaine* (1994; Quarantine) and a genuine literary sensation, Arnon Grunberg's black-comedy *Blauwe maandagen* (1994; Blue Mondays).

For some writers the passage of time has brought acceptance and an inner reconciliation, for others the realization of an experience that is sealed in its own inaccessible place, and for still others a distant time and place that can be viewed only from a detached and thoroughly ironic perspective.

Immediately after the war, many of the established writers of the prewar period regained their reading public. The grand master Simon Vestdijk continued to produce weighty novels full of penetrating analysis on an almost endless variety of topics: *De koperen tuin* (1950; The Garden where the Brass Band Played). Writing in this postwar period reflected the disillusionment and cynicism of the social atmosphere as things settled back into their dreary prewar patterns. Anna Blaman, whose overriding themes of loneliness and alienation had become familiar well before the war, continued with works such as *Op leven en dood* (1954; A Matter of Life and Death) but now had numbers of new allies in the writers in an existential vein. In a period when the rigid system of *verzuiling* was reaching its peak, many writers struggled with the stranglehold of religion on life, and a sense of revolt against religion began to appear.

A break with the past came somewhat differently in poetry than it did in prose writing. It is something of a tradition in the Netherlands to regard the literature's achievements in lyric poetry as its highest. Poetry reached high points in the Middle Ages and once more in the 17th century. With the reform movement of 1880 it again became an adventure, and after the war yet again seemed ready for fresh beginnings. The *Vijftigers* ('Fifties') were a group of young poets in the 1950's who followed the tradition of all reformers by making a bold break with tradition, and who incorporated all the experimental elements of 20th century poetry into their movement. Poetry was supposed to leave off being quiet reflection and become an exuberant activity of the spirit. They were eventually nudged aside by others who reacted against what some suggested was a flamboyance out of step with the matter-of-fact Dutch style. Lyric poetry has continued to respond to international trends, though it has never gone so far as to abandon the underlying Dutchness of its inspiration and perspective. The Dutch landscape still speaks powerfully to society.

The meager amount of good writing in the '60s is sometimes attributed to the absence of a challenge in this period of general contentment and prosperity. It was not until the '70s that a number of new voices appeared on the scene. Many of these were women writers, who have continued to claim a large share of literary production ever since. The social challenges may have been one of the stimulators of a flood of new writing, and yet curiously, many of the large issues that filled the late '60s and the '70s such as militarism, drugs, racism or rebellions against the established order are hardly reflected in the literature at all.

Of the many novelists who began in the '40s and '50s, four have emerged as universally recognized masters. The productive and many-sided Hermans and Mulisch have already been mentioned. A third, Gerard Reve, attracted national attention in 1947 with *De avonden* (The Evenings), which captured the colorless drabness of the time and set a tone for many other writers. He has gone on to explore difficult topics such as sadism and homosexuality. While all three of these writers have not hesitated to break taboos, they remain conservative in not setting out to be iconoclasts or revolutionaries. The fourth, Jan Wolkers, built up a reputation especially among younger readers with his bold style that disregarded some social niceties without being truly revolutionary. The most rebellious writer was Jan Cremer, whose *Ik Jan Cremer* (1964; I Jan Cremer) was an entertainingly narrated picaresque novel that set out to provoke by breaking every taboo in sight. It caused a furore in the already turbulent '60s, and cleared the way for other rebels.

Fig. 16.4
Boekhandel De Kler,
Leiden

Dutch writers today live in a healthy climate that is often envied abroad. Public book consumption is the second highest in Europe, and there are large numbers of small independent publishers, all of which makes for the appearance of large numbers of titles. There are a great many literary prizes, literary magazines are subsidized, and published authors even receive a royalty from distribution of their works by lending libraries.

To take a look at how the present-day Dutch world is mirrored in what its literary writers are thinking and saying, let us make a quick survey of the range of literary production in the past ten or a dozen years. Where possible these novels have been chosen from works that have been translated into English, a short selection of which is provided at the end of this chapter. Many of them have appeared on the Dutch bestseller lists.

Dutch writers are still as open as ever to international currents, from the purely esthetic to the socially involved. A small sample would be

- Outer form, experiment, esthetic style, the writer's own process of creation.
    Cees Nooteboom, *Rituelen* (Rituals) and *Een lied van schijn en wezen* (A Song of Truth and Semblance)
    Willem Brakman, *Late vereffening* (Late Adjustment)
    Lidy van Marissing, *Twee vrouwen die één keel opzetten* (Two Women who Raise One Roof)
- The irrational, psychological, the private inner world of fantasy and dream.
    J. Bernlef, *Hersenschimmen* (Phantoms of the Mind)
    Renate Dorrestein, *Noorderzon* (Northern Sun)
- Exploration of the borders of reality, of time and space.
    A.F.Th. van der Heijden, *Het leven uit een dag* (Living from One Day)
    Vonne van der Meer, *Zo is hij* (That's the Way he is)
- Man in modern society, the problems of the personality in today's world, and the sense of emptiness and disillusionment.
    Jeroen Brouwers, *Zomervlucht* (Summer Flight)
    Margriet de Moor, *Eerst grijs dan wit dan blauw* (First Gray then White then Blue)

Themes such as alienation and isolation that are part of the international cultural climate can be found in an endless variety of different types of works. Some writing deals with themes that are seen from a distinctly Dutch perspective.

- Relationships between men and women.
    Marja Brouwers, *De lichtjager* (The Light Hunter)
    Willem Jan Otten, *De wijde blik* (The Broad View)
    Renate Dorrestein, *Het hemelse gerecht* (The Heavenly Dish/Tribunal)*
- The specifically female perspective, a vigorously explored set of themes that ranges through all styles. The above two women in their playful irony have given women's writing a new voice. Two others are

---

* Since the Dutch have a fondness for titles that revolve around a play on words, many of the titles cited here are impossible to translate satisfactorily. Dorrestein's *gerecht* means 'dish' and at the same time 'tribunal', a pun she cleverly exploits in the plot.

Tessa de Loo, *Isabelle*

Hella Haasse, *Berichten van het Blauwe Huis* (Reports from the Blue House)

- A gay and lesbian perspective.

Gerard Reve, *De vierde man* (The Fourth Man)

Helen Knopper, *In de kamer van Fien Kristal* (In Fien Kristal's Room)

The West Indies voice has long been heard through the work of well-established writers such as Boeli Leeuwen, Cola Debrot, and Frank Martinus Arion. This is still a vigorous tradition, and the new ethnic minorities have also been making their special voices heard.

CURAÇAOANS

Jules de Palm, *Lekker warm, lekker bruin* (Nice and Warm, Nice and Brown)

Tip Marugg, *De morgen loeit weer aan* (The Morning comes Screaming in Again)

SURINAMESE

Joanna Winters, *Zuigend moeras* (Treacherous Bog)

MOLUCCANS

Frans Lopulalan, *Onder de sneeuw een Indisch graf* (Under the Snow an Indies Grave)

INDO'S

Marion Bloem, *Vaders van betekenis* (Fathers that Meant Something)

TURKS

Halil Gür, *Gekke Mustafa en andere verhalen* (Crazy Mustafa and Other Stories)

MOROCCANS

Naima El Bezaz, *De weg naar het noorden* (The Road North).

Hans Sahar, *Hoezo bloedmooi* (What do you mean, Pretty as a Picture)

These are the first Moroccans to be heard from, both in 1995.

Much of the writing centers on and reflects experience that is unique to Dutch society, a strong theme still being works inspired by the Indies, and reflecting on the Netherlands' relation to the Indies.

Margaretha Ferguson, *Angst op Java* (Fear in Java)

Hella Haasse, *Heren van de thee* (The Tea Merchants)

Marion Bloem, *De leugen van de kaketoe* (The Cockatoo's Lie)

We now find echoes of the Indies experience in writers too young to have first-hand knowledge.

Adriaan van Dis, *Indische duinen* (Indies Dunes)

Koos van Zomeren, *Het verhaal* (The Story)

Other themes reflect specific social conditions, such as contemporary events that form the stage or background for narrative.

A.F.Th. van der Heijden, *Advocaat van de hanen* (Attorney for the 'Mohawks'), part of his multi-volume cycle *De tandeloze tijd* (Toothless Time). Capturing the '80s.

Helen Knopper, *De pretentie* (The Pretense). A picture of the '90s.

Joost Zwagerman, *Vals licht* (False Light). What is real to the current younger generation.

- Religion and morality are only beginning to fade from center stage in literary writing. Dutch writers have gone through a long period of coming to terms with the heavy hand of religion on their culture, but by now most have achieved a comfortable distance from which to view the subject with mild irony, and more and more even with a renewed sense of identification.

    Maarten 't Hart, *De jacobsladder* (Jacob's Ladder)

    Jan Siebelink, *De overkant van de rivier* (The Other Side of the River)
- The child's or young person's small world and struggle for identity, problems of upbringing within the family.

    Thomas Rosenboom, *De mensen thuis* (The People at Home)

    Nicolette Smabers, *Chinezen van glas* (Glass Marbles)

    Freek de Jonge, *Neerlands bloed* (Our Own Pure Blood)

Dutch writing of recent years would not be faithful to its distinguished tradition if it did not devote a great deal of attention to society itself, and if it did not reflect on the world in characteristically Dutch styles.

- Social criticism and satire, a form of literature that is still enjoying a vigorous life in novels and in essays and newspaper columns later published as collections.

    Willem Frederik Hermans, *Ik draag geen helm met vederbos* (I'm not Wearing a Helmet with a Plume)

    Gerrit Komrij, *Met het bloed dat drukinkt heet* (With the Blood that is Called Printer's Ink)

    Rudy Kousbroek, *Anathema's* (Anathemas)

    Jan Blokker, *Mag het ook zwart?* (Is Black All Right too?)

Writing under the pseudonym 'Tamar', Renate Rubinstein in her columns and collections of essays was one of the most important social critics of the past twenty years. With her unique mixture of the intensely personal and the political, she took a boldly individualistic look at all fads, and had a large and devoted following.

    Renate Rubinstein, *Overgangscursus* (Transition Course)

The popular Kees van Kooten continues to satirize contemporary society, holding up a mirror to all its banalities, clichés, insecurities and the games people play with each other.

    Kees van Kooten, *Verplaatsingen* (Transpositions)

Closely related to this is the satiric mirror regularly held up to society by its ever-popular cabaret artists. One of the most characteristic features of cabaret in the Netherlands is its dependance on play with language, something the Dutch are inordinately fond of. Freek de Jonge and Youp van 't Hek are the most recent practitioners of a long and rich satiric tradition. Both appear regularly on radio and TV, and bookstores are never without numerous collections of their songs, monologs and sketches.

The wide range of colors in this ten-year spectrum seems to belie the frequent accusation from critics that literature in the Netherlands has something small and domestic about it, that too much of it has the ring of juvenile complaining, and that it declines to get down to the grubby level of the street. Such points can be well taken in general and still be a bit exaggerated.

Recent Dutch writing is still conspicuously personal in nature, as if writers are reflecting a culture concentrating on shocks felt by the inner personality rather than those administered to society in general. It reflects no trace of the nationalism that pervades literature in many countries.

A sort of national preoccupation with the individual personality and with relationships rather than with larger social realities may, however, be a less serious limiting of vision than it first seems. The strongly personal tone could be an unconscious mythmaking that has more to do with Dutch uncertainty about national identity in the modern world than with the miseries of adolescence. The search for maturity can have symbolic meaning on several levels at once. Having said that, it can be added that it is at the very least a logical manifestation of the Dutch public's historic fascination with children, something their 17th-century artists preserved over and over again in paintings.

The question of why the literature of the Netherlands has never contributed to world literature in the way that, for instance, Norwegian literature has through Ibsen is an endless debate. The inaccessibility of the language can hardly be the answer, in view of the innumerable works in other languages that have survived translation. The answer is usually found in the preoccupation of Dutch literature with its own world, what some call its provinciality or insularity. Dutch literature throughout its history has made very few ventures into the depths of evil, the dark passions or the demonic, or into the heights of passion or beauty, all of them themes that are well understood everywhere. The literature speaks very much with an urban voice that is controlled and ironic, and it reflects a people with a liking for observing and regulating but with a distrust of the uncontrolled and unpredictable. Possibly the very success of Dutch society through the centuries in creating the social structure for an orderly existence has denied it a literature that mirrors a world of peril and struggle.

But another reason can be the Dutch people's long-standing lack of interest in promoting their culture, and therefore their literature, to any of the world outside their borders. They evidence a low level of national cultural consciousness, where 'Dutchness' is all too apt to be associated in the popular mind with 'provinciality' and 'mediocrity'. To see one of the reasons for the world's indifference they need look no farther than their own characteristic undervaluing of their culture.

The place occupied by Dutch literature in translation on the world stage has until now been a very small one, but Dutch literature has experienced a breakthrough of sorts as more and more authors find their way into the international scene. Fortunately the world does not seem to be agreeing with their own unflattering assessment that their literature breathes the cramped kitchen's 'odor of sprouts' as they like to put it. Foreigners have in fact expressed fascination with the Dutch reverence for the ordinary, and praised their vision of the 'splendor of domestic life' as a unique contribution to European culture. The Dutch may still have to resign themselves to the fact that intense and scrupulous observation of a small world, however constantly leavened with playfulness, may never make the larger world sit up and take notice. On the other hand, nobody can predict where the next contribution to world literature might come from.

Other arts

It is something of a truism to say that literature allows us to keep a finger on the pulse of a society in a way that no other cultural expression does. Its primary purpose is, as we were reminded at the outset of this chapter, dealing with some of that society's ongoing realities and giving direct expression to its people's experience. But it would be shortsighted indeed to neglect the many other forms of artistic expression that give a society prominence in the world—even where that society's unique signature is less easily discernible.

Today the theater is a thriving enterprise, producing both native work being written for it and translated material. There are many active companies from national down to local, from the classical to the experimental. The unique Nederlands Werkteater, creating and performing plays on commission, has a reputation far beyond the borders. Modern dance, both performers and choreographers, is known around the world. That the Netherlands is home to a large share of the modern music world hardly needs to be pointed out. The names of many orchestras, performers and composers are international currency. Perhaps less well known in some circles is the role the two largest cities play as meccas for small, experimental popular-music groups. Present-day architecture is so well established in international consciousness (recall the comment in Ch. 4 about Rotterdam being an 'architectural showcase') that a lavish yearbook annually presents its achievements. And if Ch. 13 inadvertently left the impression that the Dutch lost interest in painting back in the 17th century, that can be corrected herewith. There have been vigorously active and experimental artists right up to the present day. Dutch film (including documentaries), Dutch film-makers and actors are familiar around the world.

The most thorough and balanced critical annual presentation of all this is to be found in *The Low Countries: Arts and Society in Flanders and the Netherlands*, listed in Ch. 1 above.

DUTCH LITERATURE TRANSLATED INTO ENGLISH
Works by a few of the writers mentioned above are

Bernlef, J. *The Phantoms of the Mind.* London: Faber & Faber, 1988. Published in the U.S. as *Out of Mind.* Boston: Godine, 1988.

Blaman, Anna, *A Matter of Life and Death* (Library of Netherlandic Literature, vol. 3). New York: Twayne, 1974.

Bredero, G.A., *The Spanish Brabanter: A Seventeenth-century Dutch Social Satire in Five Acts.* Tr. and introd. by H. David Brumble III. Binghamton, NY: Center for Medieval and Early Renaissance Studies, 1982.

Couperus, Louis, *Old People and the Things that Pass* (Bibliotheca Neerlandica). Leiden: Sijthoff/London: Heinemann, 1963.

Cremer, Jan, *I Jan Cremer.* London: Panther, 1971.

Van Eeden, Frederik, *The Deeps of Deliverance* (Library of Netherlandic literature, vol. 57). New York: Twayne, 1975.

Emants, Marcellus, *A Posthumous Confession* (Library of Netherlandic Literature, vol. 7. Boston: Twayne, 1975.

Hermans, Willem Frederik, *The Dark Room of Damocles*. London: Heinemann, 1962.

Hillesum, Etty, An *Interrupted Life: The Diaries of Etty Hillesum 1941-43*. New York: Washington Square Press, 1983.

Minco, Marga, *Bitter Herbs: A Little Chronicle*. New York: Pergamon, 1969.

Minco, Marga, The Glass Bridge. London: Owen, 1988.

Nooteboom, Cees, *In the Dutch Mountains*. Baton Rouge: Louisiana State Univ./London: Viking, 1987.

Nooteboom, Cees, *Rituals*. Baton Rouge: Louisiana State Univ., 1983.

Reve, Gerard, *Parents Worry*. London: Minerva, 1990.

Rubinstein, Renate, *Take it and Leave it: Aspects of Being Ill*. London/New York: Marion Boyars, 1989.

Van Schendel, Arthur, *The Waterman* (Bibliotheca Neerlandica). Leiden: Sijthoff/London: Heinemann, 1963.

Vestdijk, Simon, *The Garden where the Brass Band Played*. New York: New Amsterdam, 1989.

Wolkers, Jan, *Turkish Delight*. New York and Boston: Seymour Lawrence and Delacorte, 1974.

DUTCH LITERATURE ON THE INDIES TRANSLATED INTO ENGLISH
A small sample

Most of the works that are currently available are those that are being published or reissued in the series *The Library of the Indies* (E.M. Beekman, general editor), Amherst: University of Massachusetts Press. *The Canadian Journal of Netherlandic Studies*, vol. 12 no. 1 (spring 1991) contains a complete bibliography of Dutch literary works about the Indies in English translation.

Alberts, A. *The Islands*. 1983.

Beekman, E.M. (ed.), *Fugitive Dreams: An Anthology of Dutch Colonial Literature*. 1988.

Breton de Nijs, E. (R. Nieuwenhuys), *Faded Portraits*. 1982.

Couperus, Louis, *The Hidden Force*. 1985.

Daum, P.A., *Ups and Downs of Life in the Indies*. 1987.

Dermoût, Maria, *The Ten Thousand Things*. 1984.

Du Perron, Edgar, *Country of Origin*. 1984.

Multatuli (E. Douwes Dekker), *Max Havelaar, or the Coffee Auctions of the Dutch Trading Company*. 1982.

Nieuwenhuys, Rob, *Mirror of the Indies: A History of Dutch Colonial Literature*. 1982.

Van Schendel, Arthur, *John Company*. 1983.

Vuyk, Beb, *The Last House in the World*. H.J. Friedericy, *The Counselor*. 1983.

Other titles not in this series are

Moore, Cornelia N., *Insulinde: Selected Translations from Dutch Writers of Three Centuries on the Indonesian Archipelago* (Asian Studies at Hawaii, no. 20). Honolulu: University Press of Hawaii, 1978.

Nieuwenhuys, Rob, *Memory and Agony: Dutch Stories from Indonesia* (The Library of Netherlandic Literature). New York: Twayne, 1979.

Brems, Hugo, and Ad Zuiderent, *Contemporary Poetry of the Low Countries*. Rekkem: Stichting Ons Erfdeel, 1992.

Eerste druk. Overzicht en bespreking van Nederlandstalig literair proza dat voor het eerst verscheen in het jaar— Apeldoorn: Walva-Boek [A survey appearing annually, under the name of different editors; the subtitle is apt to vary somewhat].

Goedegebuure, Jaap, and Anne Marie Musschoot, *Contemporary Fiction of the Low Countries*. Rekkem: Stichting Ons Erfdeel, 1991.

Holmes, James S, and William Jay Smith, *Dutch Interior: Postwar Poetry of the Netherlands and Flanders*. New York: Columbia University, 1984 [Contains a list of Dutch poetry that appeared in out-of-the-way places].

Meijer, R.P., *Literature of the Low Countries: A Short History of Dutch Literature in the Netherlands and Belgium*. Cheltenham: Stanley Thornes/The Hague: Nijhoff, 2nd ed. 1978.

Schram, D.H., 'An unfinished chapter. The Second World War and the Holocaust in Dutch literature'. *The Low Countries*, 1994-95.

Six Books from Holland and Flanders. Amsterdam: Nederlands Literair Produktie- en Vertalingenfonds [A periodic bulletin; from the same source comes *Nieuwsbrief Letteren*].

17 North and South

An indispensable component in our attempts to understand the Dutch is how they relate to the Dutch-speaking people just south of them.

In the present day one crosses the southern border of the Netherlands into Belgium without noticing entry into another country. There is no geographical feature, or even any noticeable change in the landscape. Signs, advertisements, newspapers, and the stock on bookstore shelves bring some different names but are all in the same language, as are radio and television. People speak the language with an accent that is not strikingly different from that of Noord-Brabant or Limburg. It is in the centers of the old cities south of the border that the familiar northern scene has been left behind. Gent, Bruges, Ypres, Courtrai or Louvain all show in their architectural exuberance evidence of a past opulence that is very different from the restrained elegance of a city like Amsterdam.

The original heartland of Dutch culture lies in the South (meaning, for the rest of this chapter, 'Flemish Belgium', while 'North' will refer to the Netherlands), in the medieval manufacturing and trading centers where a prosperous urban class was first able to rival the power of the aristocracy and develop its own cultural style. City halls, guild houses and bell towers all over Belgium and far into northern France all testify to its self-confidence and wealth. In the 15th century it was Brussels that replaced Dijon as the center of gravity of the Burgundian realm. In the 16th century, the Reformation movements got their strongest start in the South; the residence of Prince William of Orange was in Brussels, and the Pacification of Gent, the first agreement of all seventeen Netherlands provinces to resist the Spanish, was signed in 1576 in a southern city.

Ironically in view of later developments, the revolt in its origins was a southern rather than a northern initiative. It was only when the Spanish military power in the South could no longer be resisted that there was a mass migration of protestants to the North. Amsterdam had to tear down its walls and expand the city to accommodate all the immigrants, and in the early 17th century Middelburg in Zeeland had a population that consisted of about 60% Flemish immigrants. The North was on its way to a 'Golden age', but not without major help from the South.

In the South, the provinces that remained under Spanish control, this amounted to an extreme example of what today we would call a 'brain drain'. The port of Antwerp was cut off from the sea by a blockade by the North, a situation perpetuated by a treaty, and the Catholic South never experienced the 17th-century flourishing of economy and culture that the North did. The style of its culture was that of the Counter-reformation given artistic form by Rubens and seen in the Baroque churches in cities such as Antwerp. Two distinct life styles and sequences of historical experience developed next to each other but in isolation from each other, a separate northern and southern cultural identity.

Fig. 17.1
The Flemish city of Louvain (left) and Brussels

Over two centuries later, North and South were rejoined in the United Kingdom from 1815 to 1830, but these fifteen years were full of antagonisms that have affected relations between North and South ever since. The separation brought for the North a humiliation in the eyes of the world and a retreat into indifference toward the South that is still one of the barriers to cultural harmony. The sudden independence of Belgium for the first time in history coincided with the peak of the Romantic movement in Europe, which brought with it all the idealism and outward trappings of 'national identity'. Belgian statehood was steeped from the start in the Romantic nationalism that is so conspicuously missing in the North.

Belgium occupies the interface of three major language areas, and is socially one of the most complex regions of Europe. The historic cultural region known as 'Flanders' is part of three modern states (Belgium, the Netherlands, and France), and the historic 'Brabant' now straddles the national border and in Belgium is divided once again by the language boundary. State borders offer little indication of cultural and linguistic realities.

The population figures for modern Belgium by language are

		%
Flemish *(Dutch-speaking)*	5,739,700	57.7
Walloon *(French-speaking)*	3,143,685	31.6
Brussels *(bilingual)*	994,780	10.0
German	69,635	0.7
	9,947,800	

The word 'bilingual' for Brussels, one of the three constitutionally fixed autonomous 'regions' of Belgium (a term to be explained further below) simply means that the capital has both a Dutch-speaking and a French-speaking population. By law no language count is made here, though it is generally assumed that the French speakers are in the majority—some estimates run as high as 85%. Coordination of any language policy is rendered much more difficult by the fact that Brussels is not a 'city' in the modern sense but a medieval-style agglomeration of nineteen autonomous municipalities.

The figures show that the two major language groups are not wildly incomparable in size. The Dutch-speaking Flemish population is distinctly in the majority, but until the last decade or two the French-speaking half more than made up for its numerical second-place through its cultural dominance. The confrontation with and eventual turning around of this ancient dominance is the key to the whole Belgian problem.

The central issue in Flemish society is the language question. The medieval Flemish cities fought off the domination of the French aristocracy, events still commemorated by Flemish nationalists. But from the Burgundian time on, historical happenings have continually reinforced the domination of French. It has been the language of administration, the church, education, and later the armed forces and the world of banking and business. The common English names of all but one of the Dutch-speaking cities of *Gent, Brugge, Ieper, Kortrijk* and *Leuven* listed at the beginning of this chapter are French. For centuries the dominant written language of the country was French. The native language of over half the population was the variety of local and regional dialects, for which there was no standardized form like the one coming into being in the North as early as the 16th century. Flemish consciousness was strongly tied to local region. Today the native language of the majority of Flemings of all classes is still dialect, and they continue to follow an instinct for congregating by region.

Consciousness among Flemish people of a separate cultural identity and consequently of the right to use and cultivate their own language was stimulated by the same Romantic movement that underlay the ideal of Belgian statehood. Through the 19th century, the emancipation of the Flemish from French domination was led by the *Vlaamse Beweging* (Flemish Movement), an effort which still continues today. The Movement's activity was focused on the legal and political area, where by slow and painful steps equal rights were gradually secured. But the primary reason for its existence was always seen in terms of the language. The people's right to use their own language meant that the Dutch language had to be recognized as equal to French in the schools, courts and in government. The novelist Hendrik Conscience, the poet Guido Gezelle, and later the novelist Gerard Walschap, created a new Flemish literature in Dutch. In 1930 the University of Gent, well inside the Dutch-speaking area, was finally officially declared a Dutch-language institution.

The Romantic nationalism that was the force behind the Flemish Movement left it vulnerable to the influence of more extreme forms of political idealism, and during both World Wars it was not able to withstand the temptation to identify its cause with the 'Pan-Germanic' and anti-French rhetoric of the occupiers. In *Het verdriet van België* (1985; The Sorrows of Belgium), the Fleming Hugo Claus paints a brilliant portrait of life in Flanders, and spells out remorselessly the many small ways in which the slide of Flemish identity into collaboration took place. This continuing tinge is said to be one of the greatest misfortunes of the Flemish emancipation enterprise. Though the Dutch with their banner of 'resistance' are apt to use this as yet another reason for looking down on the Flemish, in reality the level of collaboration in Belgium was no higher than in the Netherlands.

Reference a moment ago to the use of 'the Dutch language' by the Flemish in the 19th and 20th centuries sounds quite straightforward, as if it were entirely parallel to the use of 'the French language' in Brussels. But like everything else in Belgium that has to do with language, the reality is much more complicated. The Flemish Movement took root among a people speaking dialects who had no real consciousness of a standard form of their language that could stand up to standard French. The Netherlands across the border to the north was a remote place, a different world with a language that had an alien sound. Flemish reformers tried to stimulate the development of a form of speech that was not identified with just one region, but they were without any model that was prestigious enough. The result was that the Flemish were dependent, like it or not, on the North with its secure standard language. The debate began, and still continues, about just what should play the role of standard language for Flemish speakers. It might be northern speech just as it is (an ideal Flemish speakers could aim for but with the knowledge that they would always fall short of sounding like a 'Hollander'), or their language could be a recognized Flemish variant rather like the English and American versions of a common language.

Efforts to promote the use of the Dutch standard language in the South have been systematic and determined for a long period of time, but success has never been complete. Flemish speakers need a language that has unquestioned prestige and that can serve as a reference point in resisting 'Gallicisms', that is French words and idioms. But many ordinary speakers feel insecure about standard usage. Only the more well-educated Flemish speakers are truly certain whether a word or an expression is acceptable as part of the normal variation within a standard language, or whether it stigmatizes them as dialect speakers. Ever since the 19th century, this has led to a series of determined efforts by the Flemish to create the means for joining with the Netherlands in the enterprise of cultivating and mutually reinforcing the common language. To allow the Flemish identification with the North to make better sense, though, we need to return once more to the relation in Belgium to the French language.

The map (Fig. 17.2) shows that the three language groups in Belgium, two major and one minor, are not scattered among each other but occupy neatly-bounded regions. The linguistic boundary between Dutch-speaking and French-speaking divides the country into two approximately equal halves north and south of each other. Among the many bilingual countries in the world, Belgium is unique in being shared by two language groups so nearly equal in numbers and area, but even more in the extent to which bilingualism has been minutely regulated by legislation. In 1962 the language boundary was officially fixed, and the reciprocal rights on both sides of it were spelled out.

LINGUISTIC REGIONS IN BELGIUM

74.86

Ostend
Bruges
Antwerp
Ghent
Mechelen
Aalst
Louvain
Hasselt
Kortrijk
VOEREN
BRUSSELS
COMINES-WARNETON
Nivelles
Liège
Eupen
La Louvière
Verviers
Namur
Mons
Charleroi
Arlon

Population by linguistic region (%)

57.6 DUTCH

0.7 GERMAN

9.9 BILINGUAL

31.8 FRENCH

```
23.84   WEST-          OOST-        B R A B A N T              NEDER-
      VLAANDEREN  VLAANDEREN   Wemmel  Kraainem              LAND
Mesen              Spiere-    BRUSSEL  Wezembeek-Oppem  LIMBURG
                   Helkijn Ronse  Drogenbos HOOFDSTAD        Voeren
Komen-                        Linkebeek Sint-Genesius-  Herstappe
Waasten    Moeskroen Vloesberg Bever    Rode
FRANKRIJK          HENEGOUWEN Edingen       B R A B A N T    L U I K
                                                    0  km  20
```

To the north of the boundary, the language is Dutch, the exclusive language of all the street names, advertisements and so on. Road signs pointing to French-speaking cities south of the boundary may use only the Dutch name of a city, so a traveler needs to know that *Luik* refers to *Liège*, *Namen* to *Namur*, *Doornik* to *Tournai*, *Bergen* to *Mons*, and so on. Dutch is the language of schools and administration. French speakers from the South are free to speak French as long as they can find people to accommodate them, but they cannot claim any right to French-language education for their children or to be addressed in French in city offices.

To the south of the boundary the situation is exactly the reverse. When one drives along, at the otherwise invisible boundary all the signs and ads suddenly become French and may not be otherwise, road signs point the way north to *Malines, Anvers, Grammont* or *Courtrai* but do not mention the Dutch-speaking cities whose local names are *Mechelen, Antwerpen, Geraardsbergen,* and *Kortrijk.* Dutch speakers may work and even live in large numbers south of the boundary, but they can claim no legal right to use of their language by French speakers.

But a closer look (Fig. 17.3) shows that, once again, the situation is more involved than this. All along the boundary there is a string of 'facility' communities, and these are a result of a delicate balance, painstakingly put together, between the two language communities. A facility area north of the boundary has a 'protected French-language minority' and one to the south has a 'protected Dutch-language minority' meaning that in these designated areas certain language rights for the minority group are guaranteed by law. This meticulous spelling out of equal rights is part of the Belgian way of life. Nothing arouses passions quite like language rights and restrictions, and these agreements were necessary in order to prevent the dissolution of the state into two mutually hostile language groups.

The extent occasionally reached by this reciprocity is well illustrated by the way the division of the University of Louvain was handled in 1968. The presence of a French-language university inside the Flemish area had become unacceptable, and it was divided into the University of Leuven in its original city and *Louvain-la-neuve* to the south. The library was divided fairly and equally between the two, by the simple means of sending all even-numbered books in one direction, and all odd-numbered books in the other.

The primary focus of friction between the two language groups today is Brussels. Geographically the city lies well within the Dutch-language half of Belgium, but socially it is overwhelmingly French in its orientation. The same legislation that set the language boundary declared the capital a region separate in status from all the rest, a fully bilingual area with several French-language 'facility' areas around its perimeter. The guarantee of equal rights for Dutch speakers did not prevent Brussels from remaining predominantly French-speaking. It is only in the past few years that the Dutch language is at last well on the way to being accepted as an equal route to advancement in the worlds of government or business. The power of Brussels to radiate and extend French influence is still a source of constant anxiety to the Flemish, and the greatest fear is that the Dutch language corridor to the south of it will be overwhelmed and declared French, allowing Brussels to join the French South and depriving the Flemish of a share in their own capital.

Many Belgians in Brussels and both north and south of the boundary live in a trilingual world, moving effortlessly back and forth between dialect, Dutch and French. But in the day-to-day life of most people, the other language community hardly exists or is regarded with suspicion. French speakers by long tradition make few efforts to accommodate speakers of any other language, and in fact scarcely trouble to distinguish between Flemish and German speakers. Texts in Dutch are often clumsily translated French, even when commercial interests are involved.

In recent years Dutch has been rapidly overtaking French in prestige, as economic realities are at last bringing about what the Flemish Movement's long struggle was unable to achieve. Dutch is now becoming the prestige language of Belgium, as the 'burden' of bilingualism changes sides. More and more French speakers are learning Dutch (as knowledge of French among Flemish speakers decreases dramatically), and in the national parliament French-language representatives are increasingly becoming proficient in it.

And this brings us back to attitudes in the Netherlands toward their Dutch-speaking Flemish cousins to the south. In an endless variety of subtle ways, and often in blatant ways, Flemings are made to feel that their command of the Dutch standard language is never quite good enough. To a Dutchman from the North, Flemish speech may suggest a relaxed 'southern' lifestyle, or it may sound quaint or amusing, or like a vaguely outlandish attempt to speak Dutch. Northerners who try to imitate Dutch as it is spoken in the South, and even those who make pronouncements about it on the scholarly level, invariably exaggerate the differences. There is a strong strain of condescension in all these attitudes. An attempted cooperative Dutch-language production of the children's TV series 'Sesame Street' by the Netherlands and Belgium failed when Flemish voices were not accepted by viewers in the North, although Flemish children had no trouble with the Amsterdam accents.

The common Dutch attitude of condescension that sends messages of inferiority to the Flemish goes well beyond the area of the language. For instance, it has been documented many times that the treatment of Belgium in the Dutch press is still dominated by the old stereotypes. The Dutch tend to be ever ready to think of Flemings as aberrations from familiar Dutch ways, and satiric actors from the South usually find they get their best laughs by playing up to the northern expectations of Flemish ineptitude. The surrealistic Flemish style of humor is not well understood, and they find it difficult to be taken seriously.

The innumerable *Belgenmoppen* in circulation (always called 'Belgian jokes', never 'Flemish jokes', probably because the first is lower in prestige) almost without exception revolve around the theme of stupidity, which often includes inability to understand the language. The Flemings reciprocate with an equally creative assortment of *Hollandermoppen* (the Dutchman is always a 'Hollander', never a *Nederlander*) which invariably emphasize northern miserliness and narrow-minded smugness. Recently a Flemish cabaret artist referred to the Dutch obsession with order and punctuality as 'Calvinistic fascism'. We should be aware, though, that the very popularity of all these jokes is evidence of an underlying—though probably unconscious—sense of cultural solidarity between the Dutch and the Flemish.

A 'Belgian joke'

A Belgian goes into a store in Holland and, with a thick Belgian accent, tries to buy something. Everyone laughs.
He goes away vowing to learn perfect Dutch so they can't laugh at him.
He keeps taking courses until he can speak like a Dutchman. Back in Holland, he goes into a store and says, in his best Dutch, 'I'd like a loaf of whole-wheat bread'.
'You're a Belgian, aren't you?' says the storekeeper laughing.
'But I speak perfect Dutch', says the Belgian, 'how did you know?'
'You came in here and asked for bread. But this is a butcher shop.'

A 'Dutchman joke'

A Belgian and a Dutchman are sitting in a station waiting for a train. To pass the time, they play games.
'Let's see who can tell the most improbable story', says the Dutchman.
'All right', says the Belgian, 'you start.'
'Once upon a time there was a generous Dutchman ...' he begins.
'Stop where you are', sighs the Belgian.
'You win.'

So for the great majority of northerners, the Flemish South is a remote place that exists mainly in the form of stereotypes. The average Dutch visitor has no real understanding of the Flemish struggle for emancipation, and does not feel the area south of his border but north of the language boundary to be simply another province in his own cultural region. Most call the language *Vlaams* rather than *Nederlands*. Many attempt to speak French to everyone in Brussels, and some begin doing this as soon as they cross the national border. The massive indifference on the part of the Dutch to Flemish identity and to the cultural needs of the population is by far the greatest frustration in the cultural relationship between the two communities.

The vision of the underlying cultural unity of the Low Countries is one with a very long history. It has gone by a number of different names, a few of which became tainted in the 1930's and 1940's with vaguely fascist political associations. The most common general term came to be *Groot-Nederland* (the Greater Netherlands), used in the 19th century and still current. The idea is often expressed more simply in the less politically-loaded term *De Nederlanden* which means something like 'all the Dutch-speaking Low Countries'.

The Flemish movement in the 19th century turned toward the North for the model of a prestige standard language, and also for moral support along a wide cultural front. The vision of a joint cultural identity was a strong one, and many of the most concrete moves toward cultural integration were either initiated in the South or received their strongest support there. The term *Nederlands*, which since the 17th century had become the way to refer to the language and culture of the North, began being used to refer to language and culture of both North and South together. The *Woordenboek der Nederlandsche Taal* (Dictionary of the Dutch Language), a huge 37-volume project —claimed to be the world's largest dictionary—begun in 1851 and only now nearing completion*, was a joint effort from the outset. In English-language publications the term 'Flemish' has been abolished as a reference to the language or culture as a whole, and been replaced by 'Dutch'.

Since 1956 there has been a prize in literature awarded jointly by both countries, the *Prijs der Nederlandse Letteren*, and since the founding of the private-initiative cultural quarterly *Ons Erfdeel* (Our Heritage) in 1957, subsidy and editorial responsibility has been shared by both countries. In its subtitle it uses the common term *Algemeen-Nederlands* (*algemeen* is 'general' or 'common', but the name as a whole resists comfortable translation into English). From its inception this cultural magazine has treated North and South as a single cultural unit, a policy that is also being followed by the new English-language annual *The Low Countries: Arts and Society in Flanders and the Netherlands*.

The climax of all integration efforts up to the present moment is the creation of the *Nederlandse Taalunie*, ('Dutch Language Union', or perhaps better though more clumsily 'Greater-Netherlands Language Union'). This is the result of an agreement signed by both countries to entrust responsibility for all cultivation and advancement of the language and the literature to a single organization acting for the two countries. As such it is a unique example of

---

* The entire dictionary has recently appeared on CD-ROM.

renunciation of an important area of sovereignty by two independent states. It is, besides, the first political structure that has ever comprised all of, but only, the Dutch-speaking area. It is the first tangible reality of the cultural commonwealth of the Netherlands. The *Taalunie* is responsible for annual conferences, for the awarding of the literary prize mentioned above, for all questions having to do with spelling and orthographic reform, as well as for a variety of other cooperative efforts in literature and the mass media. Outside the Netherlands and Belgium, the *Taalunie* is concerned with the status of the Dutch language within the European Union, and the support of the study of Dutch language and culture abroad.

There is wide agreement that the most important fruit of cooperation so far is the *Algemene Nederlandse Spraakkunst* (General Dutch Grammar) of 1984. It is a practical reference grammar of a type that had never existed before. Forms, meanings and syntactical arrangements that are current mainly in Flemish Belgium are no longer stigmatized with that patronizing word *Zuidnederlands* ('Southern', understood as code for 'unacceptable in the real Dutch language'), as they used to be in dictionaries, but simply called 'regional' along with such variation in all other parts of the area. The appearance of the ANS is a milestone for the Flemish community, a reminder that the common language is no less southern than northern. On the more popular level, a recent highly-regarded TV quiz series on usage, meanings, spelling and various other language questions always pitted a Dutch team against a Flemish one, and showed that the Flemings had no trouble winning at least half the time.

To look one last time at the Dutch attitude: people in the Netherlands do not feel they particularly need the *Taalunie*, or broader cultural cooperation in general, in the same way as the Flemish do. Cultural integration is an idea that arouses feelings among the Dutch that are somewhere between suspicion and massive indifference. With its long tradition of non-interference either abroad or in the many semi-autonomous sub-societies at home, the Dutch tend to be content with their own familiar, inviolable corner and see little additional prestige coming from an expansion into the Flemish side of their common culture.

But many influential voices in both North and South continue to insist that a single language should not obscure the fact that there are, in fact, two distinct cultures needing elbow room. There is, for instance, clearly a gap between the world of writers in North and South. Writing in the Netherlands in the last few decades has had a strong tendency to turn inward, and it has not shown any primary involvement with large social issues. With all its ills, Dutch society is in a state of relative contentment, and writing there includes few real rebels. Belgian society is still struggling with more fundamental inequalities, and writers accept the responsibility to fight for social causes such as emancipation, and against corruption and militarism. The youngest generation of popular writers has adopted a brash, cynical tone and there is talk among literary critics of a 'Flemish Renaissance' as these writers continue to attract wide attention in the North.

There is evidence in many areas that the sharing of a common cultural heritage is a high-minded ideal that refuses to turn into reality. Dutch aloof-

Fig. 17.4
Using a familiar metaphor, this editorial cartoon shows Belgium now neatly federalized into three largely autonomous 'houses'

ness is still perceived as cold among the Flemish, but the Dutch point out the futility of trying to 'restore' a cultural unity that never existed in the first place. The provinces of the Low Countries have throughout their history been particularistic and gone their many separate ways. North and South are now settling into an attitude that recognizes a single common language and at the same time two distinct cultures whose differences are accepted and respected. The two cultures are still in the initial phase of learning how to present a united voice to the new federated Europe.

The Belgian state began its life as an uneasy alliance of French and Flemish against the domination of the North, and ever since then its two halves have been drifting toward a polarization. As the Flemings have won more and more rights to their own institutions, the increasing number of parallel French-Flemish administrative bodies has amounted to the evolution of a federation of two semi-autonomous states. But Belgium would not be itself if the organization of this were not rather complex. At present, Belgium consists of three autonomous REGIONS (gewesten)—Flanders, Wallonia, the Brussels agglomerate—responsible for geographically-based matters such as physical planning, energy and employment, and parallel to this three autonomous COMMUNITIES (gemeenschappen)—Flemish, French, German—concerned with language-based matters such as the language itself, education, and other cultural policy.

   This federalization has now been firmly fixed by constitution. The centralized state of previous times has been progressively hollowed out, and what little unity remains (for instance, in foreign policy) is symbolized by the monarchy. There are now voices calling for its final dissolution as the two halves are absorbed in the foreseeable future into a European federation. Others call for complete autonomy and close cultural and political ties of Flanders with the Netherlands. But since autonomy without Brussels—itself well advanced in evolving into a general European city-state—is unworkable, the federalization of Belgium will probably proceed little further.

The carillon

The sound of the carillon, the music of ornamented melodies played on bells usually in a tower in the heart of a city, is an inseparable aspect of urban life in the Netherlands and Belgium. Most towns have one, used for occasional popular concerts and on market day, and most carillons have a mechanism that plays tunes automatically on the hour or of-tener. The music is usually a well-known folksong or popular song, though it may just as well be an adaptation of a classical piece. A great deal of music has been written for the instrument itself.

Carillon music consists of a basic tune accompanied by elaborate ornamentation, usually on the higher bells. This is a style that was developed for the instrument, and one that is characteristic of performing in the Low Countries. It is a cascade of sound that can be heard over a wide area. The bells produce sets of overtones that, in combination with each other, sometimes require some effort to learn to listen to.

A carillon is a chromatic series of bells that have been cast in special foundries and carefully tuned. Most carillons consist of three or four octaves; a series of 47 bells is more or less standard. Some carillons in the Netherlands and Belgium still use bells cast in series like these in the 17th century. Delicate accentuation can be given, making the carillon a challenge for virtuoso performers. There is a carillon school in Mechelen in Belgium and in Amersfoort in the Netherlands.

Bells were used in the Middle Ages for tolling and sounding an alarm, and at some point melodies began being played on tuned series. This proved attractive to citizens who were engaged in the developing city life, and the idea caught on and spread. The bells are stationary and not struck directly but by way of a set of staves arranged in the form of a keyboard. The keyboard and its mechanism were given their form, which they still preserve today, by 1610. The evolution of the carillon is intimately connected with the rights of self-government won by the medieval cities, and the bells were proudly installed in the towers that were the mark of the city's identity.

The carillon began in Flanders and spread to the North. Today it is known all over the world, but it is still very much a Low Countries instrument and should by rights be their symbol rather than the well-worn ones.

See André Lehr (and others), *The Art of the Carillon in the Low Countries*. Tielt: Lannoo / Baarn: Tirion, 1991.

It is often pointed out that cooperation between two small cultures is the only possible survival strategy in the rapidly-developing new European system dominated by much larger countries. But this idea enjoys only slowly growing popularity in the North. Still, one can expect informal unity to keep increasing. The Catholic versus protestant chasm that for centuries was the key issue keeping them apart, has receded into the background.

FURTHER READING

Boudart, M. et al. (eds.), *Modern Belgium*. Palo Alto, CA: Society for the Promotion of Science and Scholarship, 1990.

Donk, Albert (ed.), *In Vlaanderen*. Baarn: De Kern, 1990 [12 Dutch authors write their views of Flemish culture].

Hermans, Theo et al. (eds.), *The Flemish Movement: A Documentary History 1780-1990*. London: Athlone, 1992.

Van Istendael, Geert, *Het Belgische labyrint. Wakker worden in een ander land*. Amsterdam: De Arbeiderspers, 9th ed. 1993.

The Nederlandse Taalunie (Dutch Language Union): What it is and what it does. The Hague: Nederlandse Taalunie, 1990.

18 The international perspective

In contrast to the other European languages, English has no single noun that means 'all countries except one's own', a vocabulary gap that perhaps reflects the Anglo-Saxon habit of regarding all foreign countries as remote and uninteresting, and that calls anything very strange 'outlandish'. In the Netherlands the word is *het buitenland*, and it begins only a short distance from anywhere in the country. The importance of what the neighbors do across the border and the North Sea, in Europe and the rest of the world, is a reality that hardly any aspect of life in the Netherlands can ignore. The Dutch take their relations to *het buitenland* seriously because, as one of them put it, 'it is so large compared to us'.

While the Second World War was still in progress, the Netherlands government in exile began consulting with the Belgian government to plan postwar economic integration that would create as large a market as possible for reconstruction. The result of this political coordination together with Luxemburg was *Benelux*, which came into official existence in 1944. Benelux took the first postwar step toward European integration in 1948 when customs barriers among the three states were abolished and a common tariff structure toward the outside was agreed upon. This was expanded still further in 1958 by the Benelux Economic Union. The Netherlands was vigorous from the start in its promotion of the Benelux idea, and integration would undoubtedly have developed into other areas if it had not been overtaken by the creation of the European Community.

Within the larger framework of European integration, Benelux as it celebrates its 50th anniversary continues to exist and to pursue its own steps toward political and economic cooperation. The GNP of the union is the world's eighth, and it is the fourth largest trade power in the world. Traditionally Benelux led a 'low-profile' existence in Europe, partly for the pragmatic reason that speaking too insistently with a single voice could lead other European countries to raise the question why three separate delegations are needed in European councils. One of the many effects it has is that of slowing the complete division of Belgium into separate sovereign states, and another role is taking the initiative in the current development of an integrated European market.

Although its main successes have been in the economic area, the European Community, officially termed the 'European Union' since the Treaty of Maastricht, has steadily developed a cooperative political machinery to continue the process of integration. The Netherlands has built up a reputation in the EU for a high level of European-mindedness, which is not undeserved but often comes less from idealism than from practical necessity: over 50% of the national income comes from foreign trade. The Union is indispensable to the Netherlands for economic prosperity. In addition to this economic motive for their support of European integration, the Dutch have a strong political one as well. After four centuries, they at last see themselves freed from the disagreeable and hazardous alternative of forever 'choosing sides' among their powerful neighbors England, Germany and France. Polls taken by the EU and published in the annual *Euro-barometre* regularly show that the Dutch have the most or a more favorable view of it than the other member countries. But this idealism is not always matched by confidence in EU institutions. Voter turnout for the European Parliament elections has been dropping steadily since 1979, and at 35.6% it is now among the lowest in Europe.

World rankings for comparison	
	The Netherlands is number
Total surface area	117
Population	47
Gross National Product	14
World Trade	7
Agricultural exports	2 or 3

Within the EU context, through not part of its organization, the three Benelux countries along with four others form the West European Union. The WEU was originally formed in 1954 as a united front for presenting a strong European identity toward the United States, especially on defense matters. More recently it has adopted as its domain the whole area of peacemaking and European mutual security, functioning as the defense arm of the EU.

Nothing in the EU structure precludes special relationships between states. The close relationship of the Netherlands with England, for instance, goes back to the period in which the Dutch revolt was closely followed and discussed in England, and it helped influence English political life. Later in this same 16th century the United Provinces relied on the English for support in gaining their independence, and it was an English nobleman who was summoned to exercise sovereignty in the United Provinces for ten years before they decided to run the country themselves. This relationship was not seriously damaged even by the four English Wars in the 17th and 18th centuries. In 1688, in the 'Glorious Revolution', the stadhouder William III and his wife Mary Stuart, who was the daughter of the king, were called to England as king and queen to replace a Catholic monarch. There he took the first steps in turning an absolute monarchy into a constitutional one. Today the relationship is a close one, not only culturally but through joint companies such as Unilever and Royal Dutch Shell.

The Netherlands' relationship with Germany is of a different type, and one with special difficulties. In the late Middle Ages the culture and language of the Low Countries had a strong influence on its neighbor to the east, and this was true once again in the time of the powerful Republic in the 17th century. But since then, the influence has more often been in the opposite direction. German cultural influence was strongest toward the end of the 18th century and all through the 19th, when German literature was popular and large numbers of German words entered the language. By the late 19th century and on into the 20th this influence was economic and political as well.

During the '30s the National-Socialist movement in Germany found at least modest support across the border. Today Germany is the Netherlands' foremost trading partner, the greatest share of the entire horticultural food production going there, and the two states cooperate closely in an endless variety of ways. This would seem to suggest that all is smooth now.

Centuries of being overshadowed by a large neighbor is never really welcome, and it inevitably generates suspicions and fears. But the Netherlands has learned to live with this, partly by maintaining its own economic independence and partly by pursuing a policy of neutrality. In 1940 this policy was ignored by the Germans, and the Netherlands was subjected to the humiliation and destruction of five years of military occupation. It is hardly surprising that, just under the surface, the relationship to Germany has not been quite the same since. Immediately after the war, in the Netherlands the air was full of talk of annexation, seen as an act of punishment and repayment and also as a shield against future aggression. But in the same period the Netherlands was preoccupied much more urgently with the East Indies, and the reality amounted to the annexation of two small enclaves along the border, both of which were subsequently returned to Germany.

Considerations such as repayment and protection were overtaken immediately by a matter of higher priority, the urgent need for restoration of normal relations with Germany in order to get recovery under way. Postwar prosperity, in fact, has been to a great extent possible because of close cooperation with Germany. This highly positive side, however, masked the problem that remained underneath. Strong national feelings had to be ignored, there was no time for any redress of grievances, and frustration found expression in small outbursts of hostility. The Dutch public watched a strong Germany growing after the war, and resentment was given extra fuel by the unwitting insensitivity of German tourists who flooded the country and turned some of the seaside resorts into German-speaking communities. This resentment has remained strong, long after fear of a repetition of German aggression has faded.

A telling example of the expression of pent-up feelings is provided by the Dutch public's reaction to the country's victory over the German team in the semi-finals of the world soccer championship in 1988. When the game was won, the normally reserved Dutch burst out in a frenzy of 'patriotic' celebration, as newspapers printed headlines and congratulatory ads in orange, the team was received by the queen, and bewildered German tourists had to endure an unaccustomed level of aggressiveness. This abnormally passionate celebration was widely seen as a safe release of these long-smoldering anti-German feelings, as the nation finally found a civilized public way to 'get even'.

Some of this frustration has also been taken out on the *Drie van Breda*, three German military officers serving sentences in the military prison at Breda for war crimes. Every hint or even rumor of their possible release after serving long sentences stirred up outraged protests among the Dutch public, and the remaining two were until recently the last Nazis still in prison outside Germany. After an emotional debate and against widespread protest, the last two were released in 1989 by the government in an effort to put to rest one more painful aspect of the past.

Many people in the Netherlands still look with mixed feelings at the growing strength within the EU of their next-door neighbor, and economic cooperation with Germany is strong though never smooth. An example is the recent proposal to merge the Dutch Fokker Aircraft with the German DASA, which stirred up considerable public resentment about 'selling' an important national symbol* to a powerful and occasionally arrogant rival. The Dutch are even more skeptical about increasing political integration with Germany.

Difficulties in the way of smooth relationships between the Netherlands and Germany have origins that go much deeper, and farther back in time, than the trauma of the Second World War. They are states that have been formed around two distinct cultures, and are the products of two very different national experiences. The ideal of a 'German Nation' is strong in Germany, whereas national idealism is weak in the Netherlands. Authoritarian exercise of power and a strong competitiveness have made it difficult for democratic traditions to take strong root in Germany, whereas accommodation and compromise are central to the pattern of Dutch society. The militaristic tradition is an important factor in German history, but militarism has never had any significant appeal in the Netherlands. And the list of contrasts goes on and on.

Traditionally the Netherlands was committed to the view that the way to European unity lay in the creation of a world economic order which all benefit by. When this order was firmly established, political union would follow. Today this progressive ideal of a supernational Europe has somewhat faded in favor of a more Gaullist 'Europe of states' in which old-fashioned nationalism again plays a strong role. With many of the economic goals in place, Europe is now moving toward a European Political Union. But domestic patterns of thought can narrow a country's vision. The 1991 Treaty of Maastricht, signed during the Netherlands' normal 6-month term as chairman of the EC, once again attached a Dutch city's name to an international agreement. But the treaty did not adopt the Dutch plan, which proposed a close-knit interactive structure, including significantly broadening the authority of the European Parliament, all with the ideal of deliberation and consensus at its center. The treaty was based instead on a plan which more soberly came to terms with the power realities of Europe and the continuing strength of nationalism.

The idea of a world social order based on the free play of economic interests has been a favorite Dutch theme since Hugo Grotius in the 17th century, and in modern times the Dutch thinkers who have received most international attention have been economists. The best known of these is the late Jan Tinbergen, recipient of the first Nobel prize in economics, who in many books preached an international level of organization, social conscience with practical goals. Tinbergen showed his Dutchness in effectively combining the roles of economist and missionary.

---

* After 77 years as an airplane manufacturer, the Fokker company went out of business in 1996.

A few EU figures for comparison

Satisfaction with life: 'very' or 'rather satisfied' (1990)   *in percentages*

Denmark	97	United Kingdom	87
Luxemburg	93	France	80
Netherlands	93	Italy	77
Belgium	90	Spain	77
Ireland	90	Portugal	73
Germany	88	Greece	65

Satisfaction with the democratic system in one's country (1990)

Luxemburg	79	Portugal	60
Germany	78	Ireland	59
Netherlands	73	United Kingdom	55
Belgium	63	Greece	49
Denmark	61	France	44
Spain	60	Italy	29

Percent of energy derived from nuclear power (1990)

France	33.4
Belgium	23.1
Germany	12.0
United Kingdom	7.2
Italy	1.7
Netherlands	1.4

Trading Partners (1990)

	Import from	Export to
Germany	26	28
Belgium/Luxemburg	14	15
France	8	11
United Kingdom	8	10
Italy	8	4

Percentage of land cultivated vs. forested (1988)

	Cultivated	Forested
Ireland	82	5
United Kingdom	77	10
Greece	70	20
Denmark	66	12
Spain	61	31
Netherlands	59	9
France	57	27
Italy	58	23
Germany	49	30
Belgium/Luxemburg	46	21
Portugal	36	40
World average	36	31

The protection of commercial interests, the guarantee of national security and the advocacy of an international order within which these could operate, have traditionally formed the cornerstone of Netherlands foreign policy. On its recognition in 1648, the Republic began a policy of non-involvement and non-alignment, relying on friendly relations and commercial treaties on all sides. Although the political realities of the 17th century did not allow much peaceful aloofness, the Netherlands did succeed in avoiding most European entanglements and became the mediator in a series of disputes. The Hague became the seat of the International Court of Justice. The neutrality that was preserved through the First World War but violated in the Second was replaced by a far-reaching involvement in international political matters, but one which still did not disturb the basic reliance on commercial interests, and included an aversion to nationalistic power games.

For decades the Netherlands has supplied officials at or near the top of a wide variety of European and global organizations, such as the European Parliament, NATO, the International Monetary Fund, and the Organization for Economic Cooperation and Development. It was also one of the first countries to adopt a proposed 1% of GNP as a norm for annual expenditure for development aid. The foreign policy of the Netherlands is characterized by a strong current of international idealism, which has taken on many new forms with the postwar abandonment of the policy of neutrality. A considerable share of this impulse comes from the most fundamental level of Dutch society, the independently-formed *actie*-groups. There are a hundred important public-interest groups of this sort, active with ad and poster campaigns and fund-raising on behalf of political and economic needs abroad. They not only keep an idealistic vision before the public, but put constant pressure on government to plan along similar lines.

The Dutch have not given up the attitude that the Netherlands may have some moral role that makes up for its small size. Foreign policy is shaped by an awareness of the limited means available to a small power to influence world affairs, and it tends to emphasize the persuasiveness of the moral and the legal. Dutch diplomats are often perceived at home—as well as abroad—as making sharp divisions between good and bad, seeing progress in terms of elevated goals, and in general adopting the role of missionaries who seek to set an example in the world. It is not without some justification that the Dutch so often refer to their country as a *gidsland*, by which they mean something like 'country of moral leadership', though this translation fails to capture the usual mocking connotation. This international position, a combination of practical helper and moral conscience, is part of the Netherlands' search for a role in the world.

The Dutch sometimes seem obsessed with the thought 'but we're such a tiny country!' (one inadvertently thinks of the tremendous popularity of the 1/25 scale-model city *Madurodam*). In fact, one often gets the impression that they find their moral role so congenial that they insist on smallness as a justification for it. This mentality has such a pervasive way of diverting Dutch attention from their rightful place on the world stage (recall the map showing economic scale, Fig. 5.1) that the sociologist Abram de Swaan has been urging his compatriots for years to finally recognize, and declare to the world, that the highly urbanized Netherlands is not a country at all but a huge world metropolis—with a hereditary mayor*. Regardless of whether one considers this idea frivolous or not, in what other country would anyone even have thought of it?

The uncertainty about the country's role on the international scene is closely related to consciousness of the national identity. The Netherlands could, it is claimed, become another Brittany, picturesque but surrounded by dominant neighbors and with little voice of its own. They are well aware of their talent for assimilation, and fear above all else an undifferentiated European culture ('melting pot' is a bad word in the Netherlands) dominated by the large countries. As we will see in the final chapter, questions of 'national identity' are being raised with increasing intensity. Many Dutch commentators are pessimistic that their own countrymen will learn to value their own language and culture in time for the vigorous international promotion that is going to be necessary, although part of this may be yet another example of the Dutch instinct for 'complaining about their culture'.

This brings us almost up to the point of taking on that most elusive of questions, the Dutch national cultural identity and their view of it. It is especially characteristic of the Netherlands that its relationships with the rest of the world are seen as a direct extension of domestic conditions. Foreign policy is not based on concrete external ambitions, and consequently the approach to it takes the same form as social and political life within the country. The view of international politics as a non-dominating—and even non-influencing—balance of many independent positions is basic to the Netherlands' approach. Let us take a closer look at how Dutch society is put together, especially the crucial question of the individual's place in it.

---

* Abram de Swaan, *De Olympische hoogte: Amsterdam en de spelen van 1992.* Amsterdam: Meulenhoff, 1985, and *Perron Nederland.* Amsterdam: Meulenhoff, 1991.

FURTHER READING

Van den Bos, B., *Can Atlanticism Survive? The Netherlands and the New Role of Security Institutions.* The Hague: Instituut Clingendael, 1992.

Everts, P. (ed.), *Nederland in een veranderende wereld: De toekomst van het buitenlands beleid.* Assen: Van Gorcum, 1991.

The German Factor: *A Survey of Sensitivity and Vulnerability in the Relationship between the Netherlands and the Federal Republic. Summary of the 23rd Report to the Government.* The Hague: WRR, 1982.

Hellema, D. A., *Buitenlandse politiek van Nederland.* Utrecht: Spectrum, 1995.

Voorhoeve, Joris, *Peace, Profits and Principles: A Study of Dutch Foreign Policy.* The Hague: Martinus Nijhoff, 1985.

19 Dutch society

The Dutch have a preference for imposing a visible, familiar structure on any kind of social interaction, down to the most casual. In the Netherlands, in other words, association of any type is a natural extension of the value the culture places on careful organization. Leisure activities offer some good examples of this.

Much of leisure-time activity grew naturally out of the nature of the landscape itself, for instance skating and a variety of kinds of recreation in and on the water. Fishing in the canals, 'poor people's hunting', sometimes individual and sometimes in organized groups, has been popular for a very long time though it is now being restricted by pollution. At the edge of any large city, often crowded together into otherwise unusable patches of land near railroad embankments and in manufacturing areas, are the neatly laid-out *volkstuinen* or individual gardens. These were originally means of raising extra vegetables, which many are still used for, but in suburbanized areas they have become places to relax in a carefully-tended flower garden. The little garden houses (owners must belong to an association, and the houses may normally not be occupied as permanent residences) stand in the same neat rows as the family homes themselves.

It was probably the invention of the bicycle that more than anything else transformed both leisure and transportation. It is well adapted to the flat Dutch landscape and the relatively short distances in the population centers. Leisure riders have also transformed the countryside. It was they who through an effective organization brought about not only the development of early paved roads but the system of signs, maps and the marking of highways. The organization that motorists rely on today is still called the *Algemene Nederlandsche Wielrijdersbond* (ANWB), *wielrijders* being a word for 'cyclists'.

Organized sports had their origin in competitive activities that grew out of agrarian life, such as *korfbal*, which uses a basket on a pole, and the Frisian *skûtsjesilen*, races in the traditional-style canal sailboats (which in the everyday world have, of course, long since become motorized) and *fierljeppen*, vaulting with a long pole over a canal. All these have been enjoying a revival in recent times. Urban middle-class sports, though, are largely inherited from abroad, mainly England. Football (or 'soccer' in the US) was introduced in 1879 and now has developed into the most popular sport. And there are of course other international competitive sports in the leisure mix.

Sporting activity does not have a direct connection with the school curriculum or with 'school teams', and very little is done on a purely informal 'let's get a few players together' basis. Amateur sports activity is organized into *clubs*—often using the English word—and this includes children's sports as well. The club will usually have an appropriate name, insignia, officers, rules and bylaws. Probably the majority of them are dependent to some extent on municipal financial support. These clubs are coordinated into larger organizations, and the whole structure culminates in three national sports federations, the *Nederlandse Culturele Sport Bond*, the *Nederlandse Katholieke Sport Federatie*, and the *Nederlandse Christelijke Sport Unie*. About a third of the population between the ages of 4 and 74 is a member of some type of sports association.

Voetbal (or 'soccer') is played by almost innumerable clubs organized into their own associations or leagues. A distinction is made between amateur and professional sports, though the line is not a sharp one. The largest and best-known of the professional organizations is the *Koninklijke Nederlandse Voetbal Bond*, which coordinates nationally-known local teams. *Ajax* in Amsterdam and *Feijenoord* in Rotterdam are the two teams that generate the most intense rivalry. It is the teams at this level that play in international competitions.

Another popular form of leisure activity is the *muziekvereniging*, amateur music groups of many types that are organized in ways similar to the sports clubs. Musical activity includes orchestras, chamber groups, choirs and the like, and also brass bands, mixed wind groups, drum bands, accordion ensembles and other combinations. The really native Dutch forms are the highly popular *fanfare*, usually made up of brass and saxophones, and the *harmonie*, usually made up of these two plus woodwinds. In some communities, mostly less urbanized Catholic ones, the activity around the *muziekvereniging* is still an important aspect of community social life. Typically such groups have their own uniforms, banners and all the other attributes of group identity. It is, in other words, not that such groups exist that is unusual, but the style and high degree of organization of them.

There are also large numbers of amateur music societies undertaking performances of more 'serious' music, independent and not sponsored by any church or school. Such groups will always have an executive committee to implement the society's decisions about performance schedules, and at a concert the committee's chairman may act as master of ceremonies, even welcoming the conductor to the podium. Community groups will normally be members of national coordinating federations. A typical name of a music society might be *Christelijke Oratorium Vereniging Exsultate Deo (aangesloten bij de Koninklijke Christelijke Zangersbond)* 'Protestant Oratorio Society 'Exsultate Deo' (Affiliated with the Royal Protestant Choral Association)'.

The Dutch word for this important aspect of social organization is *vereniging*, a word that does not have an exact match in English. It is both more formal and often more serious in intent than 'club', which usually emphasizes the leisure aspect, but more personal than the usually high-minded 'association' or 'society'. The word covers an almost unlimited variety of activities, from sports and music on to organizations of animal fanciers, card-players, hobbyists, gardeners. But the same word also includes similarly-organized women's groups, scouts, senior citizens, public-interest and pressure groups.

As recently as a generation ago, this vast array of voluntary organizations was rigidly separated into the ideological 'blocs' discussed in detail in chapter 11. To a great extent these invisible social walls have come down. Though many of the names still survive (note the names of the sports federa-

VERENIGINGEN

Oranjevereniging Oegstgeest
Secr.: A. Koerten, Pres. Kennedylaan 224, 2343 GX, tel. 173492.

Sociëteit De Harmonie
Secr.: W.L. Hofman, Pres. Kennedylaan 21, 2343 GG, tel. 172670.

Dante Alighiere
Contactadres: Prof. A.W.A. Boschloo, Rhijngeesterstraatweg 6, 2342 AL, tel. 155714.

Vereniging Vrienden van het Lied, afdeling Oegstgeest
Contactadres: Mw. Thea Ekker-van der Pas, Lange Voort 44, 2341 KB, tel. 172448.

Cappella pro Cantibus (jongerenkoor)
Contactadres: P.P. Hanssen, Aert van Neslaan 102, 2341 HH, tel. 170506.

SPORTVERENIGINGEN

Badmintonclub Oegstgeest
Secr.: G. Versmissen, Rozenlaan 14, 2343 TG, tel. 172867

Basketballvereniging Oegstgeest
Secr.: Mw. M. de Wekker-Stikvoort, Irenestraat 6, 2351 GL Leiderdorp, tel. 894070.

Stichting Biljartcentrum Oegstgeest
Gebouw: De Voscuyl 40, 2341 BJ, tel. 173838.

In dit centrum spelen de volgende verenigingen:

— Centraal
— De Poedelaars '83 (bejaardenbiljartvereniging)
— De Voscuyl
— Sport

Informatie: H.J. Mulder, Terweeweg 82, 2341 CT, tel. 175308.

Oegstgeester Bridgeclub O.B.C.
Secr.: Mr. IJ.S. de Wilt, Grunerielaan 16, 2343 AM, tel. 173827.

Bridgeclub Rijnland
Secr.: E. Cancrinus, Van Griethuijsenplein 2, 2341 CE, tel. 173532.

Oegstgeester Gymnastiek- en Atletiekvereniging O.G.A.V.
Secr.: N.W.C. van Bentem, Oude Rijnzichtweg 41, 2342 AT, tel. 171324.

Handbalvereniging Mercasol Saturnus
Secr.: Mw. P. Klop-van der Hulst, Bosdreef 102, 2352 BD Leiderdorp, tel. 891380.

Vereniging van Handboogschutters Attila
Secr.: G.A. Brandt, Clematislaan 65, 2343 VK, tel. 174386.

Leidse Mixed Hockey Club
Secr.: Mw. C. Liera-Verheij van Wijk, Laan van Oud Poelgeest 34, 2341 NL, tel. 171157.

Korfbalvereniging Fiks
Secr.: Mw. G. de Best, De Kempenaerstraat 80, 2341 GP, tel. 171549.

Korfbalvereniging K.N.S.
Secr.: Mw. M.C. Stammers-Harteveld, Brahmslaan 26, 2324 AN Leiden, tel. 312489.

Schaakclub Oegstgeest '80
Secr.: J.F.M. van Maris, Richard Holpad 6, 2343 NZ, tel. 174723.

Nederlandse Skivereniging Kring Leiden
Secr.: Mw. I. Hiel-Piët, Noordbuurtseweg 36, 2381 EV Zoeterwoude, tel. 01715-2250.

Tafeltennisvereniging Oegstgeest
Secr.: Mw. M. van Laere, Witte de Withlaan 4, 2253 XS Voorschoten, tel. 768101.

Oegstgeester Lawn Tennis Club
Secr.: Mw. C. Beker, Piet Heinlaan 41, 2341 SH, tel. 173542.

Fig. 19.1

Some *verenigingen* in the small municipality of Oegstgeest

tions and of the music society mentioned above), they are no longer felt to be exclusive and people associate much more freely in organizations.

A concrete example will serve to illustrate something of the Dutch style of organizing social activity. In 1975 one of the TV broadcasting associations started a series of programs called *Kerkepad* (Church Path), consisting of short documentaries on three or four historically interesting churches chosen for forming a geographical group. Viewers were invited to visit them. This much is hardly unusual. The visits were to be made not just any time but on two prearranged successive Saturdays. The careful viewer could 'subscribe' to the whole series of that year by mail, and received a brochure with maps and timetables, pictures and explanatory notes. The visitor to any one of the three churches on the day's 'route' would find an identifying flag waving on the tower, throngs of people milling about in a festival atmosphere, coffee and tea readily available—often in the church itself—and meals for sale close by. Just inside the door of each church would be a long table in front of which visitors could line up to get an official stamp on their card certifying that they had made that point on the 'route'. *Kerkepad* is now in its twentieth year and shows no signs of diminishing in popularity.

In its careful planning, smooth operation and provision for certifying participation the *Kerkepad* merely copies a style that was well established in other leisure areas, particularly sporting events. In winters cold enough to freeze the canal system, there will be not only a great deal of casual skating but an almost endless number of shorter or longer routes set up, where the point is not competitive racing or breaking records but simply finishing the whole course, demonstrated by the stamps collected at points along the way. The national super-marathon in skating, the *Elfstedentocht,* is one that thousands of amateurs participate in, and it follows the same pattern. A medal is the reward for all who finish the 200-kilometer course within the fairly ample time limits. Some interesting cultural aspects of this same marathon will come up in the next chapter. Another example of organized participation is the popular *Vierdaagse*, a four-day walk in the vicinity of Nijmegen, again organized on a set day, well prepared, and participated in by tens of thousands who are interested in 'having done it' together, rather than beating the clock.

Many organizations that use the name *vereniging* set up to deal with social questions are really an *actiegroep* or *actiecomité*, forms of organization discussed in chapter 14. As the wide applicability of this word suggests, the society perceives a structure in an exceptionally wide variety of social activities that to an outsider might look entirely spontaneous or merely casual. The concept of *actie* is one that has developed in relatively recent times, and it always implies a focus on a single issue selected from society's many needs. But this singleness of focus is merely the contemporary form given to a habit that is well-rooted in Dutch society, that of public responsibility for all the rest of society.

The best-known example of such a private, non-governmental initiative along a broad social front is probably the *Maatschappij tot Nut van 't Algemeen*. The translation 'Society for the Public Welfare' does not catch the umistakable idealism of its original name. This society was founded in 1784 for the purpose of educating, helping and in general raising the cultural level of the least privileged classes—in other words, a typical fruit of the Enlightenment. It played an active role for 200 years in founding schools, libraries, savings banks and other services not adequately provided by the government. Today the society still exists in the form of small local groups meeting local social needs, but mainly it has fallen victim to its own success. The services it provided have long since been accepted as basic for all. Though today the name has mostly disappeared, it is an example of the

Fig. 19.2
A listing of actie-groups of a variety of types

way social responsibility was, and is, perceived as being spread around in society.

The Dutch word *vergadering* is another one that is difficult to translate accurately, because it implies a specific and well-understood mode of social behavior not quite covered by the more vague 'meeting'. In the Netherlands pursuing even relatively casual aims is apt to lead quickly to the construction of a visible organization headed by a chairman and set of officers, and meetings are seldom attempted without a prearranged agenda. This cautious formal preparation is generally perceived as necessary to ensure orderly democratic procedure, the keeping of domination to a minimum, and the guaranteeing of a reasonable level of unity. Real dissent, when it arises, is apt to lead to a split and the formation of a new minority group. The society as a whole, in other words, shows a marked preference for creating a context for polite, urbane discussion in which all are given opportunity to demonstrate familiarity with good manners.

All the forms of organization seen in this chapter so far amount to well-developed means for handling a great deal of difference in as socially orderly, polite and unemotional a way as possible. Individual aggressiveness and open expression of emotion are not highly valued, which, coupled with the society's commitment to striving toward consensus in the customary *vergadering* form, gives life a markedly deliberate pace. High value is placed on group solidarity, and social conformity is imposed not from above but within the group itself. As opposed to rivalry within groups, rivalry—even contentious—between groups (with sports teams as a model) or between a group and constituted authority (with the actie-groups as a model) is not only accepted but expected as natural.

All this emphasis on politeness, democratic acceptance, smooth procedures, and a public reserve adds up to an urban, urbane style of life. A certain polite reserve is coupled with a broad tolerance of differences and maintained by a well-developed set of social forms. This is a firmly rooted tradition in the Netherlands, inherited from a city culture that reached a peak of development in the 17th century. The ideal of a calm, orderly life, in which manners were polite and any excessive show was avoided, speaks plainly from the hundreds of genre paintings that have fixed our ideas about social life in the Dutch 17th century. Today Dutch people still tend to be distrustful of too-conspicuous individual achievement or any standing out, and to dislike anything perceived as excessive display of affluence. They maintain a discreet public reserve that meticulously respects the privacy of others, accepts outsiders, and cherishes the forms of social organization that help assure all this.

Once these lines have been established, however, the individual is free to take liberties with another individual—for instance asking personal questions—in a way that often strikes foreigners as aggressive or presumptuous. Similarly, public figures being interviewed on radio and TV are regularly expected to hold their own and maintain an urbane exterior while being subjected to sharp, aggressive questioning.

The Dutch style in greeting and leavetaking (involving a great deal of handshaking), public reserve and observation of personal privacy, and in the refuge taken in organization, has changed very little. Dutch people still find it as difficult as ever to start casual conversations with strangers, and the sight of ten to twenty people sitting in a railroad-station waiting room, or thirty crowded together at a bus stop, for a quarter hour without anyone saying a word is still perfectly common. But all observers agree on one point. Though social life preserves its fundamental forms intact, society has become much more informal and casual, and there is no returning to the stiffest of the old ways. As everywhere, older people are especially apt to lament that there are 'no standards' left, but an outside observer find it rather easier to see the many invisible lines that even now are never crossed.

So we might conclude from all this that the individual is seen in this culture as a unit of responsibility rather than as an individual star standing out where possible. It is a society not so much based on individual competitiveness as it is a bargaining forum where each individual voice is respected and that proceeds by constant adjustments. We have already seen in chapter 5 how this habit of painstaking search for consensus affects the business community. The Social Economic Council described in chapter 6, as a forum for bringing together employers, workers and the government, is a typical example of the Dutch habit of seeing to it that, before any steps are taken, matters are given exhaustive discussion by all sides.

A deeply-engrained custom of outward reserve and assurance of privacy might even be seen in the way names are normally written. Both men and women still commonly write their names using only initials, thereby keeping the first name private. On forms it is still common to request 'initials' rather than 'first name'. But society is gradually becoming more flexible about this custom, and the giving of one's first name is becoming increasingly common.

Social customs in the writing of names also demonstrate the importance in Dutch society of the family and family connections. When a woman marries, custom decrees that she not drop her maiden name but write it with a hyphen following her husband's family name. The resulting hyphenated name is her 'formal' name, which most women use on any formal occasion and some use regularly. When the couple is named together, the woman's family name is again retained: *De heer en mevrouw Bakker-Van Dam*. The children of the family, however, drop the mother's name. If a family sees that a name is in danger of being lost in this way, they can legally adopt the mother's name, but in this case it is placed before the father's, and without a hyphen. The family is *Van Dam Bakker* from then on. The length of names that arise on the marriage of two people with double (or occasionally triple) names can be imagined. A long name is sometimes, though by no means necessarily, a sign of an upper-class or aristocratic family.

The use of this system can best be illustrated by the standard style used in newspaper obituaries (Fig. 19.3). Since names of survivors are normally listed in the order husband or wife, sons and daughters, brothers and sisters and their respective families, and since the hyphenation custom is always observed, in spite of the widespread use of initials it is usually not difficult to tell the exact relationship of each person listed.

Tot onze diepe droefheid overleed op 18 april 1986 mijn lieve vrouw, onze lieve moeder en grootmoeder

ALIDA CORNELIA
HARDENBERG-DE BRUYN

geboren 22 februari 1899

Amsterdam:
L. Hardenberg

Amsterdam:
L. Hardenberg
E. C. Hardenberg-s'Jacob

Dordrecht:
G. Hardenberg
C. C. Hardenberg-Bigay
Stefan
Gerrit
Ralph en Lisette

Arles (Fr.)/Amsterdam:
J. C. Golterman-Hardenberg
H. L. Golterman
Maarten en Dola
Roeland en Eliane
Karen en Jelle
Berend-Han

Baarn:
Wa. M. de Bruyn

St. John's, Canada:
Lydia Snellen-de Bruyn
Jan W. Snellen
en kinderen

Leiden:
Gerrit Jan de Bruyn
Johanna de Bruyn-Bierbrauer
en kinderen

Oisterwijk: G. M. Hardenberg-Mulder
Den Haag: M. E. Bijvoet-Hardenberg
Warnsveld: J. C. Hardenberg
Amsterdam: L. M. Slothouwer-Hardenberg
en onze kinderen
en kleinkinderen

Fig. 19.3
A typical newspaper death notice placed by the family. The names, in order, are those of the husband, sons and daughters-in-law, daughter and son-in-law, brother, sister.

Not only is the writing of the first name becoming more common, but as in other countries many people—particularly younger ones of course—do not hesitate to use first name only on initial acquaintance with strangers. Like all European languages except English, Dutch preserves a distinction in pronouns of address between 'polite' and 'familiar', *u* for the former and *jij* for the latter. In an earlier social system this distinction was one of class, *jij* being used mainly to those socially lower. By the end of the Second World War this was being replaced by a system in which *u* was used to set up polite social reserve toward anyone not well known or deferred to for any reason (such as age), while *jij* was used to signal something in common, such as family, membership in the same group, or familiarity toward those who were not yet old enough to be considered part of 'polite' adult society. For those proceeding from the 'polite' forms, the transition from polite to familiar form of address in a given relationship was, and still is, an important one involving some social niceties.

In the past few decades there has been a noticeable shift, with *u* becoming increasingly restricted and *jij* used in more and more social situations. One of the signals of the democratization of the university system is that professors do not hesitate to address students with *jij* (always implying first name as well), and if the professor is young enough, some students reciprocate. As recently as the early 1960's this would have been unthinkable. But even though the familiar *jij* is still extending its social terrain, the formal *u* maintains its ground as a needed expression of polite distance.

'Infective invective'

Dutch society in some of its moods has yet another interesting claim to distinction among modern European societies. When diseases such as cholera, the plague, typhus and leprosy were widespread, wishing them on someone disliked was a common form of cursing in Europe. Today, long after most of the diseases have as good as disappeared in the western industrialized countries, in the Netherlands this habit remains a favorite means of strong invective.

A blunt way of telling someone to get lost, drop dead or go to hell is *krijg de klere* (an old substandard pronunciation of *cholera*) 'catch cholera', or any of an assortment of other diseases such as *de pest* 'the plague', *de pokken* 'smallpox', *de tyfus* 'typhoid fever'. Calling someone a *klerelijer* 'cholera sufferer' or a sufferer from any other of the same assortment of diseases is a crude insult. Most disease names are also intensifiers, and *pokken-, klere-, pest-, kanker-, tyfus-, tering-* 'consumption' can be used—often two or three of them together—as invective prefixes in front of anything disliked. Disease names enter into a wide variety of other expressions.

It hardly needs to be added that all these strong words lead their flourishing existence well outside the boundaries of polite society.

For a fuller discussion, see W.H. Fletcher, 'Cursing can be contagious in Dutch: A survey of infective invective in Holland'. *Maledicta: The International Journal of Verbal Aggression*, vol. 12 (1993).

Statistical surveys in all western countries, including the Netherlands, suggest the same disruption and dissolution of traditional family ties and the rejection of old family values. Nevertheless, it remains in essence what has sometimes been called an 'introverted family culture'. There are two words for 'family'. The wider sense of a network of relations is *familie*, but the unit of mother-father-children, most commonly occupying a single-family dwelling, is *gezin*. Even though the family unit is no longer seen as the only option, housing patterns in the Netherlands, including the customary layout of individual houses, accurately reflect the perception of the family unit as fundamental. Interiors are normally designed following a custom which emphasizes the family circle. Living rooms usually have chairs arranged in a tight circle to make conversation maximally easy and intimate. The whole Dutch conversational style, in fact, derives from the family emphasis. Dutch families and their visitors are able to carry on lengthy conversations among six to ten people in a circle without once breaking up into individual pair-conversations (the dominant pattern in the US for instance). This particular domestic model of social contentment and fulfillment is captured in the word *gezelligheid*.

The persistence of the Dutch family network throughout adulthood is also seen in the fact that Dutch individuals are far less mobile than equivalent members of other societies. In 1990, fully 65% of all those 20-24 years old still lived in their parents' home. The individual is also apt to think of him- or herself in terms of family relationships and locality. There is even a chance that persons on first meeting will recognize some of these family connections in the other, and at times the outsider is tempted to see the whole society as 'one big family'. Going out into the world and 'making it on one's own' is not a significant cultural value. Dutch society with its emphasis on the independent responsibility of the individual on the one hand, and its strong commitment to teamwork and family cohesion on the other, represents a curious paradox.

This close family cohesion is, not unexpectedly, constantly reinforced in being immersed at times in ritualized activity. After all, the values most important to a society are given expression in its primary rituals. In the Netherlands one of the most central of these rituals is the birthday. Birthdays of family and friends are carefully kept track of, and the person celebrating is expected to maintain a sort of 'open house' for as long as practicable on that day, to receive and entertain any congratulatory guests who arrive.

The most important national holiday is *Sinterklaas,* on the evening of December 5, and it is in essence the culmination of the birthday ritual. The 6th is the birthday of *Sint Nicolaas,* a bishop who lives in Spain and comes each year on the eve of that day to enter the family celebration. It is the family holiday par excellence, and especially in families with children, the excitement builds up for weeks as everyone prepares for the saint's arrival. It is family solidarity, family fun and thus the perpetuation of traditional family values that is the central function of the ritual. Children learn that *Sinterklaas* will only reward them with gifts if they are well behaved, and the parents' manner subtly suggests that this should be taken with some seriousness. Otherwise *Zwarte Piet* (Black Peter), who always accompanies the Saint, is quite likely to take them back to Spain. Even if the child knows that the saint is really being played by father or uncle, the sense of awe cannot be escaped, and the whole ceremony has a strong flavor of group solidarity. *The Sinterklaas* celebration has some further important ritual aspects surrounding it, which we return to in the next chapter as we widen our view into the question of the Dutch national cultural identity.

FURTHER READING

The Netherlands Journal of Sociology. Amsterdam: Elsevier [A semiannual publication of translations of articles on social trends and developments that have appeared in the Netherlands].

Sport in the Netherlands. More than just Football. The Hague: Ministry of Foreign Affairs and Ministry of Welfare, Health and Cultural Affairs, 1988.

Van der Toorn-Schutte, J., *Zo zijn onze manieren.* Apeldoorn: Van Walraven, 1994.

Van Vree, Wilbert, *Nederland als vergaderland. Opkomst en verbreiding van een vergaderregime.* Groningen: Wolters-Noordhoff, 1994.

Zeegers, Wil, *Andere tijden, andere mensen. De sociale representatie van identiteit.* Amsterdam: Bakker, 1988.

Van Zoest, A., 'A master of word and image. Martin Toonder and the Bumble comic strips'. *The Low Countries,* 1994-5.

20 Cultural identity

In its rituals, a society periodically reminds itself of its values. In the Netherlands, one of the most genuine of these is *Sinterklaas*. The eve of the birthday of St. Nicholas is an important ritualized means by which the values of domestic behavior are demonstrated to the young, but its social aspects go well beyond that. The small presents exchanged by everyone in the family are, by tradition, always accompanied by a rhyme that must be read aloud first. It is in these home-made poems on December 5 that Dutch people tell each other things that for the rest of the year they can only think. In assuming the personality and tone of the Catholic bishop from Spain, on this day everyone is free to point an admonitory finger at anyone else and suggest what is right or wrong about the behavior of the recipient.

Sinterklaas is thus a classic example of the occasion, found in cultures everywhere, when all the usual rules are suspended and things can be done that are normally tabooed. The accusations in the rhymes may be blunt but the tone must always remain light and joking. Most often the content is mildly admonitory or simply reflective, and the poems tend to moralize briefly about one of an almost endless range of personal shortcomings. Many of the poems are simply complimentary. The Saint, in whose name the poems by

Fig. 20.1
Sinterklaas and Zwarte Piet

custom are written, is the ultimate observer whom nothing escapes, and he is a stern moralist but never a fanatic—his message is always lightened and seasoned with irony. *Sinterklaas* himself may be held up to ridicule, but few succeed in denying his reality and refusing to participate in the ritual. The moralizing-rhyme aspect of *Sinterklaas* has if anything been coming more to the foreground.

Although the *Sinterklaas* celebration has for a long time been central in Dutch cultural identity and the one holiday invariably celebrated by Dutch people living abroad, for a combination of reasons—which include strong commercial competition from Christmas—he has recently been declining in favor. Not only is his fatherly judging and admonishing increasingly out of step with an anti-authoritarian age, but in the present equality and ethnic diversity his accompanying servant 'Black Peter' is becoming an embarrassment. It will be interesting to see whether the society will abandon *Sinterklaas* altogether or find some way to modify him and *Zwarte Piet* into a more comfortable harmony with modern attitudes. There are some signs that the latter is under way.

The second of the primary rituals is the *Elfstedentocht* (Eleven-city race). This is a marathon skating competition held in Friesland, the province with the most elaborate network of interconnecting lakes and canals. The course is 200 km (125 mi.) laid out roughly circularly, beginning in Leeuwarden, the capital, passing through eleven towns (hence its name) and returning to the starting point. It is not held every year, but only when in the winter it has stayed cold enough for long enough to freeze all the canals to a safe depth. The cycle of the ritual is accordingly decided not by the calendar but by the uncontrollable forces of nature, and this fact along with the anticipation that builds for years (the 1985 race was the first in 22 years) gives the *Elfstedentocht* a much more powerful emotional impact than any other ritual.

Although the competitors race against the clock and winners are ultimately announced in order of crossing the finish line, the emphasis is not on beating everyone else but on completing the entire course and thus answering the challenge of nature itself. Racing skaters must withstand cold, wind, rough ice, sand, and exhaustion for an average non-stop seven hours. When the competition begins, very quickly little groups form and begin working in a choreographed rhythm, each skater taking a turn heading into the wind and—more importantly—setting the pace for the rest of the group. Enduring the course requires the smooth cooperation of these mutually sustaining but still competing groups. In 1954 the winner earned the resentment of many other competitors because he had not 'earned' his win by leading a group. In 1956 the first five came across the finish line together with their arms locked. This mixture of cooperation and competition is a perfect symbolic model of Dutch society.

The *Elfstedentocht* is run by an organization that opens competition only to its own members—18,500 of them. In late February 1986 the officers of the organization announced that the competition would be held two days hence. When the 316 competitors left the starting line at 5:00 a.m., an estimated 5,000,000 were already watching on TV. By later calculations it was said that about 91.5% of the population of the country had followed TV cov-

Fig. 20.2
The Elfstedentocht

erage for at least part of the day. When the first group neared the finish, parliament recessed long enough to follow events, and the result was announced in train stations all over the country.

But to see only the competition, even in its cooperative aspect, would be to miss the most important aspect of the *Elfstedentocht*. In the race described above, after the competitors were all on their way, the approximately 17,000 non-competing participants set out to try to complete the course, getting their cards stamped at specified points along the way. Everyone who finished before the announced closing time would be awarded a medal. About half a million spectators lined the route all day, from before dawn until well after dark, cheering all participants along with songs, music groups, flags and banners with mostly playful texts. It was a folklore festival in which the Dutch cast aside their customary reserve to celebrate with abandon.

The *Elfstedentocht* has all the elements of a genuine ritual event, and no small amount of mythic significance besides. One of the newspapers reporting the 1985 marathon captured this with the words 'All of life is an *Elfstedentocht*.' Two Dutch cultural anthropologists called attention to the striking religious symbolism they found in it. For one day the province of Friesland, where a mysterious 'rural Latin' is spoken, is declared the sacred ground for a ritual that begins and ends in darkness. It is run by the president of the organization, who is surrounded by the mystique of a chief priest as he consults with his seers about the weather. The national fascination with the tiny village of Bartlehiem along the route can reasonably be explained by an unconscious identification with a biblical name*. The TV newscaster referred to the winner of the competition as the *nieuwe ijsheilige* 'new saint of the ice'. This interpretation was unwittingly illustrated by one of the playful banners at the outskirts of the city of Dokkum (one of the eleven towns), bolstering up

---

* Yme Kuiper and Wim Hofstee, 'Hoe nationaal besef te vinden?' *Focaal. Tijdschrift voor Antropologie* No. 2-3 (April 1986), 57-71; 'De eendaagse illusie van het Herwonnen Paradijs', *NRC Handelsblad*, February 28, 1986.

the courage of all skaters, as it flashed across the TV screen: *Bonifatius heeft Dokkum niet eens gehaald* 'Boniface didn't even make Dokkum', a reference to the missionary murdered near that city by the Frisians in 754. A uniquely national experience is shared by everyone, now with the powerful aid of television.

Before we look at how the Dutch think of themselves, we might first consider what the world says about them. Though the Dutch enjoy an overwhelmingly favorable image abroad (recall Fig. 1.1), it may come as a surprise that this stereotype, a tidy little country with an industrious, permissive and tolerant people living in it, is of relatively recent invention. During most of the time there has been any people identifiable to the world as 'Dutch', the images have been rather different and often negative. Dutchmen appearing in early American literature tended to follow the round, gluttonous and lethargic image popularized by Washington Irving. The English have poked fun at Dutch coarseness and greed ever since at least the 17th century. In Othello, Shakespeare has Iago refer to the drinking feats of the 'swag-bellied Hollander'.

Sir William Temple knew the Netherlands well and did not have to resort to stereotypes. Writing late in the 17th century, he offers a balanced judgment that still does not deny some validity to a negative image:

> Though these people, who are naturally cold and heavy, may not be ingenious enough to furnish a pleasant or agreeable conversation, yet they want not plain downright sense to understand and do their business both public and private ...

Though Temple expressed elsewhere his admiration for the neatly laid-out and carefully tended gardens and fields, and the clean, apparently prosperous cities and towns, other English writers were often somewhat less complimentary about the country itself. In 1651 the poet Andrew Marvell spoke of 'Holland, that scarce deserves the name of land, / As but th'offscouring of the British sand.'

The French, who have never hesitated to give opinions about the Dutch, tended to agree with the first of Temple's observations but were sometimes generous enough to see positive sides. We find 'the Dutch are half-baked, without fire, melancholy and stale', but they are also called 'an honest, well-meaning, humane and free people, who accepted foreigners in distress in their midst with equal rights'. The Germans in the 16th and 17th centuries tended to look up to and admire the Netherlands, especially the economic success and cosmopolitan glamour of Amsterdam. Kant thought of the Dutch as orderly, industrious and practical but without a sense for the finer things of the spirit. German writers in the early 19th century saw in them a decadent trading people with few redeeming qualities, least of all their language. During the 19th century, attitudes tended to be increasingly negative and patronizing toward a neighbor that was perceived as slow and phlegmatic.

The Italian Luigi Barzini in the chapter of *The Europeans* called 'The careful Dutch' offers a string of opinions that are a grand mixture of acute observation and uncritical stereotype. Geography has made the Dutch patient, industrious, adventurous and rich. They were and are 'strict Bible-reading Calvinists' (he was claiming this at late as 1983), and are stolid, hard-working, parsimonious, earnest, unimaginative and slow-thinking. They have long pursued pacifism not as a heroic adventure but as a benefit to their commercial interests (not without some truth, but is there something wrong with that?). The Dutch—still according to Barzini—feel themselves to be an island of sanity, exercising a high moral authority in international relations.

The Portuguese Rentes de Carvalho in *Com os holandeses*, translated into Dutch but not into English, sees the Dutch today as having a good life but not knowing how to enjoy it. They are obsessed with planning, regulating and organizing: nowhere else in the world are there so many *verenigingen*, *actie* groups and *vergaderingen*. In *The Dutch Puzzle*, first written in 1966 by the Spanish Duke de Baena and popular enough to have been kept in print in successive editions, many of the same observations about the Dutch are voiced. They are full of paradoxes: they are independent but fill life with petty tyrannical conventions, they have a monarchy but think with a republican independence, they are sentimental but rude, thrifty but generous, tolerant but fanatic, international but parochial, and they have both the sensuous side of Jan Steen and the puritanical side of Calvin.

One of the more recent voices is the American Derek Phillips, in an essay in *De naakte Nederlander* (1985, The Naked Dutchman). Although the Dutch pride themselves on their individualism, their social climate is one that, instead, strongly favors a collective style of thinking and a group conformity. Even with the weakening of much of *verzuiling*, the Dutch still like to organize themselves in small, closed groups which are relatively indifferent to other groups. Individuals who distinguish themselves too conspicuously are treated with suspicion, higher value being placed on the smooth functioning of the group.

After this barrage of opinions that the Dutch have had to endure for centuries, we come back to what the Dutch say about their country, and following this what they think about themselves. Possibly no other people in the world has had such a love/hate relationship to its physical setting. The 18th-century poet Bernard de Mandeville referred to his former native country as 'that contemptible spot of ground'. For sheer ill temper, no statement has ever matched the splendid outburst of the 19th-century De Genestet's *Boutade* 'A sally', the opening line of which in the Netherlands everyone can quote. The first stanza goes

O land van mest en mist, van vuile, koude regen,
Doorsijperd stukske grond, vol kille dauw en damp
Vol vuns, onpeilbaar slijk en ondoorwaadbare wegen
Vol jicht en paraplu's, vol kiespijn en vol kramp!

O land of manure and mist, of dirty, clammy rain, /Soggy patch of ground, full of chilly dews and damps, / Full of musty, bottomless mire and unwadable roads, / Full of gout and umbrellas, of toothache and of cramps!

And the last line offers the thought that 'it wasn't at my request that you were wrested from the sea'.

To take just one further example, the modern novelist Frans Kellendonk has one of his characters say

> Well, what do you expect. The landscape is flat ... You can't tell any more that it was once nothing but marsh, but you still feel it: it sucks at our feet, it pulls our brains down and it holds our hearts ... in the right place for so long that they petrify there.

But the dyspeptic side is easily matched by the strong attachment many Dutch feel for their landscape. The poetess Henriëtte Roland Holst spoke of '... troops of clouds all fleeting, / flown to us here from the far fields of heaven, / you have horizons lying soft and even / from east to west ...' As a later poet put it, 'the polder with its swishing trees stretches / out wide, the wind sweeps spots of sunlight over it / gulls screech in the wide open space.' The Marsman poem and its parody, quoted at the end of chapter one, reflect some of this same ambivalence.

The most thoughtful and even-handed evaluation of the people that occupy this patch of ground might still be that of Erasmus, written nearly a century before there was any country the Dutch could call exclusively their own.

> As to that accusation of boorishness ... which people has not been uncultured at one time? ... If you look at the manners of everyday life, there is no race more open to humanity and kindness, or less given to wildness or ferocious behavior. It is a straightforward nature, without treachery or deceit, and not prone to any serious vices, except that it is a little given to pleasure, especially of feasting ...*

A cataloguing of descriptions of themselves by the Dutch can be a dreary experience. Today they tend to agree with the centuries-old images of the Dutch and call themselves over-serious, heavy-handed and unable to enjoy life with abandon. They see each other as addicted to complaining and arguing, but most of all they see their thriftiness as degenerated into a tight-fisted, niggling miserliness. This is summed up in the Dutch term *krenterigheid* (a word that curiously applies only to the Dutch, rarely members of any other culture). It is this quality that their cultural cousins to the South, the Flemings, think of as summing up the 'Dutchness' of Holland.

But the litany by no means ends here. Criticism of all kinds, from the most informal on through satire and cabaret and then further into serious essay, regularly takes aim at the rational, orderly passion for reducing all of life to rules. Their seeing themselves as narrow-minded is expressed by the common *Nederland op zijn smalst* 'The Netherlands at its narrowest', which properly (though far less frequently) refers to a former narrow neck of land in the province of North Holland. Closely related to this is the domestic insistence on practicality and usefulness, and, in turn, the reduction of everything to business and profitability, the ineradicable instincts of the trader.

The Dutch look at their nation divided up into endless little groups, which has created a national state of mind (even after the fading of *verzuiling*) called *hokjesgeest*, the spirit of the *hok*, which among other things means a 'pigeon-hole'. Each group is seen as exercising its right not only to exist but to preach its own brand of religious or secular morality, extending into the

* 'Auris Batava', *Adages*, 1508.

realms of politics, business or international relations. The strong hold of 'Principle' on all aspects of life, and the finger raised in admonition at home and abroad, is apt to be the first thing the Dutch see in the mirror. 'Calvinistic' in its modern senses of 'meddlesome, dogmatic' is one of their favorite ways of describing themselves even today, though this vague concept tends to be blamed for nearly everything.

The Dutch are able to go on cataloguing their faults. They have an expression *Doe maar gewoon, dan doe je al gek genoeg* 'Act normally, and you're conspicuous enough'. This puts into aphoristic form the predominant perception among Dutch people that for all their international orientation and progressiveness, they have never forsaken the mentality of the village or small town. One's image is important, and an eye must always be kept on what the neighbors are doing and what they might think. Anything that breaks out of this comfortable small-scale pattern is to be treated with suspicion. The Dutch value orderliness, and show a national dislike for the conspicuous. In a word, they perceive themselves to be bourgeois to the core.

The question, of course, is what senses we should attach to that word. We might mean the range of virtues normally accepted as belonging to a contented, orderly, hard-working, unheroic life-style usually called 'middle-class'. Accepting this general meaning, it is not hard to demonstrate that social life in the Netherlands has been of a strongly middle-class character since at least the beginnings of political independence in the 16th century. Histories often point to the development of a prosperous middle class in the cities of the Low Countries as early as the Middle Ages. Dutch literature consistently reflects this, and styles in painting that depended on dramatic effects, from Caravaggio's play of light and dark in the 17th century down to the French Impressionists in the 19th, were subtly rendered more well-mannered to suit Dutch tastes.

Fig. 20.3
An artist's view of Dutch 'moralists' at work

A picture of the worst excesses of this middle-class mentality was put into almost classic form by the poet Slauerhoff in a famous poem entitled simply *In Nederland*. He begins 'The Netherlands is not where I want to live, / you always have to keep your urges in check / for the sake of the good neighbors, / who peer eagerly through every crack / ... You always have to be striving for something, / thinking of the well-being of your fellow man. / Only on the sly may you give offense ...' The final stanza is

In Nederland wil ik niet blijven,	The Netherlands is not where I want to stay, / I would grow into a thicket and turn rigid. / Everything is too calm for me, too proper, / People speak slowly there, never become vehement, / And never dance on the slack rope. / Though the defenseless are tormented, / Never is one of those coarse peasant heads lopped off, / And never, no never is there a lovely crime of passion.
Ik zou dichtgroeien en verstijven.	
Het gaat mij daar te kalm, te deftig	
Men spreekt er langzaam, wordt nooit heftig	
En danst nooit op het slappe koord	
Wel worden er werklozen gekweld	
Nooit wordt zo'n plompe boerenkop gesneld,	
En nooit, neen nooit gebeurt er een mooie passiemoord.	

The word 'bourgeois' is the English equivalent of the Dutch word *burgerlijk*, but it is not in nearly as common use and it does not have quite the same negative connotations as the Dutch word has acquired. *Burgerlijk* has come to suggest, in everyday usage, whatever is narrow-minded and mindlessly conformist. On the other hand, the 'decalvinization' of the present consumer society is occasionally seen as evidence of a return to the (supposedly) more hedonistic life style of the 15th and 16th centuries. It remains to be seen whether a relaxation of the most rigid standards is any evidence of fundamental shifts in the habits of a culture.

The Dutch have a great national fondness for holding a mirror up to themselves. But they do this much more effectively, and for us as observers more revealingly, by the indirect means of parables told to the society by its artists. Cees Nooteboom's whimsical novel entitled simply *In Nederland* is set in an indefinite 'past' time when the Netherlands was supposedly much larger than it is now. The familiar country of today was connected to a large, wild and untamed South, more or less where the Balkans are, by a long, narrow strip running roughly diagonally between them. There is more to the title than first meets the eye. It is a conscious evocation of the devastating view of Dutch society in Slauerhoff's poem *In Nederland* mentioned just above. This alone created difficulties in finding a title for the English translation, since a mere translation of the title would miss this reference. The solution was 'In the Dutch Mountains', which suggests the wildness without capturing the acidity of Slauerhoff.

In Nooteboom's novel, the North is an 'orderly human garden', where the people worship Reality and are smug, greedy and hypocritical; they bore into each other with their phosphorescent eyes and weigh each other's souls. The climate of good will is suffocating. The people of the 'southern Netherlands' speak a bizarre mixed language and they are uncouth but live freer lives. The land itself is desolate and primitive, full of caverns that intimidate northerners. The story is about two people from the North who live and travel in the South, and what this means to their personalities. Through the person of the observer in the novel, a Spanish civil engineer called Tiburón (shark), Nooteboom plays the role of moralist and makes sure the instructive points get made.

Marten Toonder's comic strip *Tom Poes* is so popular, especially among the educated, that it can safely be called a national institution. It has appeared daily since 1938, interrupted only by the war years. When Toonder decided to retire a few years ago and said farewell to his faithful readers, the end of Tom Poes was announced on the first page of the NRC *Handelsblad* where it had been appearing, and on the TV newscast. The paper immediately began rerunning previous stories, so that there was no interruption in the strip's appearing daily. The 'strip' is really an illustrated story in daily installments, a cleverly-told tale full of ironic play with the language and inventive with new words, several of which have become a permanent part of the language. The pictures are drawn in a detailed, carefully realistic style that creates an immediately recognizable special world. This world looks un-Dutch at first sight but, like the characters thinly disguised as animals, very Dutch immediately beneath the surface.

Tom Poes en de Kniphoed
door Marten Toonder

2568. Op de middag van die dag zat heer Ollie rustig in zijn gemakkelijke stoel een goed boek te lezen, toen de bediende Joost aanklopte en binnentrad.
„Excuseer, heer Olivier", sprak de trouwe knecht, „er is een heer aan de deur om u te spreken".
„Wat is dat nu vervelend", zei heer Ollie klaaglijk. „De schurk staat net op het punt zijn masker af te zetten. Ik kan niet gestoord worden, Joost! Als ik werk, ben ik niet thuis, als je begrijpt wat ik bedoel!"

Doch het was reeds te laat. De bediende werd opzijde geschoven en in de deuropening verscheen een gebogen gedaante, die een kristallen bolletje in de hand droeg.
„Goeie dag", kraste de oude. „Uw pad zij schemerig en vol smook".
„Wablief?", vroeg heer Bommel ontdaan.
„Ik kom hier schuilen", vervolgde de grijsaard. „Mijn hoed is afgewaaid

en nu heb ik geen bescherming meer. Ik, oude man, kan niet goed tegen dit ruwe weer".
„Ruw weer?!", riep heer Ollie uit. Hij keek vol verbazing naar buiten, waar de zon scheen en de vogels zongen en toen kwam er een lichte ontstemming in hem op. Maar voor hij uit kon vallen, hernam de oude knikkend:
„Juist! De zon! Een ruw element, waarde heer! De zon verstoort de fijnere invloeden van tah en Zazel en daarom kom ik bij u schuilen. Ik heb in mijn kristallen bol gezien, dat mijn hoed bij u terecht komt en daar wil ik nu even op wachten. Het was een boze middag, vol warmte en lauwe Zuidenwind. En die wind woei mijn hoed weg — zóver, dat ik hem niet vinden kon in mijn kristallen bol. Maar hij wordt teruggebracht, dus dat is in orde. U kunt gerust zijn!"
Zo sprekende zette de grijsaard zijn koffertje neer en keek goedkeurend rond.

2574 — „Het is jammer!", mompelde de grijsaard. „Je hebt dus niets om aan mij te verkopen? Geen oude waarden? Geen eigenwaarde? Het is jammer en ongewoon. Maar goed, dan niet. Ik dring niet aan, want ik ben niet ondankbaar. Je hebt mijn kniphoed voor me gevonden en daarom ga ik verder. Lawaai en klatergoud op je pad!"
Met deze vreemde woorden wendde hij zich om en schuifelde snel weg. Tom Poes bleef aarzelend staan, in tweestrijd of hij de oude verder zou volgen of niet. Op dat moment verscheen heer Bommel echter in de kromming van de weg.
„Zo jonge vriend", sprak deze, „ik zag, dat je met die oude heer stond te praten. Wat wil hij eigenlijk? Wat heeft hij die opschepperige markies gedaan? Niet dat ik nieuwsgierig ben, hoor. Maar ik wil het graag weten. Men treft zo zelden iemand met gevoel voor schoonheid, als je begrijpt wat ik bedoel".

„Hm", zei Tom Poes. „Hij is een koopman in oude waarden, zegt hij. Maar ik vertrouw hem niet. Er is iets raars met hem en zijn kniphoed".
„Een koopman in oude waarden?", herhaalde heer Bommel ontsteind. „En hij gaat naar de markies om dingen te kopen? Zou hij soms denken, dat die meer waardevolle dingen heeft dan ik? Dat is sterk, dat zal je moeten toegeven!"

„Laat die oude toch lopen", zei Tom Poes. „Ik ben blij, dat u geen zaken met hem hebt gedaan".
„Het gaat niet om de zaken!" riep heer Ollie uit. „Geld speelt geen rol voor een heer van mijn stand. Maar het gaat om het principe! Iedereen weet dat ik de meeste dingen van waarde heb en toch gaat hij naar die waardeloze Cantecler. Dat kan ik niet nemen!" Met deze woorden zette heer Bommel zich in beweging en snel liep hij achter de grijsaard aan.

Fig. 20.4
Two episodes from the Tom Poes strip. We see the opening of a new adventure, Heer Bommel's customary reckless pursuit of the mysterious stranger into dangers, and the cautious, observant role of Tom Poes.

Bommel, a bear, has a sovereign imperturbability as he seeks to maintain his image of dignified respectability. Tom Poes (*poes* is 'pussycat', though his name is really a pun on *tompouce*, a popular confection) is the seer with wide-open eyes, the intellect who figures everything out and gives advice. Each complete story consists of about 60 daily installments, and it brings home a specific moral lesson in a whimsical but transparent way. In one, a villain came and stole everyone's *eigenwaarde* 'self-esteem'. The problem Heer Bommel and Tom Poes were called upon to solve was the 'reduction of all values', and the adventure concluded with the traditional dinner at which the moral lessons were reviewed.

Toonder's mythical Rommeldam is well established in Dutch folklore, and it is the world of one of the society's most widely recognized myths. Many of the strip's main characters are readily recognizable prototypes, figures nestled deep into the Dutch social consciouness. Toonder has provided his culture with more of these than any other Dutch writer in history.

With all these firmly-established traditions shared by the whole society, it ought to be easy to sum up a Dutch 'national identity' sensed by those born and raised there (which is very different from generalizing about 'national character'). In actual fact, this is one of the most difficult questions of all to answer. 'Identity' is a rather vague, slippery idea, one that might even be said to have taken on a certain trendy tone now. The concept of a 'Dutch nation' is one that has always been weakly developed, and it is pointed out occasionally that the state that came into being in the 16th and 17th centuries was a quirk of history that does not fit most reasonable definitions of a 'state'. The fact that the official name of the country (*Koninkrijk der Nederlanden* and its translations in other languages) is still plural, and that *de Nederlanden* is still used to refer to the Low Countries in general, is sometimes seen as putting a finger on the problem.

The Netherlands has taken its place among the modern nation-states, but with hardly a trace of the Romantic nationalism that has created a strong sense of identity in many European countries, or of a 'national destiny' that could carry a people into imperialistic adventures. Occasional attempts to claim descent from the ancient Batavians are not taken seriously, and identification with the special Dutch landscape runs into the awkward circumstance that physically the land inside the national borders is indistinguishable from the coastal region all the way between France and Denmark.

The Dutch debate about where—if anywhere—their national identity is to be found is a perpetual one. Some have even claimed that the most strongly articulated national identity among the Dutch consists precisely in the insistent denial that any such thing exists at all. It has been pointed out that whenever national unity has been threatened, the discussion of Dutch identity has intensified. The current realities of the development of a multi-racial society and the challenges it poses to a sense of identity have reopened the discussion. We might note at this point that the Dutch have two words for 'society', *maatschappij* and *samenleving*. The first matches all the meanings of the English term, whereas the second is sometimes synonymous but emphasizes the interactions between individuals and groups on an ordinary level.

In many countries the language is a powerful means of reinforcing a sense of national identity, but this too would not seem to be a very promising place to look in the Netherlands. The Dutch, as was pointed out above, are raised with the realization that their language is not understood outside their borders and counts for little among world languages. They accordingly take pride in adapting, and their ready use of other languages is a matter of prestige few can afford to ignore. Their sense of denying any value to their language outside their own native circle is so strong that foreign visitors who want to speak it are given little chance. Apparently the extremes of self-denying adaptability are not new in the Netherlands. In the 1670's Constantijn Huygens wrote in a letter to England about 'our honest citizen, Mr Leeuwenhoeck, or Leawenhook, according to your orthography' (try to picture any Englishman writing 'Mr Sjeekspier, according to your orthography'!). And yet, the other side of this is that the Dutch language does in fact have a strong cultural-identity component to it. It has something of the nature of a secret code shared in by 'us' and nobody else. Most Dutch people think of their language as 'terribly difficult' for anyone else to learn, and the reaction to someone who does learn is invariably one of astonishment. Chapter 8 brought out something of the fears they sense for the viability of their language in a new federated Europe.

The place where the source of a sense of national identity can most confidently be found is the shared experience of history. The Revolt in the 16th century and an accompanying sense of being a people passing through trials has never faded completely away, and when the trial of the Second World War came, this whole set of national feelings was reawakened. The constant reliving and reinterpretation of the German occupation for the past half century shows what an important part of the culture's identity this experience has become. National identity resides in the experiences themselves and not in national symbols. The annual commemorations of the Liberation, including the fortieth and fiftieth, were and are quiet and reflective, without any appeals to nationalism.

The Revolt brought about the bond with the House of Orange that by stages has been constitutionally secured ever since, creating in the color orange itself the one universal symbol of national identity that does exist. The sense of moral specialness that has its roots in the revolt still regularly draws the fire of society's critics, but should not be underestimated as part of that identity. It is an important ingredient, whether one happens to agree with it or not, in the Netherlands' search for its own role in the modern world. The current experience of forming a new multiracial, multicultural society is one that, for all its jolts and discomforts, is being carried on and will continue to be carried on in a distinctly Dutch way. This too is a shared experience that is making its contribution to the national identity.

With the evolution of Europe into increasingly integrated phases, the Dutch debate about their national cultural identity has come to occupy center stage once again. They value their internationalism and talent for assimilating, but see clear dangers in what they perceive as an undifferentiated European 'melting pot', and have been one of the small countries insisting that the European system should include some strong form of cultural charter.

This still leaves the troubling question: what identity is it that is to be preserved? Ironically perhaps, this very agonizing about cultural identity has something characteristically Dutch about it, so that the ongoing discussion itself has the engaging role of giving the culture a unique form of continuity. Indeed, it seems reasonable to claim that the Dutch 'inferiority complex' expressed in scorn heaped on their own culture (recall that pithy aphorism *Nederlandse cultuur is klagen over de Nederlandse cultuur* 'Dutch culture is: complaining about Dutch culture' quoted at the beginning) is itself a perverse form of chauvinism. Perhaps it is even an unacknowledged form of guilt at admitting how strong the national pride—expressed in their sense of moral superiority—really is. The characteristic Dutch pride in the absence of any aggressive nationalism is itself a central part of their national cultural consciousness.

Social life in the Netherlands has a well-developed attachment to the domestic, middle-class way and a moralizing stance, but at the same time it has an overwhelmingly strong international outlook. It is following patterns that were laid down long ago. Nearly five hundred years ago, the Dutchman Desiderius Erasmus was writing exclusively in Latin yet managed to build up a popular reputation throughout Europe by putting out book after book full of practical, sensible advice and lively depictions of everyday life, such as the ones mentioned a few pages ago. He shrank from taking sides (in the Reformation, in his case), preferring instead a quiet and patient working toward peaceful consensus; he was reserved with a strong suspicion of expressions of passion, he had an instinct for putting things into a playful ironic perspective and loved games with words. He had a strongly international instinct, with a curious alienation from his own country. If there is such a thing he might even be called the 'quintessential Dutchman', because the Dutch today are still following all the same cultural patterns. These are the ones that will continue to provide the channel for evolution toward the future.

FURTHER READING

Baena, Duke de, *The Dutch Puzzle*. The Hague: Boucher, 5th ed. 1975.

Boissevain, Jeremy, and Jojada Verrips, *Dutch Dilemmas: Anthropologists Look at the Netherlands*. Assen: Van Gorcum, 1989.

Horst, Hans van der, *The Low Sky: Understanding the Dutch*. Schiedam: Scriptum / The Hague: NUFFIC, 1996.

Joustra, Arendo (ed.), *Vreemde ogen. Buitenlanders over de Nederlandse identiteit*. Amsterdam: Prometheus, 1993.

Vuijsje, Herman, *'t Is niet de bedoeling te verwijten, Het zijn gewoon wat blote feiten. Sinterklaasdichters in Nederland*. The Hague: Nijgh en Van Ditmar, 1984.

White, Colin, and Laurie Boucke, *The UnDutchables: An Observation of the Netherlands. Its Culture and its Inhabitants*. Montrose, CA: White and Boucke, 3rd ed. 1993.

Index

Illustration credits

G.B. Trudeau, pg. 10
Compact Geography of the Netherlands (IDG, Utrecht, 1996), pg. 12, 14, 22, 24, 30, 41, 43
A short History of the Netherlands, by Ivo Schöffer, pg. 17
Topografische Dienst Nederland, pg. 18 (below), 20
Gates and operating system for the Eastern Scheldt storm surge barrier, pg. 25
IDG, pg. 29, 35
NS-Design, pg. 36
Fotopersbureau Dijkstra, pg. 45, 47
Collectie Gemeentearchief Rotterdam, pg. 48
Tom de Rooij Fotografie, pg. 49
Peter van Straaten, pg. 50
Director of the Amsterdam Physical Planning Department, pg. 51
Bert Niehuis, pg. 53
Resources, no. 84, pg. 55
Philips, pg. 57
Arend van Dam, pg. 61
Ministry of Education, Culture and Science, Zoetermeer, pg. 69
Dutch. The language of twenty million Dutch and Flemish people (Stichting Ons Erfdeel vzw,
    Rekkem, 1996), pg. 77, 80, 82
ANP Foto, pg. 87, 94, 96, 141, 142, 205, 207
Trouw, pg. 119, 123
de Volkskrant, pg. 123
NRC Handelsblad, pg. 123
De Telegraaf, pg. 123
Algemeen Dagblad, pg. 123
Het Parool, pg. 123
José Melo, pg. 146
Ministry of Social Affairs and Employment, The Hague, pg. 147
Boekhandel De Kler, Leiden, pg. 170
Vlaams Commissariaat Generaal voor Toerisme, pg. 179
Marten Toonder, pg. 213